STRATEGIC HUMAN RESOURCE MANAGEMENT

Kenneth A. Kovach

University Press of America, Inc.
Lanham • New York • London

Copyright © 1996 by
University Press of America,® Inc.
4720 Boston Way
Lanham, Maryland 20706

3 Henrietta Street
London, WC2E 8LU England

Library of Congress Cataloging-in-Publication Data

Kovach, Kenneth A..
Strategic human resource management / Kenneth A. Kovach.
p.   cm.
Includes bibliographical references.
1. Personnel management. 2. Strategic planning. I. Title.
HF5549.K6662   1996   658.3--dc20   96-13813 CIP

ISBN 0-7618-0331-9 (pbk: alk. ppr.)

⊖™The paper used in this publication meets the minimum
requirements of American National Standard for information
Sciences—Permanence of Paper for Printed Library Materials,
ANSI Z39.48—1984

Table of Contents

Readings

Cases

Selection

Cases

Cases

Cases

Improving Employee Motivation
in Today's Business Environment

**A wide gap exists between what workers want and what
management thinks they want from their jobs.**

In today's complex business world with rapidly changing technology,
crumbling traditions, and growing pressures from labor unions,
stockholders, consumer groups, and militant minority groups (both within
and outside the organization), employee motivation has become both more
difficult and more important than ever before.

People today are subjected to a more varied and less stable set of
influences than in the past. Local traditions and conventional wisdom are
no longer the chief determinants of most people's ideas. Although basic
human nature has not changed, the information available to us for shaping
our ideas about ourselves and our jobs has increased explosively. As our
ideas have become less predictable, so has our behavior.

Ever since 1972 when workers at the General Motors plant in
Lordstown, Ohio, walked off their jobs for 22 days to protest the monotony
of their work, American concern with worker discontent has grown.

Evidence of this discontent was found by Studs Terkel while developing
material for his book, *Working*. Terkel conducted literally hundreds of
interviews with working men and women all over the country. When
asked to condense into a few words the result of these interviews, his
response was "loneliness and boredom." "The price our nation is paying
from manifestations of work alienation is staggering: underproduction,
poor quality, sabotage, turnover, absenteeism, and alcoholism are but a
few of them."[1]

Keeping employees motivated so as to accomplish company objectives
in the face of growing obstacles is one of the major keys to business
success. Consequently, over the past several years a great deal of research
has been conducted by both managerial and behavioral scientists on the
subject of motivation. A wide range of theories and differing viewpoints
have evolved. The purpose of this article is to compare some of the more
significant theories and viewpoints on motivation and suggest some
practical steps which, if followed, should improve motivation in any
organization today.

1

Definitions and Theories of Motivation

Disagreements and conflicting definitions frequently appear in the literature on the subject of motivation. Many writers, however, conclude that the various theories on motivation are not really incompatible but deal with different aspects of the entire motivation process.

Motivation theories can generally be classified as either process theories or content theories.[2]

Process Theories

Motivation in the more traditional sense refers to the process of stimulating people to act and to accomplish desired goals. In other words, motivation is a function that a manager performs to get subordinates to achieve job objectives. Process theories of motivation generally are based on the assumption that behavior which leads to rewards tends to be repeated, while behavior which does not lead to rewards will not be repeated. These theories consider pay as the major motivating factor. Expectancy theory and equity theory are among the significant types of process theories.

Expectancy theory assumes that people have certain built-in beliefs (reinforced by management attitudes) regarding their expected roles within an organization and that their behavior must conform to these roles. If they conform, they then expect a certain level of compensation. Expectancy theory holds that individuals perceive their compensation to be just or unjust based on its relationship to their performance.

Equity theory assumes that each individual is most concerned with personal contribution and expected outcome (for example, income) compared to one's peers. Equity theory holds that the individual's compensation-performance comparison for themselves is only deemed just or unjust when it is compared to this relationship for others.

Content Theories

Instead of viewing motivation as a management process, it can also be looked at from the standpoint of the individual being motivated. People act differently because of different personal experiences. These differences, in turn, cause each person to view the work situation in a manner not quite identical to fellow employees. Content theories of motivation focus on individual motives that relate to job performance. A few of the more popular content theories are discussed below.

  - The *achievement motivation* theory hypothesizes that individuals who derive satisfaction from resolving difficult problems, influencing others, making decisions, and achieving results possess achievement motivation. This theory tends to explain the motivation of higher-level executives.
  - *Need hierarchy* and *self-actualization theories* assume that employees have a hierarchy of needs, and that as more basic needs - such as food, shelter, and security - are fulfilled, they become more concerned with higher-level needs such as self-actualization.
  - The *two-factor theory* divides motivation into intrinsic, or job content factors, and extrinsic, or hygienic factors.[3] Under this theory, the hygienic factors like wages and working conditions do not actually motivate, they merely minimize dissatisfaction. On the other hand, intrinsic factors such as "full appreciation for work performed" contribute to real job satisfaction and serve as motivators.

Process Versus Content Theories: Two Sides of the Same Coin

  Dwight Eisenhower is credited with saying that "leadership is the ability to get a person to do what you want him to do, when you want it done, in a way you want it done, because he wants to do it." [4] This quote is representative of the process approach to motivation. Rensis Likert termed motivation the core of management and concluded that "the nature of human motivation shows that every human being earnestly seeks a secure, friendly, and supportive relationship which gives him a sense of worth in face-to-face groups which are most important to him...a superior should strive to treat individuals with dignity and a recognition for their personal worth." [5] This quote is representative of the content approach to motivation.

What People Want from Their Work

  To some people, their jobs while pleasant (or at least not distasteful) are, nevertheless, merely a means to secure sufficient funds to purchase necessities or luxuries for themselves and their families. To others, work while not an end in itself, is in a very real sense, a way of life. To those latter persons, the complex relationships of the job situation - social as well as economic - are quite as satisfying as the economic rewards accruing to the person who engages in work solely as a means of earning a living.

Numerous surveys have been conducted to determine what employees want from their jobs. One of the most widely known surveys was published in *Foreman Facts* by the Labor Relations Institute of New York in 1946. White-collar, non-supervisory employees were asked to rank ten job factors in order of their motivational value to themselves. Then these same employees' immediate supervisors were asked to rank the factors as they thought the employees had. The results are presented in Table 1.

Table 1

What People Want from Their Work

Employee Ranking		Supervisor Ranking
1	Full appreciation of work done	8
2	Feeling of being in on things	10
3	Sympathetic help on personal problems	9
4	Job security	2
5	Good wages	1
6	Interesting work	5
7	Promotion and growth in the organization	3
8	Personal loyalty to employees	6
9	Good working conditions	4
10	Tactful disciplining	7

The ranking of items is not necessarily the important thing to observe since conditions have changed since 1946 when the survey was taken. The significant point is the wide variance between what workers consider to be important in their jobs and what their supervisors think workers feel is important. Research, presented in the next article, indicates that a wide gap still exists today between what workers want from their jobs and what management thinks they want.

Wages and Motivation

Traditionally, wages have been considered to be the primary motivating force behind employee action. Wages, however, operate like a price mechanism to distribute the labor supply among employers but do not affect job performance in any lasting or significant way.

Money can motivate or influence action only when the increment is large enough relative to existing income.[6] Most salary increases, bonuses, profit sharing plans, and many commission and incentive pay plans, do not provide an increment that is large enough to motivate any action other than the purely passive action of remaining in the organization.

Employees tend to expect pay increases as something they are entitled to, rather than something they must earn. When the time at which the increase is expected is still remote, the prospect of the increase serves to motivate continued membership in the organization, provided the expected increase is considered to be equitable.

If the increase does not occur on schedule, that fact will generate disappointment and feelings that the system is unjust. If the delay is prolonged, the employee may search for another job or be motivated to complain, not necessarily about money alone, but about all the petty annoyances ordinarily tolerated. Work performance will probably suffer as a result.

When the size of the increase becomes known and it is less than expected, the worker may feel deceived. Although expectations may have been unrealistic, it is likely that the individual will become cynical and mistrustful of the organization.

If the increase is about equal to what was expected, an employee will simply see the company as having purchased continued membership at a fair price. The person will also be reassured that the system is fair; however, *such reassurances only satisfy, they do not motivate.*

If the increase exceeds expectations, productivity may increase somewhat, or the feeling may exist that compensation is being given for work already performed.[7]

There can be serious problems associated with the rapid growth of income, especially when the job is not sufficiently satisfying to the individual. There is a tendency for some workers in repetitive, unchallenging jobs to demand wage increases that bear little relationship to the work being performed. They tend to demand whatever the traffic will bear and support militant union leaders who press management for the largest possible wage settlement. These workers can hardly be said to be motivated by their incomes in the sense of deliberately producing at a higher than usual rate.

Such situations suggest that the monetary drives of some may really have psychological origins, that is, money may be a sort of "revenge" against management, a way of hitting back at an adversary where it presumably will hurt most. The tendency of these individuals to see management as an adversary has less to do with feelings of inadequate pay than with feelings of alienation. Present day management has done little to change this situation.

Human Goals

People are diversely motivated. Each individual's heredity, environment and experience shape attitudes, motives, behavior, and goals in life. The basic needs of people are classified as: physiological needs, safety needs, social needs, and egoistic needs.[8] Although these needs are found in all people, each person places them in a differently prioritized hierarchy, and this hierarchy can change over time. This explains why each employee acts differently and views the work situation in a manner not quite identical to other employees.

Although psychologists are not in complete agreement, there are several generalizations regarding human behavior on which most agree:

1. Individuals strive to satisfy needs on the job. The twelve most important factors affecting job satisfaction are: security, interesting work, opportunity for advancement, recognition, working conditions, wages, supervision, social aspects, opportunities to learn or use ideas, hours, ease of job, and fringe benefits.

2. Individuals differ greatly in the importance they attach to the satisfaction of various needs. Their attitudes also change with time and circumstances and are heavily influenced by the attitudes of their colleagues and superiors.

3. Needs may be unconscious and unspoken or they may be expressed as aspirations or goals. Motivation is weakest when the individual perceives a goal as either unattainable or too easily attainable. Motivation is strongest when the goal is perceived as both a challenge and attainable.

4. Individuals are receptive to changing their ways of doing things only when they personally recognize the inadequacies of the present method

or when they are given an opportunity to participate in the development of the new methods.

5. Individuals resist change when they perceive it as a threat to any of the twelve motivation factors listed in number one.

6. Individuals tend to accept evidence of their performance more willingly and use it more constructively when it is presented in a manner that they regard as objective, i.e., without personal bias, and when the information is perceived as coming from a valid source.

7. Beyond a certain point, pressure for improved performance accomplishes nothing and may, if continued, reduce performance.[9]

Organizational Goals

Organizations were created as a device to satisfy needs that individuals working alone could not satisfy. Organizations were designed to serve people, not vice versa. Once established, however, they tend to become entities with goals of their own. Their goals consist of growth, efficiency, productivity, profits and survival. As organizations grow, there is usually a separation between their ownership (stockholders) and control. The stewardship for operating business organizations is usually entrusted to a group of professional managers. Because of the interdependency of individuals both within and outside the organization, these managers are in a position of great power and influence.

Managers today, as never before, have to maintain the balance between satisfaction of human needs and the accomplishment of organizational goals. The following are a few of the changing conditions that management must adapt to while trying to maintain this delicate balance: ever changing human needs, changing organizational goals, the population increase, rapid transportation, improved communications, mass education, automation, development of more bureaucracies, urbanization, more government controls, increases in non-skilled workers, technological unemployment, higher wages, more leisure time, standardization, and increases in the number of administrative personnel.

To the extent that an individual accepts organizational objectives as being desirable, fulfilling them becomes a need. Understanding and accepting objectives, both organizational and individual, is necessary to work productively.[10]

A Current Trend: Job Enrichment

Job enrichment permits workers to plan and control more of their work, even to the point of encroaching on management decision making. More and more companies think it may be a way to overcome absenteeism, high turnover, and lagging worker productivity, as well as a way to challenge workers, especially the restless younger ones.

As a case in point, American Telephone and Telegraph encourages their supervisors to grant technicians greater autonomy and make each of them responsible for maintaining the telephones in entire neighborhoods. Chrysler Corporation involves workers in departmental decisions, and in some cases, workers are allowed to run their own departments when supervisors are on vacations. General Electric gives machine operators in its Lynn, Massachusetts plant a greater role in scheduling work and devising work rules.[11]

Job enrichment is, however, a controversial concept. Even though it seems to be working in some locations, it has collapsed at others. Among urban blue-collar workers, it has fallen into disrepute.

Frederick Herzberg, who is widely regarded as the originator of job enrichment, believes that workers become motivated when their jobs are seasoned with motivators like recognition, a sense of achievement, and personal growth. Once these conditions are met, Herzberg's *motivation-hygiene theory* implies that employees will become far more industrious.

Critics argue that enrichment efforts are based on a faulty view of human nature. Charles L. Hulin observed that "the assumption behind job enrichment is that everyone can be made to think that his job is his life. That simply isn't always the case."[12]

Motivation Under Different Political/Economic Systems

Motivation appears to be a worldwide problem. A. S. Tannenbaum conducted a study in Italy, Israel, the former Yugoslavia, Austria, and the United States to compare worker attitudes under various political and economic systems.

Although under Communism the alienated worker is supposed to become the "happy producer," Tannenbaum found that workers in Marxist Yugoslavia were no happier or more motivated than their American counterparts. An analysis of American participation indicated that worker participation in plants does make a difference, "but not nearly to the extent" that Marxists would expect. Yugoslav workers participate in more decision making than do American workers, *but their attitudes toward the plant were no more favorable* and communication was no more open.

Supervisors are not necessarily more interested in and responsive to ideas of their subordinates in plants where there is a formal worker-participation plan. Tannenbaum found that attitudes were worse in Italy under the "autocratic version of the way to run a business." [13]

Steps Toward Improving Motivation

What management needs most is not so much a revolutionary *technique* for motivating employees, but a new *perspective*. Once managers realize that the rules for motivating have changed, they can begin making progress toward discovering new and better ways of motivating workers.

Although each work situation is different, steps that managers could and should implement to improve motivation are the following:

1. *Grant individual freedom but maintain control.* Authority and responsibility should be delegated to the level closest to the problem situation. Allowing subordinates to make decisions (particularly those decisions where they are more qualified) fosters a feeling of confidence.[14] It gives the subordinate a feeling of independence and individual expression. It gives an employee a chance to learn and an opportunity to make a personal contribution. Controls can be set up which will enable the manager to take corrective action, in case things go astray. Individual freedom is basic to any motivational strategy.

2. *Create an atmosphere conducive to growth.* Management should not be expected to play the role of mother, father, minister, and psychiatrist to its workers. It should, however, create an atmosphere that affords each employee the opportunity to develop and utilize voluntarily their knowledge, skill, and ingenuity to contribute to the success of the enterprise.[15] It is in this type of atmosphere that management can derive the greatest benefits from its human resources.

Employees should feel comfortable when making suggestions. All new ideas begin in a nonconforming mind that mistrusts the popular image.

Robert N. McMurray stated that great progress can be made if top management can be led to see that (1) their points of view are not the only ones; (2) most issues are not absolutely black or white, but do have some gray areas; (3) they personally do not enjoy a monopoly on the truth; and

(4) because someone espouses a system of values which differs from theirs, that person is not necessarily ignorant, stupid, or disloyal.[16]

Most people can learn to accept and to seek responsibility. The average person has the capacity to exercise a high degree of imagination, ingenuity, and creativity if placed in a proper set of conditions.

The intellectual potential of the average individual is only partially used. The authoritarian leader, by inhibiting the intellectual growth of subordinates, denies their contribution. Management should create situations where employees' intelligence can create group goals to coincide with their individual needs. As a result, the individual, organization, customers and society will experience the benefits.

3. *Foster good communication within the organization.* Most individuals work for a business that provides their sole source of income, security, social status, and self respect. Through feedback, they want to know what their supervisors think of them.[17]

Sometimes, the supervisor may say one thing, but convey another through gesture, intonation, and expression - hence subordinates may complain that they do not really know where they stand. This is precisely where the impact of motivation can be realized. The employee is eager to have the organization confirm an internal estimate of expressed capabilities. Where the supervisor is regarded as a valid source of feedback on performance, good communication of information is vitally important.[18]

4. *Preserve competence.* Competence, after all, is a relative rather than an absolute quality. It is a matter of being able to do what is expected of one. Until recently, most employees were never really free of the fundamental pressures of job security and income.

Today, income is a less crucial problem and people tend to become concerned with such esoteric motivators as dignity, recognition, and a sense of fulfillment in their work. David McClelland stated that money is no longer the incentive it used to be, but is now the measure of one's success.[19] The tendency is to demand more of one's job and less of one's self, and the typical result is a gradual decline in output. Most jobs should not be designed in ways that minimize or deny the exercise of intelligence.[20] With the exception of relatively few people, it is much wiser to incorporate difficulty, variety, and challenge into most jobs. If employees become less competent, an attempt can be made to restore competence with refresher courses, retraining and encouragement.

Management must try to keep the problem of competence in perspective and avoid overly pessimistic conclusions about human capabilities.

5. *Change the organization's structure.* In a large organization, a position could be created for a full-time analyst of, or worrier about, motivation. This person should be a member of every planning committee and every major decision-making conference. This analyst should know as much as possible about what is going on in the organization. However, their only responsibility, or at least their chief responsibility, should be to assure that the motivational impact of all management decisions is weighed before actions are implemented.[21]

An organization that is left to its own devices will seek to run smoothly; and this is all too easily accomplished by stressing what is superficial, by ignoring what is difficult, and by discouraging dissent. The organization whose members accept its ways passively is likely to conclude that its ways are right. But the main purpose of an organization is to achieve results, not to exist merely to create harmony.[22]

Conclusion

To fully capitalize upon our existing knowledge and insights into the nature of motivation and its impact upon human performance, the manager's attitudes must be changed radically. The basic motivational deficiency in many businesses today is the lack of sufficient decision-making authority and responsibility in jobs held by people who are best qualified to make decisions.

There is no actual shortage of decision-making power; it is simply and unnecessarily monopolized by management, especially by higher organizational levels. This is due to the traditional belief that relatively few people are capable of making effective decisions and are willing to accept the resultant responsibility. Such attitudes cause managers to limit their principal task to deciding what other people should do, and then making sure they do it. This type of thinking is already antiquated and will become increasingly distant from reality in the future.

To effectively motivate the people whose work they direct, managers will need to learn to be a "bit of a behavioral scientist" themselves. At the very least, they will need to know how to use the findings of behavioral scientists in practical, discriminating ways.

It is doubtful whether behavioral scientists will ever learn enough about people to reduce the practical problems of management to a simple system that can be applied without a great deal of judgment. However, we already know enough to improve substantially both the individual's contributions to the organization and personal satisfaction in belonging to it.

Robert Townsend, past president of Avis-Rent-A-Car, put it this way:

> Get to know your people--what they do well, what they enjoy doing, what their weaknesses and strengths are, and what they want and need from their job. And then try to create an organization around your people, not jam your people into those organization-chart rectangles. The only excuse for organization is to maximize the chance that each one, working with others, will get for growth in his job.[23]

You cannot motivate people. That door is locked from the inside. You can create a climate in which most of your people will motivate themselves to help the company reach its objectives. Move decision making power lower in the organization structure so it is closer to the level of implementation. Then watch your employees' responses. Those who can handle it, reward both extrinsically and intrinsically. Those who cannot or will not handle it should be cut loose. In the long run, you will be pleasantly surprised, and the organization's bottom line will look much better.

Endnotes

[1] "No 'Heigh-Ho' It's Off to Work We Go," *Business Week*, 13 April 1974, pp. 10-13.

[2] Miner, John B., *The Management Process-Theory, Research and Practice* (New York: The MacMillan Company, 1973), pp. 297-322.

[3] Herzberg, Frederick W., et al., *The Motivation to Work*, 2nd ed. (New York: John Wiley & Sons, 1959), pp. 12-35.

[4] Boyd, Bradford B., *Management-Minded Supervision* (New York: McGraw-Hill Book Co., 1968), p. 113.

[5] Likert, Rensis, "Motivation: The Core of Management," *American Management Association Personnel Series*, 155, 1953, p. 21.

[6] Faltermayer, Edmund, "Who Will Do the Dirty Work Tomorrow?" *Fortune*, January 1974, pp. 132-138. Faltermayer believes that in the case of "menial jobs," the only way to motivate people is "more money."

[7] Gellerman, Saul W., *Management by Motivation* (New York: Vail-Ballou Press, Inc., 1968), pp. 187-196.

[8] Maslow, A.H., *Motivation and Personality* (New York: Harper & Brothers, 1954), pp. 20-35.

[9] Scott, William G., *Human Relations in Management* (Homewood, IL: Richard D. Irwin, Inc., 1962), pp. 43-68.

[10] Newman, William H., Summer, Charles F. and Warren, E. Kirby, *The Process of Management*, 2nd ed. (Englewood Cliffs, NJ: Prentice-Hall, Inc., 1967), p. 197.

[11] "Job Enrichment: Sometimes It Works," *Wall Street Journal*, 13 December 1991, p. 3.

[12] Hulin, Charles L., *New Perspectives in Job Enrichment* (New York: Van Nostrand Reingold, 1971), p. 4.

[13] Tannenbaum, Arnold S., "Rank, Clout and Worker Satisfaction: Pecking Order - Capitalist and Communist Style," *Psychology Today*, September 1975, pp. 40-51.

[14] Davidson, Gerald C., and Wilson, G. Terence, "Behavior Therapy: A Road to Self-Control," *Psychology Today*, October 1975, pp. 54-60. The authors suggest that workers should be allowed to choose their own goals: "As long as the boss sets the goals, workers will feel manipulated."

[15] Kreitner, Robert, "PM - A New Method of Behavior Change," *Business Horizons*, December 1975, pp. 79-85. Positive Management (PM) stresses learning instead of motivation. Kreitner's thesis is that managers should be trained in "proper attitudes" and that productivity increases will follow.

[16] McMurray, Robert N., "Conflicts in Human Values," *Harvard Business Review*, May-June 1963, pp. 130-145.

[17] Minicucci, Rick, "Motivating Employees in a Down Economy," *Administrative Management*, June 1975, p. 20. Minicucci believes that the key to motivation is "rapport between management and employees."

[18] "Personal Problem Roundtable: Motivating the Worker," *Administrative Management*, December 1975, pp. 26-30.

[19] McClelland, David, *The Achieving Society*, (Princeton, NJ: Van Nostrand Co., Inc., 1961), p.62.

[20] "Those Boring Jobs - Not All That Dull," *U.S. News & World Report*, 1 December 1975, pp. 64-65.

[21] Zaffarano, Joan, "Management's Leading Edge: Future Trends - Human Resources Matrixing - Motivation Control," *Administrative Management*, January 1976, pp. 31-42.

[22] Steiner, George A., *Business and Society*, (New York: Random House, Inc., 1971), p. 225.

[23] Townsend, Robert, *Up the Organization*, (London, England: Coronet Books, Hodder-Fawcett, Ltd., 1971), p. 130.

Employee Motivation: Addressing A Crucial Factor In Your Organization's Performance

ABSTRACT

One thousand employees were asked to rank order ten rewards in terms of motivational value. Immediately thereafter, the subjects' supervisors were asked to do the same, ranking the rewards as they thought the employees had. Results were compared between the two groups as well as between subgroups of employees differentiated by sex, age, income level, organization level, and job type. Cases where statistically significant differences were and were not found are discussed, possible explanations are offered, and implications for manipulation of reward systems are proposed.

Introduction

This study asked 1,000 employees to rank order ten possible rewards and found that "interesting work" was preferred in the majority of the cases. If this is the answer, then all that is necessary is to make all of the work in industry interesting and we will have happy, productive employees who come to work on time and do not leave. Unfortunately, not all jobs can be made interesting and more importantly, what is interesting to one person might not be interesting to another person.

The direct supervisors of the employees might not be able to recognize the differences between their employees and make sure that all employees were in jobs that were interesting to them. However, when these supervisors were asked their opinions on what their employees wanted from their jobs, the supervisors claimed their workers' highest preference was not for interesting work but for good wages. If the immediate supervisors are to be believed, all a company has to do is make sure it pays good wages to all of its employees.

The second solution, i.e., good wages, is probably easier to implement than interesting work, but the employees say this is not extremely high on their list of preferences. Thus, there appear to be some differences in managers' and employees' perceptions.

15

This article compares results of three surveys concerning employee and supervisory rankings of ten motivational items, discusses individual differences between groups of employees and supervisors, and looks at the manipulation of reward systems. It is hoped the information presented will shed some light on the question of why workers work and what an employer or supervisor can do to attain full productivity.

Survey Results

In 1946, employees were asked to rank ten "job reward" factors in terms of personal preference. The results were:[1]

1. Full appreciation of work done
2. Feeling of being in on things
3. Sympathetic help with personal problems
4. Job security
5. Good wages
6. Interesting work
7. Promotion and growth in the organization
8. Personal loyalty to employees
9. Good working conditions
10. Tactful discipline

A similar questionnaire was given to industrial employees in 1981 and again in 1994. By 1981, there were changes in what workers wanted compared to 1946. Interesting work was positioned in the number one slot and sympathetic help with personal problems was moved to the number nine slot. By 1994, the list looked like this:

1. Interesting work
2. Full appreciation of work done
3. Feeling of being in on things
4. Job security
5. Good wages
6. Promotion and growth in the organization
7. Good working conditions
8. Personal loyalty to employees
9. Tactful discipline
10. Sympathetic help with personal problems

The workers surveyed in 1946 came from a different environment than the workers of 1994. America had just come out of a depression and gone through a war. In 1994, after almost fifty years of relative prosperity and a rise in the standard of living beyond the imagination of the workers in 1946, it is not surprising that the list of what workers want from their work has changed.

If we consider the list of employee ratings as relating to Maslow's hierarchy of needs[2] or to Herzberg's hygiene theory,[3] it becomes fairly obvious that in the United States organizations have done a better job of satisfying the basic or "deficit" needs of the worker than they have in satisfying the ego or self-fulfillment needs.[4]

In each of the 1946, 1981, and 1994 studies, supervisors were asked to rank the list of job rewards as they believed the employees had ranked it. Their rankings remained almost the same for each year:

1. Good wages
2. Job security
3. Promotion and growth in the organization
4. Good working conditions
5. Interesting work
6. Personal loyalty to employees
7. Tactful discipline
8. Full appreciation of work done
9. Sympathetic help with personal problems
10. Feeling of being in on things

The above rankings by the supervisors show that not only had their collective perception of factors that motivate employees not changed over the last fifty years, but also that they have little realization of the importance of Maslow's hierarchy of needs or Herzberg's extrinsic and intrinsic factors in motivation. Most importantly, a comparison of employee and supervisor rankings shows that the latter group has a very inaccurate perception of what motivates the former.

Why have managers, assuming they are aware of the almost five decades of research, chosen to ignore the theories of motivation? Specifically, why do managers continually place wages at the top of their hierarchy and put the other motivators that both Maslow and Herzberg consider essential for job satisfaction at the bottom of their list? Several reasons are possible for the supervisors' apparent neglect of the conclusions drawn from behavioral scientists' research.

One reason could be that supervisors feel employees do not believe it is socially desirable to be interested in money and other basic needs and thus pay lip service to more socially acceptable factors such as interesting work, even though these are not in fact the factors that most motivate them. Or, on the other hand, it might just be possible that employees are better witnesses to their own feelings than their supervisors. Another reason for this disparity might be that managers chose the rewards they have less responsibility for, such as pay raises, which are usually determined by formalized organizational policies, as opposed to values that stem from the personal relationships between supervisors and employees, thus "passing the buck" when it comes time to fix the blame for poor levels of employee motivation.

These explanations are largely intuitive and untested. However, one theory the author believes may explain this phenomenon is what he calls "self-reference;" i.e., managers offer workers rewards that would motivate managers (that is, themselves), but this may not necessarily be what will motivate their employees. David McClelland, in his studies, found that supervisors are usually high achievers who are interested in concrete measures that reflect how well they have done - namely, money.[5] For them, it is a quantifiable way to keep score. As stated above, there is a significant difference between the supervisors' rankings of employee rewards in 1946 and employee rankings in 1946, and a significant difference between the two in 1981 and 1994. Thus, managers appear to remain out of tune with the wants of their employees. Despite a tremendous volume of behavioral research into what motivates employees, supervisors' self-reference is still as much of a problem today as it was after the Second World War. This is a sad commentary on the implementation of motivation research results in the workplace.

Differences Between Subgroups

The survey taken in 1994 also divided employees into various categories, something the earlier surveys did not do. Just as there are differences between what employees want over time, there may also be differences between categories of employees based on sex, age, income level, job type, and organization level. (See Table 1 for the subgroups studied in the 1994 survey).

Table 1 Survey Statistics

1,000 Employees	100 Supervisors* (1st and 2nd level)
Sex	Sex
(S1) M = 622	(S1) M = 76
(S2) F = 378	(S2) F = 24
Age	Age
(A1) Under 30 = 202	(A1) Under 30 = 16
(A2) 31-40 = 348	(A2) 31-40 = 29
(A3) 41-50 = 325	(A3) 41-50 = 40
(A4) Over 50 = 125	(A4) Over 50 = 15
Income Level, Annual	Income Level, Annual
(I1) Under 20,000 = 135	(I1) Under 25,000 = 6
(I2) 20,001-30,000 = 360	(I2) 25,001-40,000 = 34
(I3) 30,001-40,000 = 334	(I3) 40,001-50,000 = 39
(I4) Over 40,000 = 171	(I4) Over 50,000 = 21
Job Type	Job Type Supervised
(J1) Blue-collar unskilled = 350	(J1) Blue-collar unskilled = 31
(J2) Blue-collar skilled = 291	(J2) Blue-collar skilled = 27
(J3) White-collar unskilled = 206	(J3) White-collar unskilled = 23
(J4) White-collar skilled = 113	(J4) White-collar skilled = 19
Organization Level	Organization Level Supervised
(O1) Lower Non-supervisory = 418	(O1) Lower Non-supervisory = 34
(O2) Middle Non-supervisory = 359	(O2) Middle Non-supervisory = 37
(O3) Higher Non-supervisory = 139	(O3) Higher Non-supervisory = 29

* Supervisors surveyed are directly connected with employees surveyed.

When the subset data is analyzed against the total employee response, only two groups do not meet the null hypothesis, which specifies that the distribution of the total response is equal to the distribution of each subset. One of these groups is the under-thirty age group, and the other is the group with income under $20,000. (See Table 2 for comparison of total employee response to each employee subset response.)

Table 2 Response Distribution

	S	E	S1	S2	A1	A2	A3	A4	I1	I2	I3	I4	J1	J2	J3	J4	O1	O2	O3
Interesting Work	5	1	1	2	4	2	3	1	5	2	1	1	2	1	1	2	3	1	1
Full Appreciation of Work Done	8	2	2	1	5	3	2	2	4	3	3	2	1	6	3	1	4	2	2
Feeling of Being in on Things	10	3	3	3	6	4	1	3	6	1	2	4	5	2	5	4	5	3	3
Job Security	2	4	5	4	2	1	4	7	2	4	4	3	4	3	7	5	2	4	6
Good Wages	1	5	4	5	1	5	5	8	1	5	6	8	3	4	6	6	1	6	8
Promotion and Growth in the Organization	3	6	6	6	3	6	8	9	3	6	5	7	6	5	4	3	6	5	5
Good Working Conditions	4	7	7	10	7	7	7	4	8	7	7	6	9	7	2	7	7	7	4
Personal Loyalty to Employees	7	8	8	8	9	9	6	5	7	8	8	5	8	9	9	8	8	8	7
Tactful Discipline	9	9	9	9	8	10	9	10	10	9	9	10	7	10	10	9	9	9	10
Sympathetic Help with Personal Problems	6	10	10	7	10	8	10	6	9	10	10	9	10	8	8	10	10	10	9

NOTE: S = Total Supervisor Response, 1994; E = Total Employee Response, 1994.

When the subset data is analyzed against the supervisor rankings, all but three groups do not meet the null hypothesis, which specifies that the distribution of the supervisors is equal to the distribution of each subset. These groups are the under-thirty age group, the under-$20,000 income group and the lower organizational level. (See Table 3 for a Chi Square analysis of total supervisor response to each employee subset response and for total employee response to each employee subset response. See Table 4 for supervisor/subgroup agreement by factor.)

Table 3 Employee vs. Supervisory Responses

	E 1994 vs.			S 1994 vs.	
Subgroup	Chi-Square	Sig. Level	Subgroup	Chi-Square	Sig. Level
S1	1.28	N.S.	S1	34.28	.01
S2	3.71	N.S.	S2	41.61	.01
A1	22.44	.05	A1	8.52	N.S.
A2	4.72	N.S.	A1	31.62	.01
A3	6.50	N.S.	A3	44.79	.01
A4	9.67	N.S.	A4	86.78	.01
I1	27.18	.05	I1	9.21	N.S.
I2	2.83	N.S.	I2	39.08	.01
I3	1.20	N.S.	I3	46.12	.01
I4	4.03	N.S.	I4	69.32	.01
J1	4.65	N.S.	J1	28.92	.05
J2	9.59	N.S.	J2	24.53	.05
J3	9.13	N.S.	J3	49.01	.01
J4	3.78	N.S.	J4	46.08	.01
O1	11.53	N.S.	O1	13.36	N.S.
O2	.36	N.S.	O2	45.99	.01
O3	4.49	N.S.	O3	72.54	.01

Note: E = Total Employee Response; S = Total Supervisor Response.

Table 4 Supervisor/Subgroup Agreement by Factor -- 1994

Supv Rank	Tactic-Reward		Subgroups Agreeing	Pop.	Percent of Total
1	Good Wages	A-1	Age under 30	202	20.2
		I-1	Income under $20,000	135	13.5
		O-1	Lower Non-Supervisory	418	41.8
2	Job Security	A-1	Age under 30	202	20.2
		I-1	Income under $20,000	135	13.5
		O-1	Lower Non-Supervisory	418	41.8
3	Promotion and	A-1	Age under 30	202	20.2
	Growth in the	I-1	Income under $20,000	135	13.5
	Organization	J-4	White-Collar, Skilled	113	11.3
4	Good Working	A-4	Age over 50	125	12.5
	Conditions	O-3	Higher Non-Supervisory	193	19.3
5	Interesting Work	I-1	Income under $20,000	202	20.2
6	Sympathetic Help with Personal Problems	A-4	Age over 50	125	12.5
7	Personal Loyalty	I-1	Income under $20,000	135	13.5
	to Employees	O-3	Higher Non-Supervisory	193	19.3
8	Full Appreciation of Work Done		None		
9	Tactful	I	Aggregate	1000	100.0
	Discipline	S-1	Males	622	62.2
		S-2	Females	378	37.8
		A-3	Ages 41-50	325	32.5
		I-2	Incomes $20,001-30,000	360	36.0
		I-3	Incomes $30,001-40,000	334	33.4
		J-4	White-Collar, Skilled	113	11.3
		O-1	Lower Non-Supervisory	418	41.8
10	Feeling of Being in on Things		None		

Subgroups Finding No Common Ranking with Supervisors

A-2   Ages 31-40
A-4   Age over 50
I-4   Incomes over $40,000
J-1   Blue-Collar, Unskilled
J-2   Blue-Collar, Skilled
J-3   White-Collar, Unskilled

Males Versus Females

When one analyzes male versus female responses by the Chi Square technique, no significant statistical difference in the distribution of rewards is found between the two. However, when one looks at the ranking of values in Table 2, it is found that females rank "full appreciation of work" in first place while males rank it in second place. "Sympathetic help with personal problems" is ranked seventh by females as opposed to tenth by the males. This indicates that perhaps female employees place greater importance on interpersonal relationships and communication than male employees - a difference that should be noted by managers. Women in the workplace today do have different problems than men because many are still trying to cope with their traditional role of homemaker along with that of employee. This could cause them to seek more appreciation of work and more help with personal problems.

Age Groups

The age groups analyzed consisted of under-thirty, thirty-one to forty, forty-one to fifty, and over fifty. As mentioned above, the under-thirty group showed the greatest disparity in its distribution from the total responses of all groups, but showed the greatest similarity to the supervisors' estimate of how employees would respond. The difference between how the under-thirty group responded when compared with each of the other age groups is statistically significant. The under-thirty group chose good wages, job security, and promotion and growth as its first three choices. This could indicate that because they are new workers, they have not yet fulfilled their basic needs according to Maslow. When comparing the under-thirty group to the thirty-one to forty age group, it is noteworthy that the thirty-one to forty group still places job security high on its ranking but as one moves up through the age groups, the basic needs become less important to the respondents. Thus, industry seems to do well in taking care of the basic needs of the employees, at least for those who stay past their fortieth birthday.

The over-fifty workers have some anomalies in their ranking of rewards. They place "sympathetic help with personal problems," "good working conditions," and "personal loyalty to employees" as moderately high on their list of preferences. Again, as one ages, personal problems become more of a factor. (See Table 5 for the Chi Square analysis of the age groups.)

Table 5   Age Distribution

Subgroups	Chi-Square	Sig. Level
A1 vs A2	22.86	.05
A1 vs A3	33.67	.01
A1 vs A4	84.21	.01
A2 vs A3	14.65	N.S.
A2 vs A4	43.95	.01
A3 vs A4	12.67	N.S.

Income Group

The low income group (under $20,000) also showed a response pattern that was quite different from the total employee responses and similar to the supervisors' expectations.   The responses were also statistically different from the other income groups. As with the low-age group, the low-income group placed "good wages," "job security," and "promotion and growth in the organization" in the primary positions. The next two income levels (through $40,000) showed little difference in their responses and differed from the low-income group only in that they placed "good wages," "job security," and "promotion and growth in the organization" in a moderate position in their list of preferences.   Interestingly, the over-$40,000 group placed "job security" as third in importance. Perhaps the increased income causes a desire to retain it, thereby increasing the importance of job security. (See Table 6 for Chi Square analyses of income levels.)

Table 6   Income Level Distribution

Subgroups	Chi-Square	Sig. Level
I1 vs I2	27.69	.05
I1 vs I3	34.92	.01
I1 vs I4	60.77	.01
I2 vs I3	1.87	N.S.
I2 vs I4	13.53	N.S.
I3 vs I4	5.53	N.S.

Job Types

The comparison of the blue-collar, unskilled responses with those of the white-collar, unskilled workers showed significant differences. The unskilled blue-collar group gave top ranking to "interesting work," "full appreciation of work done," and "good wages," whereas the unskilled, white-collar worker showed a greater interest in "good working conditions," and a lesser interest in "good wages."   The unskilled, blue-collar worker was more interested in "job security" than the unskilled, white-collar worker, whereas the unskilled, white-collar worker placed more value on "promotion and growth in the organization."

When one compares the skilled, blue-collar with the skilled, white-collar worker, fewer differences are found. The most significant difference is that the blue-collar skilled do not seem to place much value on full appreciation of work done. One could assume they are intrinsically content with their work, since in the majority of cases their tasks are well-defined and self-contained, while the tasks of white-collar workers tend to be more open-ended and the worker is more dependent on supervisory feedback for the definition and assessment of the job. "Job security" was more important for the blue-collar skilled, whereas "promotion and growth in the organization" was of more importance to the white-collar skilled.

Comparing the blue-collar unskilled to the blue-collar skilled, one finds the most significant difference between the two to be the placement of "full appreciation of work done." The blue-collar skilled rated this factor sixth out of ten, whereas the blue-collar unskilled placed it as number one in importance. When one compares the white-collar unskilled to the white-collar skilled, a significant difference is found between how the two groups rated "good working conditions." The unskilled, white-collar worker placed working conditions as number two in importance, whereas the skilled worker placed it as number seven. (See Table 7 for a Chi Square analysis of the job levels.)

Table 7   Job Type Distribution

Subgroups	Chi-Square	Sig. Level
J1 vs J2	30.31	.01
J1 vs J3	17.67	.05
J2 vs J4	11.01	N.S.
J3 vs J4	16.56	N.S.

Organization Level

The organization levels were divided into lower, middle, and higher non-supervisory categories. The comparison of the lower with both the middle and the higher levels produced statistically significant differences. The largest difference between the lower organization level and both higher groups was that the lower organization level employees rated "good wages" as number one and "job security" as number two, whereas both the middle and higher levels rated "interesting work" and "full appreciation of work done" as numbers one and two. Again, one must return to the satisfaction of the basic needs before the higher needs are expressed as an important and relevant concept when evaluating employee satisfaction. (See Table 8 for the Chi Square analysis by organization level.)

Table 8   Organization Level Distribution

Subgroups	Chi-Square	Sig. Level
O1 vs O2	30.30	.01
O1 vs O3	61.92	.01
O2 vs O3	7.29	N.S.

Reward System Manipulation

All three surveys showed supervisors feel that money, i.e., high wages, is the major motivator of their employees, whereas only three of the employee subgroups rated money as the most important reward. These subgroups were the under-thirty group, the under-$20,000 income level, and the lower organization level employee.

Why do managers choose to ignore the reward responses given by the majority of the workers under their supervision? This question was addressed earlier in this article, and it was suggested that managers operate under a self-reference system. That is, they rank rewards as they would want them for themselves and assume their employees would subscribe to the same ranking. If this is true, and the author would point to the survey results to show that it is, then how can management be encouraged to base its employee policies on more objective interpretations of employee motivations?

One way to encourage more objectivity in structuring reward systems is to do attitude surveys such as the survey described herein. This survey revealed that supervisors do not know what their employees want and also revealed differences between employee subgroups that management should take into consideration when structuring reward systems. Managers need to be aware that reward practices should be designed to fit the needs of particular persons working under particular conditions. Using the present survey as an example, reward systems could be manipulated as follows for the various groupings:

Males Versus Females

Males were more inclined to prefer interesting work, whereas females seemed to need more appreciation of work well done. Efforts should be made to design the job format to provide more interest to both groups, since both marked interesting work as one of the two primary rewards. Managers should take into account the fact that female workers have more need of appreciation and should, therefore, engage in more verbal communication intended to foster such a feeling. Also, managers should be more aware of the needs of women for sympathetic help with their personal problems and thus be willing to spend more time with them on such problems than they do with male subordinates.

Age Groups

Flexible pay incentives might be used effectively with the under-thirty workers since they seem to be concerned about their basic needs, while the higher age groups could be expected to respond more positively to job enrichment and job enlargement programs. One group, the forty-one to fifty group, placed as number one "the feeling of being in on things." Systems of "top-down" vertical communication within the organization would appear to be particularly effective with this group. Perhaps supervisors dealing with the forty-one to fifty-year-old group could make an effort to include this group in discussions of policy, even if their input and ideas are not always implemented. The over-fifty group places as moderately important "good working conditions," "personal loyalty to employees," and "sympathetic help with personal problems." An awareness of these needs by the manager could make these employees more productive.

Income Groups

The lower income group is primarily concerned with "good wages" and would respond to incentive pay programs. They are moderately concerned with "interesting work," "full appreciation of work done," and "the feeling of being in on things." All of the other income groups are primarily concerned with "interesting work" and "full appreciation of work done." A job enrichment/job enlargement program would probably work for all income groups except the lowest one, while an incentive pay program (piece-rate, Scanlon plan, etc.) might be a good investment in regard to motivating lower income employees.

Job Types

The most striking difference between the unskilled, blue-collar worker and the unskilled, white-collar worker is the difference in emphasis placed on "good working conditions." The unskilled, white-collar workers judged this to be second in importance on their list of preferences and were the only group that rated this factor so high. The supervisors of this group should be able to address the physical working conditions for the unskilled, white-collar worker by simple environmental analysis and reap some motivational return.

The difference between the blue-collar, skilled and the white-collar, skilled is significant in the positioning of "full appreciation of work done." The blue-collar, skilled worker evidently has a high self-awareness of his/her job and how well s/he does it, whereas the white-collar worker has little sense of self-awareness concerning his/her job and needs outside confirmation of its worth. The blue-collar, skilled worker should be included in more decision-making activities, as s/he seems to have a need for being in on things. The skilled, white-collar worker would respond to the same stimuli as the skilled, blue-collar worker but for a different reason. For the skilled, white-collar worker, greater participation in decision-making activities gives him/her the feedback needed to define the job and better opportunities to receive the exposure needed for advancement.

Organization Level

Employees at the lower organizational level would respond to pay incentives and greater job security, and in the middle and higher levels to job enrichment/job enlargement programs. Respondents in the middle organizational level ranked job security in the number four position, the same position as the total respondent ranking. Thus, the insecurity experienced by workers in the industrial sector is a factor that should be considered seriously by management. Evidently job security matters when you do not have it, as evidenced by the under-thirty group ranking it in the number two position, and the over fifty group (a group with the most seniority) ranking it as seventh. The higher organization level group, probably those with the most security, ranked job security in the number six position. Again, one finds evidence to support Maslow's contention that fulfilled needs no longer motivate.

Attitude Surveys

With the exception of two groups, the under-thirty group and the under-$20,000/year group, all of the respondents ranked "interesting work" in one of the three top positions. Jurgensen, in a study that drew on a thirty-year practice in a large utility company of asking job applicants to rank-order job characteristics in terms of importance to the applicants, came up with a similar result.[6] Over this period of time, job security declined in importance and "type of work" increased in importance. Furthermore, Jurgensen sorted the respondents out by groups according to educational attainment and found that higher educated persons attached more importance to type of work, while those with only high school diplomas attached more importance to job security. The author would argue that since our labor force contains a higher percentage of persons with post-secondary education each year, the increasing importance of interesting work is to be expected and will continue in the future. Making work interesting is not an easy task, however; it is much easier to pay more, to make work cleaner and safer, even to insure reasonable job security, than it is to make some kinds of work interesting. As stated previously, perhaps job enlargement and enrichment are ideas worth trying in the future on a far larger scale than has been done in the past. Organizations without considerable numbers of younger, lower-paid workers may well take a long look at these behavioral concepts.

The author would never argue that attitude surveys are the only answer needed to all motivation problems, for it goes without saying that job satisfaction is a difficult thing to measure. It is tied to the expectations of the worker who answers the questions and is difficult to evaluate against a fixed scale of intensity. At what point, for example, do the cumulative negative feelings of an individual add up to an overall assessment that s/he is dissatisfied with the job? Only the individual can make such an overall judgment. However, this doesn't mean that we can't generalize from these surveys. For example, we can say that based on these surveys, it appears that in most cases the basic needs of the worker are met by today's U.S. organizations. That is, wages are not a burning issue except with the under-thirty-year-old age group, the under-$20,000-a-year pay group and the lower organizational level employees. What is important to the majority of employees surveyed is "interesting work," "appreciation of work," and the "feeling of being in on things." Obviously then, supervisors should make every effort to be aware of the importance of these particular values and encourage upper-level management to become involved in job restructuring programs and constructing better formal communication systems within the organization. They should be aware that the employees want to be appreciated and should make an effort to give credit where credit is due, and whenever possible, include all levels of employees in some form of decision making so that the employee has a feeling of belonging and participation.

The more often surveys are taken, the more likely managers will heed them and take a personal interest in the progress of programs that they have initiated. It would also enable them to spot potential dissatisfaction factors that could arise because of changes in the make-up of the work force and in the background of the employees. But above all, frequent surveys would help to impress managers with the importance of taking the needs of employees into account. To know what the specific needs are, attitude surveys are necessary, and because of today's rapid changes in our society and organizations, these surveys need to be administered often. Self-reference, a major problem in employee motivation for at least fifty years, will not and cannot be eliminated or even minimized any other way!

The results of attitude surveys should also be disseminated to the supervisors directly in charge of the employees and not held in the hands of upper-level management. This may help to dispel the false notion held by supervisors that their employees are motivated by high wages above everything else. Gellerman, in 1963, stated that "myths die hard. It is quite clear that money's reputation as the ultimate motivator is going to be a long time a-dying."[7] As the present survey shows, this myth is still alive and flourishing with most supervisors in the business sector.

Maslow would contend that under current business conditions most American employees have lower-level or deficit needs substantially satisfied. Therefore, such management strategies as increasing employee incomes or strengthening job security will not accomplish as much as is often expected. The results of these surveys both bear out Maslow's contention and yet point out that there exists a degree to which various respondents' job circumstances are or are not providing sufficient rewards in each job area. The author believes this survey serves an important function in pointing out both the problem of self-reference in motivation and the differences between subgroups of employees in terms of motivational factors and their relative importance.

It must be remembered, however, that each organization's labor force may well score differently when given the present survey. The results discussed herein may be vastly different than those obtained from a particular employer. The resulting conclusions drawn would, of course, be different in such a case.

What the author has found after twenty years of research and consulting in the area of employee motivation is that it is crucial for the organization to address this area. Employee motivation is a key factor in determining long-term employer success levels. Yet, ironically enough, it is an area overlooked by many organizations. Surveys such as the one discussed in this article must be properly structured before they are administered, and must be properly analyzed after the fact. This is not an easy job, but given its importance, it is one that should be undertaken with all deliberate speed. In most organizations (yours?), the time to address this issue was yesterday!

Endnotes

[1] Kovach, K.A., "Why Motivational Theories Don't Work," *S.A.M. Advanced Management Journal*, Spring 1980, p. 56.

[2] Maslow, A.H., "A Theory of Human Motivation," *Psychological Review*, July 1943, pp. 370-396.

[3] Herzberg, F., et al., *The Motivation to Work*, (New York: John Wiley & Sons, 1959).

[4] Filley, A.C., and House, R.J., "Some Empirical Evidence About Needs Theory, Managerial Motivation and Compensation," *Michigan Business Studies*, University of Michigan, Ann Arbor, 1972, p. 239.

[5] McClelland, D.C., "The Role of Money in Managing Motivation," *Managerial Motivation and Compensation*, 1972, p. 527.

[6] Jurgensen, C.E., "Job Preferences: What Makes a Job Good or Bad?" *Journal of Applied Psychology*, 1978, p. 63.

[7] Gellerman, S.W., "Motivation and Productivity," *AMA*, New York, 1963, p. 64.

Employee Motivation: A Blue-Collar Perspective

Introduction

Since the rise of the field of study known as behavioral science a few decades ago, as much has been written by management theorists about employee motivation as any other single subject. It has been studied, probed, and diagnosed from every conceivable direction.

The author is convinced, however, that a thorough review of the literature reveals one area in which motivation theory has an exceptionally dismal track record. When one looks objectively at the results of applying various motivation theories to blue-collar workers in general, and those located in a large metropolitan area in particular, it is obvious that the implementation of the theories leaves much to be desired. It is understandable that this sector should cause the most trouble, since the jobs are more mundane, unchallenging, etc., than those of higher organizational levels. By the same token, however, if motivation theories are ineffective in the sector where the problem of motivation is most acute, then one must question the value of the theories. The author finds this to be the case.

It is one thing to apply a theory to individuals at an organizational level where intrinsic rewards are meaningful and the organization is flexible enough to allow various reward systems to function simultaneously, and then to find that these individuals have become motivated. The jobs must have been such that they allowed for the easy introduction of motivating factors. It is here that motivational theorists have realized their greatest success. It is quite another matter to work with jobs where the job description, formal or otherwise, does not permit such flexibility, i.e., the blue-collar sector. This is not to say that there is any shortage of *theories* concerning motivation in this sector, but rather that the success when actually applying these theories has been minimal.

Reviewing the published literature, one would probably come away with the opposite impression, but the author would caution the reader to keep in mind that theorists in the behavioral sciences are more inclined to report instances where their theories have proven successful than when the opposite is true. No academician ever satisfied the "publish or perish" demand by consistently writing about failures, and no consultant ever made a name by publishing the fact that successes were seldom realized. Once in a while, such an article is acceptable, but it must be more than compensated for by numerous articles detailing instances where the theory held true. Should the reader doubt this, the author would urge them to look at a sample of research results published by any particular motivation theorist. If these people really realized the success-versus-failure ratio indicated by their articles, there would be no reason for any manager to ever tolerate unmotivated employees. All that would be necessary would be to contact one of these individuals, or easier still, apply the theory. This is obviously not the case, the reason being that failures to motivate do not get the publicity that successes do.

Take Management By Objectives (MBO), for example. Over time this has been one of the most written about theories. While it has been relatively successful among upper-level employees, it has been a dismal failure among most blue-collar employees. (Even among upper-level employees, the impact fades drastically after a short period.) Yet it is clear from a study of the literature that these failures have been skimmed over, and undue emphasis given to the original successes at higher levels.

The Cause of the Problem

As mentioned previously, the problem is particularly acute at the blue-collar level. The author believes this is so because many employees at this level have been conditioned by years of unstimulating, repetitive, unchallenging work to simply accept things as they are. They have come to expect nothing more than a paycheck from their job, and have been taught by labor organizations, peers, and company policies to view management as the enemy. To many, the relationship of employees to management is an "us and them" type of relationship, and employees seek their satisfaction, enjoyment, etc., not on the job, but through more time *away* from the job - longer vacations, more holidays, earlier retirement, etc. American businesses have no one but themselves to blame for this attitude, for they fostered it through their own company policies for generations. Rather than follow the examples of Japan, Sweden, etc., and make the blue-collar worker feel *part* of the organization, they have made the worker feel like a tool of the organization: a replaceable, interchangeable factor of production.

It is only in the last decade that we have seen any large-scale attempt to depart from this position. Here we run into the management theorists concerned with motivation. Through programs such as job enlargement and job enrichment, they have tried to motivate today's employee. As stated earlier, such theories have worked on a limited scale where such programs could be practically implemented (white-collar, lower and middle management, skilled laborers, etc.). However, they cannot, do not, and will not work to any degree among blue-collar employees, the majority of whom have internalized the attitude toward their job discussed above. In such a situation, the introduction of one program of job enlargement/enrichment will not overcome the barrier of years of conditioning. Job enlargement and enrichment programs have as an implicit assumption that the job can be made an important part of the employee's life. In many instances, this is simply not the case.

Numerous times the author has heard the argument from company executives that the reason programs such as MBO or job enlargement fail among blue-collar employees in their organization is that the employees at that level just are "not ready for it" or "are incapable of handling it." Nonsense! That is the exact type of thinking that *caused* the present situation. "People can't handle it, therefore, I will not allow them to try." While there are obviously differences between individuals in terms of intellectual capabilities, it cannot be seriously contended that blue-collar employees are mentally and emotionally incapable of handling anything more than the robot-like jobs that many of them now perform. If they had been challenged originally, their attitude might be far different now. At this point, however, it is natural for them to be skeptical of attempts to enrich their jobs.

The author must conclude, therefore, that not all the blame for unsuccessful implementation of motivation strategies at the blue-collar level lies with the theory itself. Part of the problem is management's conditioning process the employees have experienced for most of their working lives, *before* the theory was introduced.

This is not to excuse the theorists entirely, however, for the rest of the blame is clearly theirs. An intelligent practitioner or other outsider reading a cookbook of motivational theories will find that the theories fall into one of two categories: either they are so abstract and theoretical that nobody with any sense would actually attempt to operationalize them in an actual organization, or they are simply common sense approaches cloaked in academic jargon. Ninety-nine percent of motivation theories and 75% of all management theories originating from academicians fall into one of these two categories.

An additional problem occurs when the researchers study a small, select group of subjects. A look at even the most respected journals reveals that most research studies are based on less than 200 subjects.

These subjects are usually chosen because they are all in one location, or, at best, one occupation, and thus easily accessible to the researcher. When this is not the case, they are most often chosen at random. In neither instance are they chosen to represent an adequate cross-section of an industry, occupation, etc. The point is that the findings, based as they are on such a nonrepresentative sample, cannot be generalized beyond the environment being studied. At best they may give an indication of reality in the particular organization for which the subjects worked. An attempt to attribute universality to such findings must be seriously questioned. Yet, this is exactly what has happened in the motivation area over the last twenty years! Today there are particular journals where the entire publication is composed of researchers talking to other researchers through such studies. No astute supervisor with responsibility for blue-collar employees should take any of this writing seriously. Yet it is those academicians, who engage in such rhetoric to the greatest degree, that are awarded the highest scholarly honors. When honors are based on the published results of questionable methodology, it denigrates any prestige the award could convey. Should such a trend continue, the gap between practitioners and academicians can only widen.

Conclusion

In conclusion, the author contends that implementation of today's theories of motivation is useful only in select environments. He further contends that their biggest failure comes in the blue-collar sector, owing to the attitudes forced on employees at that level by long-standing employer practices.

The best applications of motivation theory cannot be found by studying academic pontifications, but by watching the day-to-day routine of first-line supervisors in a particular organization. There are no universal theories of motivation. Each organization and each subunit has its own peculiar set of values and rewards. The best way for a supervisor to decide what is appropriate as far as motivation of their blue-collar workers is to watch successful, motivating supervisors in the organization unit closest to, or most similar to, their own. In other words, learn everything possible from observing successful practitioners. Many of these practitioners, while not formally educated, have enough common sense to tell academicians that, while their applications of motivation theory may satisfy "publish or perish" requirements, they do not have a chance of large scale success in the real world. Reading motivational theories is no way to become a good motivator. Observing what has worked in situations similar to yours, and adapting to your particular situation is the only road to success. Motivating employees cannot be taught - it must be learned.

The Privacy and Freedom of Information Acts

A new issue of national concern (based on fears about the centralized use of personal information) has emerged in recent years. The issue involves the right to privacy, a poorly defined and vague concept that has been given new meaning by the Congress.

Congressional interest in privacy, reflecting a broad national concern, arose out of the fear that a directory of dossiers and data banks was developing. The misuse, and even the ordinary use, of government record systems threatened to invade our privacy.

In passing the Privacy Act of 1974, Congress specified that the privacy of an individual is directly affected by the collection, maintenance, use, and dissemination of personal information by federal agencies. The Privacy Act was the first general attempt by Congress to define individual rights of privacy by restricting government handling of personal information.

The balance of this discussion will consist of a broad examination of the growth of interest in privacy, a sketch of events that led up to the Privacy Act of 1974, an outline of the Act, a statement of the goals implicit in the Act, a discussion of the Act and the private sector, a detailed presentation of the Freedom of Information Act, and a discussion of the effects of the Act on the National Labor Relations Board.

The growth of privacy as a personal and national issue reflects, to a significant degree, the growth of technology that can collect, store, interrelate, and disseminate information. This technological ability was very limited in the early years of the United States, and interest in personal liberties was directed elsewhere. The word "privacy" does not appear in the Constitution, although the Bill of Rights does contain restrictions on governmental actions in areas related to privacy, such as speech, association, religion, and intrusion into homes, possessions, and lives of citizens.

The concept of legal protection of personal privacy developed toward the end of the nineteenth century, generated in part by an article written in 1890 by Samuel D. Warren and Louis D. Brandeis entitled "The Right to Privacy." The article was inspired by what the authors viewed as misuse of new methods of collecting and disseminating information. In particular they were concerned that, "recent inventions and business methods call attention to the next step which must be taken for the protection of the person, and for securing to the individual...the right 'to be left alone.'

Instantaneous photographs and newspaper enterprise have invaded the sacred precincts of private and domestic life; and numerous mechanical devices threaten to make good the prediction that what is whispered in the closet shall be proclaimed from the house-tops."

Other technological developments of the nineteenth and twentieth centuries had far-reaching consequences for privacy, although concern over these consequences did not surface until much later. The telegraph was invented in the mid-nineteenth century, along with the telegraph wiretap. Photographic equipment became cheaper, smaller, more mobile, and easier to use - a development that continues today. Telephones and telephone wiretaps followed along with other sound-transmitting, recording, and intercepting devices. Developments in personality assessment produced personality and intelligence tests, polygraphs, and other psychological and psychoanalytic measurements. More advanced technology brought faster communications-automobiles, improved printing processes, radio, airplanes, television, and satellites.

Negative Consequences

Many of these inventions were so useful, so capable of bringing measurable improvements to people's lives, that the negative privacy consequences did not immediately become a matter of public notice or anxiety. The use of these devices for surveillance was (and still is) tangled with issues such as law enforcement and national security - problems remote from everyday experience, especially earlier in this century. In 1958, the Supreme Court weighed some of these issues and, by a vote of 5-4 in *Olmstead v. United States*, came down on the side of law enforcement. The Court held that the difficulties in bringing offenders to justice permitted the admission of illegally obtained wiretap evidence.

In a famous dissent, Justice Brandeis discussed the importance of privacy: "The makers of our Constitution undertook to secure conditions favorable to the pursuit of happiness. They recognized the significance of man's spiritual nature, of his feelings and of his interest. They knew that only a part of the pain, pleasure and satisfactions of life are to be found in material things. They sought to protect Americans in their beliefs, their thoughts, their emotions and their sensations. They conferred, as against the Government, the right to be left alone - the most comprehensive of rights and the right most valued by civilized men."

The holding of *Olmstead* - that illegally obtained wiretap evidence is admissible - was reversed by statute, and later by a subsequent Supreme Court decision.

As the fruits of technology improved, multiplied, and came into common use, other changes in American society began to make individuals aware of privacy-invading developments that could affect their daily lives. The tremendous growth of government, beginning with the New Deal of the 1930s, resulted in greater demands for personal information. Social service responsibilities accepted by the federal government at that time required that individuals be identified, measured against economic and social yardsticks, and then categorized for purposes of determining eligibility for personal or regional assistance.

As a result of these and other programs, Americans interacted with their government in an increasing number of ways, and each new contact forced individuals to reveal additional personal data.   Expanding government intervention in the economy necessitated increasingly detailed social and economic information as input for planning and budgeting efforts. The widening scope of government activity in these areas is still apparent today.

With the rapid growth of interstate commerce, most notably in the period following World War II, the need for the collection of commercial information grew evermore. Management techniques to extract and employ this information were developed. Business planning became more important and more scientific. Industry was not only interested in its markets, products, and consumers, but also in its personnel. Large corporations developed the capability to improve the methods of employee selection and control by means of personality testing and other screening procedures. The polygraph also became a tool of some importance to business.

The post-war period was marked by an explosion of consumer credit. In the 25 years after the end of World War II, consumer borrowing increased by more than 2,000 percent. Because of the nature of the risks involved, lending is an information-intensive industry, and extensive facilities evolved to meet the need for more information in this area. Changes in banking technology enabled banks to provide checking accounts at a price that many consumers could afford. One less visible cost of this convenience was the increasing centralization of individuals' financial transactions recorded at banks. The success of the credit card industry contributed to the concentration of financial records that previously had been scattered. The next step in this development may eventually be the so-called "cashless society," where individual central accounts will be used for all personal financial dealings.

While all of these structural changes were taking place, and while people relinquished more and more personal information to governmental and private organizations, widespread concern over loss of personal privacy was slow to appear. Although many factors have contributed to the recent surge of interest in privacy, it is the ever-increasing ability of computers to store, analyze, recall, and exchange information that has focused the attention of the public on the dangers that began to develop many years ago.

The computer is viewed as the quintessential threat, despite the fact that, in general, it is not being used to extract new types of information from individuals: rather, it is being used to bring together, to coordinate, and to manage all of the information that has been collected by others. Thus, the computer could, if permitted, collect and analyze financial information from a bank or credit bureau, medical records from a hospital, tax returns from the Internal Revenue Service, employment history from an employer, educational records from schools, etc.

Virtually everything that a computer is able to do can also be done manually. Conversely, the manual collection and analysis of diverse records is not only time consuming and expensive the first time it is collected, but is equally time consuming and expensive *each* time it is done. Because of the difficulties involved, such investigations are not usually done for casual purposes. Programming a computer to collect information from other computers and to analyze the information is a complex task, but once completed, the use of the program to prepare reports on individuals may be a simple and cheap operation. It is the automatic, mindless fashion in which computers can operate that is perceived as threatening, perhaps generating more fear than is warranted by actual computer use.

Recent Events

Many events of the past three decades have highlighted privacy as an issue of continuing concern. While the effect of these events has not been uniform - some have increased privacy protections and others have established or threatened new invasions - the open discussion of privacy in the courts, in Congress, and in the press raised public consciousness in this area and contributed to the passage of the Privacy Act.

- In 1965, the Supreme Court in *Griswold v. Connecticut* struck down a state law prohibiting the use of contraceptives, because the law violated the right of marital privacy, a protected freedom. The Court found that "the First Amendment has a *penumbra* where privacy is protected from governmental intrusion." The case reactivated interest in privacy rights under the Bill of Rights.

- In 1967, after hearings conducted the previous year, the Senate passed a bill designed to protect the privacy and the rights of federal employees. Similar legislation was considered by subsequent Congresses and was approved by the Senate several times, but the failure of the House to concur prevented the proposal from becoming law. Among other things, the bill would have generally prevented asking federal employees any questions regarding personal characteristics outside those specifically permitted by law, restricted personality testing for selection purposes, narrowed the use of polygraphs, and set standards for disclosure of personal financial information.

- The Fair Credit Reporting Act was passed by Congress in 1970 to insure fairness, impartiality, and respect for consumer privacy in the reporting of credit information. The Act contains rules for treatment of obsolete credit information, disclosure provisions for credit bureau records, and a disputes procedure. However, at the same time that Congress took these steps to aid privacy rights, it also required banks to keep copies of all checks written by customers, and to report currency and foreign transactions of customers. These latter requirements increase the numbers and types of required disclosures of personal financial information.

- There have been a series of disclosures in the press and in Congressional hearings of secret activities by government agencies involving invasions of privacy of citizens. The U.S. Army conducted surveillance of civilians and maintained computerized dossiers on suspicious persons. The Federal Bureau of Investigation has been accused of illegal counter-intelligence and undercover operations. The Central Intelligence Agency has admitted to various domestic intelligence projects, as well as to monitoring and opening mail of United States citizens.

- The concept of a Federal Information Network (FEDNET) as a government-wide system of data processing and communication equipment designed to serve the entire federal community was developed in 1972 by the General Services Administration's Automated

Data and Telecommunications Service. When the General Services Administration and the Department of Agriculture began to take the first steps to implement FEDNET, a wave of Congressional opposition forced a drastic reduction in the scope of the project and an elimination of interconnection features that would have permitted computer-to-computer communications. Realization of the great potential of such a system to violate the privacy of individuals was a factor in the drafting and passage of the Privacy Act.

- In 1973, President Nixon signed Executive Order 11697 permitting the Department of Agriculture's inspection of farmers' tax returns to prepare statistical information about farming operations. When the order's existence became known, there were strong protests from Congress and, as a result, the order was modified and later revoked. The opposition was based largely on the invasion of privacy issue; information collected on tax returns for one purpose was to be used for another purpose, without the permission of the taxpayers and without any controls on the actual use of the data.

- The Crime Control Act of 1973 restricts the use of criminal history information. This Act requires that, to the maximum extent feasible, records of depositions be kept with records of arrest, that procedures for collection, storage, and dissemination be reasonably designed to insure that all information is kept current, that the security and privacy of all information be adequately maintained and that information be used only for law enforcement, criminal justice, or other lawful purposes. Also, individuals are granted a right of access to records about themselves contained in automated systems so that they may check the accuracy of the information.

- Two 1974 laws were passed limiting the use of educational records by educational institutions receiving federal funds. The effect of these laws was to make records of students available to students' parents, to provide for procedures whereby the contents of the records can be challenged, to limit generally the disclosure of student records without the consent of the parents, and to require that schools account for all disclosures that are made.

- In 1974, Congress established the National Commission on Electronic Fund Transfers to conduct a study and to recommend legislation in connection with the development of public or private electronic fund transfer systems. One of the factors that the commission considers is the need to afford maximum rights to privacy and confidentiality for the user and consumer.

All of these events (and others not included) helped educate the public and the Congress about privacy. The identification and discussion of abuses also served to highlight those areas appropriate for legislative action. The Privacy Act of 1974 was the product of these and other influences.

Because the Privacy Act is the first law of its kind, future developments in this area will probably depend largely on the effectiveness of the Act. As with the Freedom of Information Act originally passed in 1966 and not substantively amended until 1974, it is probable that Congress will not make any major changes in the law in the near future. Private sector activities and legislation by the states are likely to be delayed as well, or else based on the Privacy Act. As the Act's shortcomings become apparent, alterations and new proposals will become ripe for adoption. Therefore, the most significant privacy issue for the next several years will be the implementation of the Privacy Act and the evaluation of its provisions.

The Privacy Act

The Privacy Act of 1974, which became law on the last day of 1974, is the first attempt by Congress to legislate general government-wide standards for the protection of individual privacy. The Act was enacted to "safeguard individual privacy from the misuse of federal records, provide that individuals be granted access to records concerning them which are maintained by Federal agencies, establish a Privacy Protection Study Commission, and for other purposes." The outline of the Act that follows indicates the issues that Congress viewed as important and how Congress chose to deal with them.

The Act's restrictions on the maintenance, collection, use, and dissemination of systems of records apply only to federal agencies, except for certain minor limitations imposed on government contractors and state and local governments. A system of records subject to the Act's provisions is a group of records from which information about an individual is retrieved by name, Social Security number, fingerprint, photograph or other individual identifier. The Act applies only to records about individuals and does not cover records about corporations.

A basic premise of the law is that information about individuals should not be maintained in secret files. Agencies are required to publish at least an annual notice of the existence and character of a system of records. The notice must include a description of the categories of individuals on whom records are maintained, the categories of records maintained, the types of sources for the information, and the routine uses of the records.

Upon request, an agency must permit the subject of a record to gain access to the record and to copy it. An individual disagreeing with the contents of the record may request an amendment and the request must be acted on within ten days. If dissatisfied with the result, an individual may appeal the decision within the agency and then, if still dissatisfied, may appeal the matter to a district court or place a statement about the disagreement in the record. The agency is obliged to distribute the statement of disagreement with all disclosures of the record.

Records contained in a system of records may not be disclosed without the consent of the subject of the record, unless the disclosure is specifically permitted by the Act. There are eleven categories of permissible disclosures, including disclosures to Congress or to the General Accounting Office, and disclosures for a "routine use."

"Routine use" is a term of art in the Act, meaning a disclosure defined by the agency maintaining the system that is compatible with the purpose for which the record was collected. Since routine uses must be included in the published descriptions of systems, individuals theoretically will have notice of all uses that will be made of information supplied to the government.

Agencies are also required to keep an accounting of the date, nature, and the purpose of most disclosures, as well as the names and addresses of the persons to whom the record was disclosed. These persons must be notified of all subsequent corrections of the record and of any disputes about the contents.

Other provisions of the Act require that agencies:

- maintain only such information as is relevant and necessary to accomplish a legal purpose of the agency;
- collect information to the greatest extent practicable directly from the subject when the use of the information may result in an adverse determination;
- inform each individual asked to supply information of the authority for the request, the principal purpose for which the information will be

used, any routine uses that may be made, the consequences of failing to provide the requested information, and whether the disclosure is mandatory or voluntary;

- maintain records with such accuracy, relevance, timeliness, and completeness as is reasonably necessary to assure fairness;

- prior to the dissemination of a record, make a reasonable effort to assure that the records are accurate, complete, timely, and relevant;

- maintain no records describing how any individual exercises rights guaranteed by the First Amendment, unless expressly authorized by statute or unless the records are pertinent to authorized law enforcement activities;

- establish appropriate administrative, technical, and physical safeguards to insure the security and confidentiality of records;

- sell or rent mailing lists only when specifically authorized by law; and

- promulgate rules establishing necessary procedures.

Agencies planning to establish or to alter any systems of records must provide adequate advance notice to Congress and to the Office of Management and Budget to permit an evaluation of the impact of the proposal on privacy and other personal rights.

The Act permits systems of records maintained by the Central Intelligence Agency or other agencies involved with law enforcement to be exempted from many of the provisions of the Act. More limited exemptions are permitted for systems of records that contain classified information, statistical data, or information from confidential sources. The exemption provisions are permissive and not mandatory, i.e., they apply to a system of records only when specifically invoked by the head of an agency.

Federal, state, and local agencies are restricted by the Act in asking individuals to disclose their Social Security numbers. Unless the disclosure is required by law or by a regulation that predates the Privacy Act, no rights, benefits, or privileges can be denied an individual who refuses to reveal a Social Security number. Requests for the number must indicate whether the disclosure is voluntary or mandatory, and what use will be made of the number.

The Act also created a Privacy Protection Study Commission composed of members appointed by the President of the United States, the President of the Senate, and the Speaker of the House. The commission is directed to carry out studies of data banks, automated data processing programs, and governmental and regional information systems in order to determine the standards and procedures in force for the protection of personal information.

The Privacy Act presents many difficult questions of interpretation. The law introduces several new concepts - record, system of records, routine use - but does not define them as fully as might be desired. In practice, some requirements appear to be pointless, unduly burdensome, or both. Despite attempts by various courts to set clear standards for the interpretation of the Act, wide variations still occur.

One major area of difficulty is the coordination between the Freedom of Information Act and the Privacy Act.

Privacy Policy Goals

Because privacy is a subject that has recently undergone thorough legislative scrutiny, and because full implementation of the legislative directives has only occurred over the last two decades, it is both easier and harder to define the goals of privacy policy than it might be in the case of a subject with more of a history. It is easier, because the congressional description of goals, as revealed in the statute and accompanying materials, is recent, and because policy choices have been made and conflicts resolved in a reasonably clear and consistent fashion.

However, the task of goal definition is also harder because the lack of experience makes it more difficult to identify all the consequences, conflicts, and constraints that follow from a given policy choice. With experience, the possible can more easily be separated from the impossible and the unlikely, so that the definition of goals can be more realistic and more useful. Subject to these caveats, five privacy goals can tentatively be identified. The discussion includes a brief description of the goal, the reasons for its selection, and an indication of conflicts that are likely to arise with other desirable ends.

Limiting Systems of Records. The limitations envisioned by this goal include not only restrictions on numbers of systems, but on the contents of the systems as well. The maintenance of unnecessary records or information is unwise for at least three reasons: (a) it is expensive; (b) the information may be misused and thereby violate someone's privacy; and (c) the mere compilation of personal information is an invasion of privacy that can only be justified by some legitimate governmental need. Defining what information is "relevant and necessary" (the statutory standard) has presented substantial problems in many cases. For example, how "dangerous" must a person be before it is appropriate to be included on the list of those who may threaten the President? What financial or other information is sufficiently reliable and useful to justify its collection from potential welfare recipients to determine eligibility?

Eliminating Secret Record Keeping. The abuses resulting from the maintenance and use of secret records were a strong factor contributing to the passage of the Privacy Act. Without any notice of the existence or use of a record containing personal information, individuals may be and have been denied a right, benefit, or privilege for unstated reasons. Unaware of the reasons for the denials because of the secret nature of the records, it is virtually impossible for an individual to react.

Openness of record keeping also provides a check on the substantive activities of government agencies. It may be more difficult for agencies to engage in activities of questionable legality, because the existence of the underlying records (although not the contents) is public information. However, this goal is not absolute, and some law enforcement and national security record systems should be kept secret. Identifying those systems whose existence is properly hidden has presented a major line-drawing problem.

Protecting Records from Misuse. In the context of this goal, "misuse" must be very broadly defined. It includes such things as unauthorized access to records, use of records for purposes other than those for which the records were collected, improper sharing of data, etc. This goal is important, because if successfully met, it will alleviate many of the fears engendered by the existence of large and numerous record systems. Individuals will have more control over personal data because they will know how and when the information is to be used. The constraints in this area are the cost and difficulty of proper physical security of records, the cost of administrative controls over users of records, and the possible interference with substantive functions because of restrictions on the use of records.

Permitting Individuals Access to Their Records. The advantages of this goal benefit both the keeper and the subject of the record. Accessibility not only contributes to an individual's control over personal data in the possession of others but also to the accuracy of the record keeping process. In many cases, the subject of the record will be able to correct errors resulting from clerical mistakes, mechanical errors, and other shortcomings inherent in the collection of data. Even when disputes cannot be resolved, both sides of the issue can be presented to users of the record.

The sense of fairness that follows from compliance with this goal is not without costs, both financial and administrative. To the extent that those who compile records are inhibited from including material that legitimately belongs in the record, then the right of access imposes a limitation on the usefulness of the records. Maintaining the facilities of access has required massive revision of existing record-handling procedures over the last two decades.

Assuring the Accuracy of Records. This goal is very similar in many respects to the previous one, differing primarily because the burden of assuring accuracy is on the record keeper and not the subject. The setting of standards for accuracy, timeliness, and completeness of records should not only improve the quality of the records but should also help to create and maintain the appearance of fairness. Because the affirmative responsibility on record keepers and compilers is much greater than for the fourth goal, the costs of compliance have necessarily been greater.

The Privacy Act and the Private Sector

It is well to remember that the Privacy Act was not enacted in response to actions taken by members of the private sector, but rather out of concern over the misuse of information about private citizens by the Federal government. The expressed intent of the law does not have as its focus the private sector.

Members of the private sector began to anticipate and formulate responses in 1973 and 1974 to the then pending legislation which is now the Privacy Act. In June of 1973 and again in November of 1974, *Business Week* dealt with several probable impacts of the privacy legislation. Their concern developed out of a recognition that much of the Act was concerned with controlling record keeping functions, specifically, automated data retrieval systems designed to provide access to numerous data concerning specific individuals.

It was well recognized in the private sector that the issues of the intended bills did more than give slight attention to the invasion of privacy implications inherent in massive and rapid input and output data retrieval systems. It was also well recognized that such systems were being used extensively throughout the private sector. These systems housed massive amounts of information pertaining to the financial, medical and personal activities of individuals and their interactions with the business community. It was also of no small concern to many within the private sector that vast income streams were being provided by developers of the technology for such data bases, utilizing these data bases as products themselves or providing some service or marketing capability for some group of products.

The intended legislation represented an economic threat to the private sector. Concern over the economic implications of the Act had already been expressed within the government itself. The Office of Management and Budget estimated that it would cost some $200 million a year in operational expenses for the various agencies within the government to maintain compliance with the proposed provisions of the Act. It requires little speculation to imagine the concern which developed within the private sector for the possible economic implications of the Act.

Notwithstanding long established precedence, including all that has passed before us in the arena of government regulation of business activity, it is the author's position that much of the anticipated impact on the private sector has not been forthcoming. This position is developed out of an examination of several key elements associated with the socio-political environment within which the bill was made law, the political mechanisms operating among the United States Senate, United States House of Representatives and the Executive Branch during the formulation of the legislation, and the expressed omission of several proposed provisions of the Act.

Separate privacy bills were passed by the United States Senate and the United States House of Representative on November 21, 1974. A major provision of the Senate bill would have established an independent privacy protection commission empowered to develop guidelines and assist agencies in implementing the law, and to receive and investigate charges of violations. House members opposed the creation of such a commission and the Ford Administration finally agreed to establish a two-year, seven-member Privacy Protection Study Commission to give attention to problems in state and local governments and the private sector. One senatorial staff member commented that the failure to establish an overall enforcement agency significantly weakened the bill. The last twenty years have shown this to be an unwarranted criticism.

It is also important to note that the appointed commission membership was composed of five people appointed by the House and the President. This insured the blunting of this commission's activities, as both House and Executive Branches were opposed to its creation.

It was the concern over the purported mission of the Privacy Commission that sent shock waves through local governments and private businesses. However, a thorough examination of the *Congressional Quarterly* and the *National Journal* reveals no comments or articles pertaining to the activities of the commission. It is apparent from the immediate political activity surrounding the enactment of the bill, as well as subsequent impotence on the part of the commission, that a thrust into the private sector was never seriously contemplated, and in fact the issue has not come up since.

The final version of the Act agreed to by both the House and Senate deleted two Senate provisions governing the collection of records by business. The first would have permitted citizens to remove their name and address from a business' mailing list. The second would have prevented a business from discriminating against people for refusal to disclose their Social Security numbers. Both of these provisions have subsequently been added to the Act through amendments.

Although a great deal of legal and historical precedent has been provided to enable the provision to this Act to be brought to bear in the private sector, the political process, as well as expressed deletions from the Act itself, and the weakening of the primary vehicle for implementation outside of government, i.e., the Privacy Commission, served to blunt considerably the Act's possible impact on the private sector.

The Freedom of Information Act

The Freedom of Information Act is the base legislation for the Privacy Act. In fact, the Freedom of Information Act is Section 552 of Title V of the United States Code and the Privacy Act is Section 552 a. of the same title. The Freedom of Information Act was signed into law on July 4, 1966, to become effective on July 4, 1967. This Act is an amendment to Section 3 of the Administrative Procedures Act which first attempted to legislatively address the "right to know" of the public.

There were problems with Section 3, however. The wording of the section allowed withholding of information if, in the judgment of the agency concerned, the information was such "requiring secrecy in the public interest," or "required for good cause to be held confidential." In addition, Section 3 allowed for no appeal or judicial review of the agency's decision. Section 3 was being used to *increase* secrecy instead of opening up the records of government. The problem was that Section 3 was written in broad terms and attempted to provide a guideline for release of information to the public. The text of Section 3 is short and is produced here in its entirety.

SECTION 3 - Except to the extent that there is involved (1) any function of the United States requiring secrecy in the public interest, or (2) any matter relating solely to the internal management of an agency:

(a)   RULES - Every agency shall separately state and currently publish in the Federal Register;

(1)   a description of its central and field organization including delegations by the agency of final authority and the established places at which, and methods whereby, the public may secure information or make submittals or requests;

(2)   statements of the general course and method by which its functions are channeled and determined, including the nature and requirements of all formal or informal procedures available, as well as forms and instructions as to the scope and contents of all papers, reports, or examinations; and

(3)   substantive rules adopted as authorized by law, and statements of general policy or interpretations formulated and adopted by the agency for the guidance of the public, but not rules addressed to and served upon named persons in accordance with law. No person will in any manner be required to resort to organization or procedure not so published.

(b)   OPINIONS AND ORDERS - Every agency shall publish or, in accordance with published rule, make available to public inspection all final opinions or orders in the adjudication of cases (except those required for good cause to be held confidential and not cited as precedents) and all rules.

(c)   PUBLIC RECORDS - Save as otherwise required by statute, matters of official record shall in accordance with published rule be made available to persons properly and directly concerned, except information held confidential for good cause found.

There were many abuses of Section 3. The ambiguity of the two general exemptions, "secrecy in the public interest," or "matter relating solely to the internal management of an agency," allowed for wide interpretation. Some of the information kept secret under these exemptions were telephone books, the names and salaries of government employees, and the amount of the bids for bidders who were not awarded government contracts.

If all else failed, there was the all-encompassing exemption of Subsection C stating that the information could be withheld "for good cause." Rather than opening government records, Section 3 was cited as reason to *withhold* information - a direct turnaround from the intent of the law! The Freedom of Information Act attempted to remedy this by the use of very specific language and by specifying exemptions to the Act.

The Freedom of Information Act breaks down into several subsections. The first subsection restates Section 3(a) pertaining to publishing in the *Federal Register*. This was not a problem under the original Section 3, except for complaints about the volume of information required to be published. The Act allowed information to be published by reference, if the source data was "... reasonably available to the class of persons affected thereby."

The Act also changed the sanction for not publishing from "...no person shall in any manner be required to resort to organization or procedures not so published" to: "except to the extent that a person has actual and timely notice of the terms thereof, a person may not in any manner be required to resort to, or be adversely affected by, a matter required to be published in the *Federal Register* and not so published." It is possible for a person to be "adversely affected" without having to "resort to" the agency. This implies that the agency cannot use the lack of publication as a defense against someone unfavorably affected by unpublished material, another incentive for publication.

The next subsection of the Act stipulates that the information must be made available for "public inspection and copying," for in most cases, unless the data can be copied for future reference, its value is severely diminished. This subsection states certain classifications of information which must be made available:

(a)   final opinions, including concurring and dissenting opinions, as well as orders, made in the adjudication of cases;

(b)   those statements of policy and interpretations which have been adopted by the agency and are not published in the *Federal Register*; and

(c)   administrative staff manuals and instructions to staff that affect a member of the public.

It does allow an agency to delete identifying details from the information "...to the extent required to prevent a clearly unwarranted invasion of personal privacy." Although the Freedom of Information Act is specific in other areas, this area was left largely undefined until the passage of the Privacy Act.

This subsection also requires that agencies index information "...as to any matter issued, adopted, or promulgated after July 4, 1967." This index requirement meant that agencies could not withhold information simply by preventing anyone from having knowledge of its existence, and thus being unable to ask for it.

Subsection 3 establishes judicial review of agency decisions to withhold information under the Freedom of Information Act and places the burden of proof on the agency to prove that the information should not be revealed. It also specifies that the case should be considered *de novo*, i.e., from the beginning, with no reference to past cases. This section also enlarged on the old Section 3(c) by specifying that the material must be made available to "any person" and not just to "persons properly and directly concerned."

The fourth subsection requires that agencies composed of more than one member shall keep a record, and make it available to the public, "...of the final votes of each member in every agency proceeding."

Exemptions

There are nine exemptions provided in the law for withholding data. It is important to note that the wording of the Freedom of Information Act permits, rather than requires, withholding data within these categories.

- Exemption 1 pertains to matters "specifically required by Executive Order to be kept secret in the interest of the national defense or foreign policy." There is a conflicting interpretation here, however. If it is interpreted that only material relating to the national defense or foreign policy and covered by Executive Orders can be withheld, then there are some documents covered by Executive Orders which must be released under this law. This could be construed as an attempt to limit the powers of the President and as a violation of the constitutional provision of separation of powers. If it is intended to permit exemption of all Executive Orders, then the agencies could cite some vaguely worded Executive Order as authority to withhold information. Since the courts have shown great reluctance to enter into disputes between the executive and legislative branches, they will probably allow the agencies great latitude in this area.

- Exemption 2 concerns matters "related solely to the internal personnel rules and practices of an agency." Basically this refers to information intended to guide agency personnel which, if disclosed, would impede the function of the agency.

- Exemption 3 is for matters "specifically exempted from disclosure by statute." This exemption is important, because the ability to obtain judicial review under the Freedom of Information Act allows a person to challenge situations where sovereign immunity was previously cited as a defense. The Freedom of Information Act also shifts the burden of proof to the agency claiming exemption by statute.

- Exemption 4 involves "trade secrets and commercial or financial information obtained from a person as privileged or confidential." This explanation is self-explanatory.

- Exemption 5 is for "inter-agency or intra-agency memoranda or letters which would not be available by law to a party other than an agency in litigation with the agency." This exemption was included so that agencies could have a free flow of information and exchange of views without being subject to scrutiny during the decision making process. It is only after a policy or decision is made that it (the policy or decision) must be made public. There are some problems with interpretation of this exemption. Items like legal memoranda, staff analysis prepared for internal use, and recommendations of experts or consultants are clearly covered, but what about a purely factual report with no opinions expressed? The latter is not protected.

One interesting sidelight is the problem of interagency communication involving Congress. Since Congress is not considered an agency (it is expressly excluded from the definition of an agency by the Administrative Procedures Act), transmittals between Congress and an agency of government are not protected by the Act. It is doubtful that Congress meant to exclude itself from protection under this exemption, but the fact is it did.

- Exemption 6 concerns personal privacy, specifically, "... personnel and medical files and similar files, the disclosure of which would constitute a clearly unwarranted invasion of personal privacy." This exemption is self-explanatory. It was intended to prevent personal information, which a person was required by law to provide, from being available to anyone. It was not intended, and has not been interpreted, to prevent someone from seeing his own personnel or medical files.

- Exemption 7 concerns "investigatory files compiled for law enforcement purposes, except to the extent available by law to a party other than an agency." The intent of this exemption was to prevent any earlier or greater access to government investigatory files than would have been previously available. This exemption includes investigations leading to administrative action, as well as criminal action.

- Exemption 8 concerns matters that are "contained in or related to examination, operating, or condition reports prepared by, on behalf of, or for the use of an agency responsible for the regulation or supervision of financial institutions." This is somewhat of a restatement of Exemption 4 since that exemption protects "commercial or financial information" from disclosure. The restatement was primarily to emphasize the importance Congress placed on protecting this type of data from disclosure. This has had its major effect on the Federal Home Loan Bank Board, the Comptroller of the Currency, and the Federal Reserve System.

- Exemption 9 covers "geological and geophysical information and data, including maps, concerning wells." This exemption also is somewhat superfluous, since the information could be considered covered under the "trade secrets" and "commercial or financial" language of Exemption 4.

The Effect of the Act on the NLRB

The National Labor Relations Board must certainly be included among those organizations upon which the Freedom of Information Act has had a profound effect. The Board's involvement with the administration of the National Labor Relations Act has caused it to be concerned with many of the issues addressed by the Act. Basically, the Board's concern is with the use of the Act for purposes of discovery when litigation is, or may be, involved. The Board can invoke the Act for discovery of information known to private employers, and at the same time these private employers can and do invoke the Act to discover information known to the Board. At any given time, there are anywhere from twenty to forty cases in District Courts involving the Board, in which the Freedom of Information Act is invoked. Thus, much time and money (an estimated $900,000 in 1995) is spent by the Board to assure its compliance with the Act.

Yet, more important than the monetary investment necessary for compliance, are the psychological implications of the Act's interpretation on the parties involved. For instance, if individuals' names are to be disclosed as part of the pretrial publicity, what are the implications of this policy on the willingness of these individuals to testify? Is the opportunity for intimidation of witnesses not enhanced by such disclosure? The author would contend that it is. Most personnel managers will assert that, since the mandatory disclosure to employees of the content of personal and work reference checks by prospective employers, an increasing number of sources have either (1) refused to give any reference, positive or negative, or (2) taken to giving all very positive or neutral references.

We have seen the same two reactions from those individuals asked to testify before the NLRB, since mandatory early disclosure of witnesses' names became the norm. Some of the impact in this area has been limited by court rulings in *Title Guarantee v. NLRB*[1] and *Goodfriend Western Corporation v. Fuchs, et al.*,[2] in which it was held that affidavits obtained by the Board in connection with an unfair labor practice proceeding were protected from disclosure under Exemption 7(A).

Another major concern of the board is the tendency of certain parties at NLRB proceedings to view the Act as a vehicle for obtaining information that is not otherwise available. In the case of *NLRB v. Sears Roebuck and Company*,[3] the Court ruled exempt from discovery documents not otherwise available in such proceedings, i.e., under Section 5, "...intra-agency or inter-agency memoranda or letters which would be available by law to a party other than the agency in litigation with the agency."

Also under the *Sears* ruling, the Board was required to provide memoranda in cases where the ultimate decision was to not issue an unfair labor practice complaint, but was not required under the Act to provide similar information where the decision was to issue such a complaint. This holds even though *Sears* contended that their status as a charged party gave them an interest greater than an average member of the public. This ruling will hopefully remove some of the problem of intimidation of witnesses, since mandatory early disclosure will not occur in cases where it is known that a complaint will be, or has been, issued.

The Act has also necessitated administrative changes at the Board. For example, responsibility for answering information requests under the Act has been decentralized to the regional offices, to comply with the ten-day response time limit as called for in a recent amendment to the Act. A set of guidelines has since been issued to the regional offices, instructing them in procedures for responding to requests made of the Board under the Act.

It can be seen then, that the Freedom of Information Act has had an impact on the National Labor Relations Board in a number of ways. The General Counsel of the NLRB has said that, for the board to use the Act to better enforce the NLRA, the coming years must "...produce a final resolution of the question of whether some form of discovery should be permitted in Board proceedings. To answer this question, consideration must be given to the feasibility of meeting four conditions which are essential prerequisites of establishing a workable system of pretrial disclosure." [4] The four conditions are:

(1) disclosure must speed, rather than delay, board proceedings;
(2) disclosure must result in more actual settlements;
(3) such disclosure must insure against the intimidation of witnesses; and
(4) such disclosure must be available to the General Counsel, as well as private parties.[5]

Endnotes

[1] (CA-2, 1976) 78 LC § 11,363.
[2] (CA-1, 1976) 78 § 11,409.
[3] 421 US 132 (US 1975) 76 LC § 10,803.
[4] Irving, John S., General Counsel for the NLRB, speech at the 29th annual New York University Conference on Labor Law in New York City entitled "The Right to Privacy and Freedom of Information: The NLRB and Issues Under the Privacy Act and the Freedom of Information Act."
[5] *Ibid.*

Comparable Worth Moves Into The Private Sector

Kenneth A. Kovach
Peter E. Millspaugh

Pay equity has been an issue of considerable discussion in the United States for decades. This discussion has led to such legislative and judicial initiatives as the Equal Pay Act of 1963, the Bennett Amendment to Title VII of the 1964 Civil Rights Act, and the *Gunther* and *State of Washington* court cases. Comparable worth is the most current area of pay equity to be addressed, yet major concerns have been expressed over the practicality of implementing this concept. The validity of such concerns is now being tested in the province of Ontario, Canada. For the first time in this hemisphere, an aggressive comparable worth law has been enacted which is applicable to both the public and private sectors. All Ontario employers are now attempting to achieve compliance. To say that proponents and opponents of comparable worth are watching the unfolding drama with intense interest would be a drastic understatement. The implications of the success or failure of this pioneering legislation are self-evident and enormous. Practical support for the validity of proponent or opponent arguments will emerge, and such support may well prove crucial in determining the future course of comparable worth in the U.S. and elsewhere.

Overview

Simple economic justice dictates that wages in the workplace be the same within similar jobs for both men and women. Legislation in pursuit of this ideal was first content to strive for equal pay for equal, or substantially similar, work as it took form in the United States. In recent years, however, strong advocates have urged that wage equity between the sexes not be confined just to similar jobs performed by both, but expanded to include jobs that are dissimilar, but of comparable value. This extension of the pay equity concept has gathered a considerable following over the last two decades in this country and become widely identified as the theory of "comparable worth."

An imposing literature has evolved over the years addressing the subject of comparable worth pay equity from diverse perspectives. Although there have been applications of comparable worth theory through legislation in the United States, these have been confined to state and local jurisdictions, and applicable to only the (government) public sector work places. There have been no instances where a political jurisdiction has imposed the application of comparable worth policies on its private sector employers. Canada has likewise exhibited the same reluctance to move comparable worth dictates into the private sector, until the province of Ontario stunned many observers by breaking ranks.

This article will explore the implications of this Canadian initiative by first sketching the evolution and applications of comparable worth policy in the U.S. The pioneering Canadian law will then be carefully examined from the broader setting from which it emerged to its final configuration and requirements. In conclusion, it will explore the broader implications of this type of legislation and offer some observations as to its applicability in the U.S.

I. Comparable Worth Policy: The United States Setting

The importance society is attaching to pay equity and gender corresponds to the emergence of women as a factor in the labor force. The rise of the feminist movement and the increasing percentage of working women have been the two major factors driving the concern for wage comparability. Demographic changes reflected in the modern American work force, in particular, are instructive.

The Demographic Underpinnings

The stereotypical family unit of a generation ago, with the male breadwinner, the female housewife and one or more children, applies to only 15% of U.S. families today.[1] While the vast majority of unmarried women have traditionally worked, at present in the U.S. nearly 50% of married women with children under two-years old are working, with 62% of all mothers working outside the home. These figures have doubled since 1973, and there is every indication that the trend will continue. In the near future, over 80% of all mothers with children at home will be working.[2]

Part of this increase comes from women seeking self-fulfillment through careers - the feminist influence mentioned earlier. The rest is the result of economic necessity. From 1960 to 1973, family income increased every year, but the level achieved in 1973 has not been matched since, despite the rapid increase in dual-income families resulting from women entering the labor force.[3] One reason for this can be found by looking at sex-segregation markets that confine women to a limited number of low-paying jobs. For example, according to the last U.S. Census, women constitute 44% of all workers, but fill 81% of clerical, 97% of private household and 61% of other service occupations.[4] Other reasons include the average number of years of professional preparation (male 4.2, female 0.4) and average years of job seniority (male 12.6, female 2.4), both of which depress the wages of women and confine them to lower paying jobs.

The earnings from jobs such as those mentioned above, now being filled by an increasing percentage of married women, are not enough to offset the decrease in their husbands' real wages caused by inflation and the technologically forced shift from manufacturing jobs to lower paying service jobs. Thus, the decrease in real family income.

Proponents of comparable worth argue that one of the reasons the above-mentioned occupations, as well as individual, stereotyped "female" jobs, e.g., elementary and high school teachers, nurses, librarians, etc., are paid at their present low level, is because most of the positions are held by women. The same proponents contend that a fairly applied standard of comparable worth would raise the wages associated with these jobs and drastically alter many of the demographic patterns evident in today's workplace.

Legislative History

Congress first addressed the problem of gender pay equity through an amendment to the 1938 Fair Labor Standards Act (FLSA). In 1962, a bill was introduced to amend FLSA requiring equal pay for jobs of "comparable worth." First the House, and subsequently the Senate voted to narrow the concept to require equal pay for "equal work." This resulted in the passage of the Equal Pay Act (EPA) of 1963. Its provisions applied to those workers performing closely related jobs, not different jobs - even though they demanded the same degree of skill, effort, and responsibility and had the same working conditions. Exceptions were recognized to allow for merit and seniority systems along with the quality of the work product.

The following year, Congress passed the Civil Rights Act. Under the language of Title VII, discrimination in employment decisions based on sex was outlawed. When concerns were raised about potential conflicts between the sex discrimination provisions of Title VII and the wage equality guarantees of the Equal Pay Act, Senator Wallace Bennett advanced an amendment designed to eliminate the perceived problem. Ultimately enacted, this amendment stated that an employer may differentiate on the basis of sex in determining pay under Title VII, if the differentiation is authorized by a fair reading of the Equal Pay Act of 1963. By limiting gender-based wage discrimination under Title VII to EPA standards (equal work, not comparable), the Bennett amendment seemed to eliminate the statutory authority necessary to advance wage discrimination claims based on the theory of comparable worth.[5]

This question was later settled by the U.S. Supreme Court in *Gunther v. County of Washington*,[6] which ruled that claims of sex discrimination in compensation under Title VII were not necessarily limited to equal work situations. A claim of discriminatory pay, the High Court instructed, is not barred under Title VII simply because the type of work associated with the jobs being compared is not identical.

Judicial sentiment for comparable worth as a viable legal doctrine was further tested in the celebrated case of *AFSCME v. State of Washington*.[7] Responding to a comparable worth pay discrimination complaint, the State of Washington ordered a study to identify female-dominated job classifications that had salaries falling below male-dominated classifications of comparable skill and responsibility. This study, the first of its kind in the United States, found numerous such classifications.

Breaking new ground, the District Court recognized the plaintiff's comparable worth arguments and ruled in their favor. This decision was subsequently reversed by the Ninth Circuit Court of Appeals. A settlement between the parties prevented an opportunity for Supreme Court review, but this widely followed litigation symbolized the substantial moral sentiment, public opinion, and interest group pressure in promoting the comparable worth approach to pay equity.[8]

In 1984, Congress enacted the Pay Equity and Management Act reflecting the federal government's interest in the comparable worth theory as it might be applied to the government work force. The Act requires that outside experts conduct a study of pay and job classifications of federal employees to determine if gender based wage discrimination is present. In 1987, the U.S. Federal Employee Compensation Equity Study Commission

Act examined and further attempted to promote equitable pay practices within the federal work force.   In search of ever greater levels of sophistication, the Congress enacted the Federal Equitable Pay Practices Act of 1988 to determine the extent that wages are affected by gender alone, across the board, and the role this may play in the formation of wage differentials between male and female-dominated occupations.

This flurry of federal activity has been matched by numerous state government actions as well. A recent survey indicated that some thirty-one states were formally examining their work forces for gender based pay equity.   Twenty states had specifically enacted legislation or adopted policies aggressively implementing comparable worth standards in the state and civil service.   Ten states simply enacted legal prohibition against unequal compensation rates for comparable jobs within their civil service ranks.[9]

Alongside the federal and state government activity must be placed similar actions by thousands of local governments throughout the country. Despite a lack of data as to the precise extent, it is clear that comparable worth pay policies are deeply penetrating the personnel systems of cities, countries and school districts around the nation today.[10] The comparable worth approach to combat gender based wage discrimination is clearly gaining acceptance in the public sector.

Despite considerable public sector acceptance and experience to date, the merits of comparable worth as a matter of broad public policy remain highly controversial in the United States. While proponents argue for the concept based on its inherent fairness, its moral underpinnings, and its impact on wage-based discrimination against women, opponents cite its lack of consideration of market forces, its impact on labor supply and demand, and the seemingly impossible task of consistent, objective and fair enforcement. These opponents contend that market forces such as inflation rates that dictate higher real wage rates for those most recently hired in a particular job, the hazardous or unpleasant nature of certain tasks within a job or group of jobs, geographic location, location-specific inflation rates, and the level of competition for labor within a particular area all make implementation of comparable worth on a wide scale impractical.

Opponents further argue that even if these problems did not prevent implementation, they would cause major labor force movements with no relation to supply and demand of labor. How then are employers to entice applicants to jobs not favored in a comparable worth system? By paying more and thus upsetting the balance again? Finally, who is to administer and enforce such a system on a nationwide scale? Few in the private sector doubt what the answer will be, but even fewer look forward to government intervention to the degree seemingly required.

Although those opposed fiercely disagree, the proponents of a comparable worth approach to pay equity contend that it is necessary not only in the public sector but also in the private sector. For this and many other reasons, the recently enacted Ontario private sector comparable worth law will be followed closely by opponents and advocates of greater pay equity. Its implications for eventually moving an aggressive comparable worth policy into the private sector in the United States need to be carefully examined.

II. The Canadian Comparable Worth Initiative

Canadian public policy concerning gender based wage discrimination has undergone the same evolution as in the United States. Defined initially as comparisons between substantially similar jobs, the working definition of "equal pay" is gradually being expanded to jobs which may be dissimilar, but of comparable value. Unlike the United States, Canadian pay equity legislation has not been confined only to the public sector.

Equal Pay Laws: Legislative Background

Equal pay legislation in Canada first began to appear in the provinces and territories some four decades ago. Following the lead of Ontario in 1951,[11] subsequently enacted legislation in all provincial jurisdictions generally mandates that women be paid the same as men for equal or "substantially similar" work.[12]

At the national level, the principle of equal pay is addressed in careful detail in the Canadian Human Rights Act. Enacted in the mid-1970s, evidence of the Canadian evolution toward a comparable worth view of pay equity appears in the language of this statute. Under the title of "Equal Wages," the legislation clearly states that wage differentials between male and female employees are illegally discriminatory if both are performing "work of equal value." This law and the provincial pay equity laws throughout Canada are enforced by the Canadian Human Rights Commission, provincial departments of labor, or human rights agencies, separately or in combination.

Despite long standing pay equity provisions in Canadian law, survey data in the 1980s suggested that a substantial wage gap between men and women persisted. For example, female average occupational earnings as a percentage of male average earnings was 59.4 percent, a full seven years after the Human Rights Act was passed, with a range across occupations of 46 to 68 percent.[13] Even comparisons between the same occupations within the same firm reflected wage disparities between 10 to 20 percent.[14] Reasons advanced to explain the lack of sufficient progress under existing pay equity law included the prevailing narrow interpretation of the laws and the extent of their enforcement. Despite the support for a comparable worth approach to attaining pay equity on the part of a growing number of lawmakers and public policy advocates, existing laws were being interpreted to apply only to the same or similar jobs within the same firm. Enforcement was found to be lacking, because most laws were passive or essentially reactive in posture - merely declaring a general prohibition against gender based wage discrimination. Cited also were impediments to meaningful litigation in the courts, such as the unavailability of class actions and a specific-intent burden-of-proof associated with enforcing some of the prevailing statutes.[15] It is largely the disappointing results experienced under the old regime that are fueling support for today's aggressive, proactive pay equity legislation utilizing comparable worth standards.

The Ontario Experiment:
Proactive Comparable Worth Pay Equity

Before its daring new comparable worth law took effect, Ontario's long-standing pay equity statute carried the title "Equal Pay for Equal Work" and predictably set up a standard prohibition against gender based wage discrimination between "substantially the same kind of work in the same establishment, the performance of which requires substantially the same skill, effort and responsibility, and which is performed under similar working conditions..."[16] Impatient with the marginal results this traditional approach had produced over the years, the government began work on pay equity legislative reform in the fall of 1985.

Drawing on legislative ideas already emerging in Manitoba, Ontario first proceeded on the notion that two separate statutes would be necessary - one for the public sector and the other for the private sector. Through a lengthy two year process that enlisted the participation of the Province's citizenry and organized interest groups, the legislative provisions applicable to both sectors were ultimately combined into a single law.

Secure in its determination and expertise to write legislation for its own employees, the provincial government concentrated on an approach best suited to private sector regulation. To stimulate public discussion on the proposition of extending an aggressive comparable worth law to cover the province's private economy, the Ontario government issued a document entitled "Green Paper on Pay Equity."[17] A panel of distinguished citizens was then appointed which conducted public hearings on the proposition all across the province, gathering ideas and gauging public sentiment. At the same time, advisory groups from business and organized labor were appointed to advise the Premier and senior government officials at regular intervals as the legislation was being developed.

The result was the enactment of the Pay Equity Act of 1987 by the Ontario Legislative Assembly, with its provisions enforced as of January 1, 1988. This precedent setting law defines male and female job classes, establishes evaluative criteria, mandates equality of pay between classes of comparable worth in both the public and private sectors, and creates two permanent government agencies to insure its enforcement. A close look at each of the law's five major parts is instructive.

Part I: Definitions and Purpose

The act's singular purpose is "to redress systemic gender discrimination in compensation for work performed by employees in female jobs" [Sec. 4(1)]. Discrimination in this form is identified by comparing each male and female job class in an organization in terms of compensation for the work performed and its value. Female job classes are defined as those comprised of 60 percent or more female members, while male job classes are considered to be those with 70 percent or more male members [Sec. 1(1)].

The formulation employed to place a value on each designated job class specifies the applicable criterion. The criterion is described as "a composite of the skill, effort and responsibility normally required in the performance of the work and the conditions under which it is normally performed" [Sec. 5(1)]. Nowhere in the law is it specified how the skill, effort and responsibility are to be evaluated. Thus far, most firms are using the point system of job evaluation to assess the level of each factor.

Once job class valuation has been completed, if the employer's work force contains a trade union, only job classes contained within the bargaining unit may be compared. The same rule holds for comparisons of job classes established within that segment of the work force falling outside a bargaining unit [Sec. 6(4)].

The act specifically prohibits employers from reducing the compensation of any employee or position to meet the new pay-equity requirements [Sec. 9(1)].

Part II: Implementation: Public Sector and Large Private Sector Employers

Where wage discrepancies appear, employers are required to prepare and post their pay equity plans in the workplace. The employer with a segment of its employees within a bargaining unit and the remainder without, must prepare a separate plan for each [Sec. 14(1)]. Employees not part of a bargaining unit have 90 days from posting to suggest changes in the employer's proposed plan. Whether these are incorporated or not is left to the discretion of the employer [Sec. 15(4)(5)].

The pay equity plan and wage adjustment posting deadlines under the new law are summarized in the following table:

Pay Equity Plan Requirements[18]

Location	No. of Employees	Mandatory Posting	Wage Adjustment
Public Sector	All	January 1, 1990	January 1, 1990
Private Sector	500 or more	January 1, 1990	January 1, 1991
	100-499	January 1, 1991	January 1, 1992
	50-99*	January 1, 1992	January 1, 1993
	10-49*	January 1, 1993	January 1, 1994

*Employers with 10 to 99 employees *may elect* to post a pay equity plan.

If an employer and the employees cannot agree on a plan, the Pay Equity Commission is to be notified [Sec. 15(7)]. A review officer is then assigned to investigate and effect a settlement. Failing a settlement, the review officer is empowered to choose the plan and order it placed into effect. Objection from either party to the review officer's disposition can be filed with the Commission within 30 days, in which case a tribunal (discussed below) shall make a final resolution of the matter (Sections 16, 17).

Part III: Implementation: Small Private Sector Employers

Formal pay equity plans for employers of more than nine but less than 100 employees are optional (Sec. 19). Should the employer choose to establish a plan, however, it would then be subjected to the same posting, amending, and formal objection requirements established for mandatory plans (Sec. 20).

Part IV: Enforcement

The creation of a formal Hearings Tribunal and a discussion of its powers are found in this section. Among the powers allocated to the Hearings Tribunal are the authority, when necessary, to order a review officer to prepare a pay equity plan for an establishment (at the employer's and the bargaining agent's expense), to order reinstatement of an employee's job and previous pay level, to order back pay and wage adjustments, and to order revisions in an employer's pay equity plan [Sec. 25(2)]. Failure to comply with any provision of the act or any order issued by the Hearings Tribunal can result in fines of up to $2,000 in the case of individuals, and up to $25,000 in the case of firms or bargaining units.

Part V: Administration

This section describes the various institutional arrangements referred to briefly in the proceedings parts of the statute. For example, the creation and establishment of a "Pay Equity Commission of Ontario" is to consist of two sub-agencies, the "Pay Equity Hearing Tribunal" mentioned above, and the "Pay Equity Office" [Sec. 27(1)(2)].

The Hearings Tribunal is similar in concept to the Industrial Tribunals introduced into British industrial relations in the mid-1960s. Pay Equity Hearing Tribunals are to be comprised of a presiding officer and deputy officer, and include representatives from employers and employees in equal numbers [Sec. 28(1)].

The Pay Equity Office is conceived as a permanent provincial agency responsible for the ongoing enforcement of the provisions of the Act and the orders of the Hearings Tribunal [Sec. 33(1)].

Finally, the pay-equity review officer, as the foot-soldier of the statute's implementation and enforcement programs, is granted unsettling powers by current United State's standards. In pursuit of investigatory authority, the review officer is empowered to enter any premises at any time, request the production of relevant documents, remove those documents for purposes of making copies, and to interrogate persons (subject to their right to have counsel or another present) [Sec. 34(3)].

Employer Experience To Date

The preceding table showed that the first group to comply did not have to take any posting or wage adjustment actions until January 1, 1990, so it is now possible to look at the experiences from those companies who were first required to meet the law's provisions.

The two large employers who are further along the road to compliance than any others are Warner-Lambert, the Canadian arm of the Morris Plains, N.J., pharmaceutical company, and T. Eaton Company, the Toronto based retailer. At Warner-Lambert, an eight factor point system was used to determine comparable jobs. The plan was posted for employees to see and there was almost no negative feedback. Donald Henley, Director of Employee Relations, attributes the ease with which the plan has advanced to the lack of labor organizations within the company. The company is pleasantly surprised at the amount of positive employee feedback from those whose jobs were not directly affected.

T. Eaton Company has 15,000 employees in 580 jobs within Ontario and in the past, had used a different evaluation system at each of three organizational levels. To comply with the new legislation, the company went to a computer scored version of the Weighted Job Questionnaire, modified specifically for T. Eaton. According to William E. Robinson, Compensation Manager, completion of this task required four full-time employees, and the results continue to cost the company "quite a few million dollars annually" in equity adjustments. On the other hand, he notes benefits of increased internal communication including a monthly bulletin devoted solely to company actions relative to the law, and an awareness of compensation inequities that had gone undetected in the past.

In at least one heavily unionized sector, all major employers have come together in an attempt to achieve compliance. In the retail food industry where all employers deal with the United Food and Commercial Workers' Union, the industry has bargained as one with the union in an attempt to arrive at one overall plan. Here again, the point system is being used, but major problems have arisen in reaching agreement about points assigned within each job factor for particular jobs. If this one situation is any indication of what lies ahead, large unionized firms or industries are going to have severe problems.

Wyatt Company, a Toronto-based consulting company, is presently working with over fifty firms on compliance with the law. Sizes range from 200 to 20,000 employees and include many U.S. subsidiaries. The major problem Wyatt clients are encountering is similar to that in the food industry - that is reaching agreement with bargaining agents over details of the plan. Those clients of Wyatt who are still struggling with formulation of their plan are those who have labor forces represented by automobile, steel and hotel workers' unions. To date, the Pay Equity Commission has received over eighty formal complaints from unions under the Pay Equity Act according to Nanette Weiner, the Commission Research Manager. Some employers have deliberately let deadlines pass without complying. The rationale here is obvious when one considers that the maximum fine is $25,000, while the difference between the plans proposed by the employer and the union is often several hundred thousand dollars. The lesson here for the U.S. is that, if such legislation is enacted in this country, economic sanctions may not be enough, and if they are all that is available, the size of the fine should serve as a deterrent to even the largest employers.

III. A Canadian Model For The American Workplace

As the Ontario Pay Equity Act went into effect, attempts were undertaken to gauge its success. With accumulated experience, the statute's impact on the political, social and economic life of the province will become more clear. In turn, this outcome will bear heavily on the influence this legislation will exert on lawmakers in the United States. For the present, there are certain particular features of the legislation that should be noted and monitored.

Perspectives on the Ontario Law

The salient feature of this law distinguishes it from previous United States and Canadian laws: its proactive imposition of comparable worth wage scales on the private sector. Less obvious, but of equal importance, is its focus on jobs, as opposed to individual employees. The evaluations and comparisons called for by the statute pertain to job classes, not the workers themselves. Because the law represents a crusade against discriminatory wages paid to female-dominated job classes, it is only these jobs which can be affected. Therefore, the workers who stand to benefit are confined to those employed in female-dominated job classes found to be underpaid in comparison with a comparable male-dominated class within the same establishment.

It is an intriguing irony that the structure of this approach to pay equity inevitably boosts the male worker minority, as well as female workers, in those female-dominated classes where wage adjustments will be required under the law. Disappointedly, the same structural limitations prevent the law from reaching those female employees who suffer from gender based wage discrimination, but fall outside a female-dominated job class. Because of these design limitations, the present Ontario legislation can never be said to ensure fair compensation for all female employees, let alone employees of both genders.

Another obscure but important feature of the law pertains to the mechanics of evaluating job classes. Beyond the statutory requirement to take the criteria of skill, effort, responsibility and working conditions into consideration, the precise type of job evaluation scheme is left to the employer's discretion. This represents an area with potential for ongoing conflict between the Pay Equity Commission and the provincial employers it must regulate. Its implementation could be extremely thorny and will bear watching.

Of far-reaching consequence is the statutory role envisioned for labor unions. In essence, implementation of the act, as it pertains to union members, is made largely a subject and function of collective bargaining. Presumably, this allows critical aspects of how the law is to be applied to this segment of the work force to be negotiated between unions and employers. Permitting key determinations of what constitutes a single "establishment" or "gender dominance" to be made through negotiation seems to put the employee who is a union member on a footing different from that of a non-union counterpart. In many respects, this feature of the new law would appear to benefit the unionized employee by virtue of the leverage which collective bargaining affords.   One can argue that organized labor lobbying may have come into play here. Were glaring discrepancies in the statute's application to begin appearing between the unionized and non-unionized employee, the credibility and full acceptance of the new law would be seriously impaired.

The final feature of this legislation which should not be overlooked pertains to the surprisingly broad categories of exempted wage discrepancies. Until some experience is gained, it is difficult to estimate the size of the hole that the exemption for wage differentials based on seniority, merit, temporary training, etc., will put in the overall legislative scheme. It is unlikely that employers will seek wholesale refuge in these exclusions, but the incentive to move in this direction is certainly present. Whether or not the exceptions ultimately overrun the rule, the swath they cut is certain to be wide.

The Ontario Law's Adaptability to the
United States

The adaptability of the Ontario legislative scheme to federal or local jurisdictions in the United States seems highly unlikely for the foreseeable future. Opposition to comparable worth policies remains vocal and well organized among business organizations and others.   The aggressive scheme adopted by Ontario might be more palatable in the U.S. if confined to the public sector where comparable worth measures are gaining some degree of acceptability.   Private sector mandates such as these, however, would predictably encounter stiff opposition in this country.

Private sector commercial interests opposed the Ontario legislation in its initial form.   This caused Canadian lawmakers to accommodate a number of the business communities' concerns in the design and language of the legislation. Fully cognizant that moving comparable worth dictates into the private sector would raise problems unequal to the public sector's, the matter was studied intently.[19]   The statutory accommodations to business interests ultimately adopted are particularly instructive to American policy analysts, since comparable worth critics in the United States cite essentially the same objections.

The Ontario framers contemplated the concern that employers may be unable to afford the required wage adjustments and that higher wages would lead to higher consumer prices and reduce much of the competitive advantage enjoyed by provincial employers. The lawmakers' response was to phase in pay equity requirements starting with those sectors most easily able to make the adjustment, i.e., the public sector and large private sector employers, followed by private firms of decreasing size. It was felt that the smaller firms could benefit with more time to learn from the experiences of the larger firms preceding them. Also, private-sector employers were not placed under a calendar-date deadline for full compliance, as long as a minimum of one percent of the previous year's payroll was devoted to wage adjustments annually.

To offset concerns that the law would intervene in labor markets as it standardized wages across the entire province, the law limited wage comparisons geographically to single establishments, even though geographically dispersed establishments may share the same ownership. Wage comparisons were also limited to prohibit the matching of union with non-union jobs, or the matching of job classes between different unions whenever possible. Wage control and standardization were further relaxed by allowing pay equity plans and their implementation for unionized employees to be worked out through collective bargaining. Also, the statutory exemptions for established practices, e.g., seniority preferences and merit pay, can be viewed as an attempt to preserve certain wage setting prerogatives important to the private sector.

IV. Observations and Conclusions

A private sector experiment with mandatory comparable worth standards has now been instituted in the Canadian province of Ontario. The neighboring province of Manitoba is preparing similar legislation. Drawn with elaborate care in an attempt to accommodate private sector interests, the Ontario legislation still carries liabilities which would be considered unacceptable by contemporary U.S. standards.   These shortcomings can be briefly summarized:

1. The problems which have long plagued the comparable worth theory of pay equity have not been overcome through this legislation. A meaningful and practical definition of "job worth" remains elusive, as does the basis for job class comparison with the requisite precision. The problems applying these amorphous concepts in the private sector will only magnify as employer, employee and bargaining agent pursue advantage, while provincial review officers and hearing tribunals attempt to mediate and enforce.

2.   The scale of intervention into labor markets and managerial operating prerogatives would be considered unnecessarily heavy handed from a United States perspective. Only less intrusive means could hope for acceptability.

3.   The benefits sought are unlikely to outweigh the costs. The direct and indirect costs associated with employer compliance would not likely be viewed as appropriate, since the legislation achieves only marginal rate adjustments in a relatively small subsegment of the labor force.

It is certain that this controversial legislative experiment undertaken by our neighbors to the north will be closely followed by both the advocates of comparable worth pay equity standards and its detractors.   The prospects of similar laws rooting in the United States will inevitably hinge to a certain extent on the success or failure of the Ontario initiative. With case studies in process, perhaps the debate concerning the efficacy of comparable worth policy in the private sector can be joined once again. To be sure, the Canadian laboratory is, at best, a rough approximation of conditions in the United States.   Much can be extrapolated from the Canadian effort, however, that will inform the debate in the future. All serious followers of comparable worth would be well-advised to become familiar with, and to follow the progress of, this piece of Canadian legislation. It may well be the most important development to date in the area of comparable worth.

Endnotes

[1] "Job Protection Guarantees for Workers," *Congressional Quarterly*, June 14, 1986, p. 1361, and Samuelson, Robert J., "Uncle Sam in a Family Way," *Newsweek*, August 11, 1986, p. 40.

[2] Giraldo, Z.I., *Public Policy and the Family: Wives and Mothers in the Labor Force* (Lexington Books, DC: Heath and Company, 1990), p. 31.

[3] Mann, Judy, "Families Need These Bills," *The Washington Post*, July 3, 1987, p. D13.

[4] Patten, Thomas J., *Fair Pay* (San Francisco: Jossey-Bass, 1988), p. 31.

[5] Patten, *op. cit.*, pp. 40-41.

[6] 452 U.S. 161 (1981).

[7] 578 E Supp. 846 (WD. Wash. 1983), 770 E 2d 1401 (9th Cir., 1985).

[8] Hunter, E.C., *Equal Pay for Comparable Work: The Working Women's Issue of the Eighties*, (New York: Praeger, 1986).

[9] Patten, *op. cit.*, pp. 74-81.

[10] Patten, *op. cit.*, pp. 97-102.

[11] *Ontario Female Employees Fair Remuneration Act*, 1951.

[12] Abella, R.S., "Employment Equity," 16 *Manitoba Law Journal* 187 (1987).

[13] Statistics Canada, unpublished data from *Survey of Consumer Finances*, 1983, cited in Abella, *op. cit.*, note 12, p. 186.

[14] Gunderson and Morley, "Work Patterns," *Opportunity For Choice: A Goal For Women in Canada,* ed. A. Cook (Ottawa: Statistics Canada, 1988), p. 120.

[15] Abella, *op. cit.*, p. 189. See Nieman, L., *Wage Discrimination and Women Workers: The Move Toward Equal Pay for Equal Value in Canada*, Bureau Series A: *Equity in the Workplace*, No. 5 (Ottawa: Labour Canada, Women's Bureau, 1984).

[16] *Ontario Employment Standards Act*, 1981, Part IX.

[17] Ontario, *Green Paper on Pay Equity*, (Toronto: Queen's Printer, 1985).

[18] Pay Equity Commission, *Pay Equity Implementation*, Series 3:1, March, 1988.

[19] Discussed by the Assistant Deputy Minister of the Ontario Women's Directorate in Todres, E.M., "With Deliberate Care: The Framing of Bill 154," 16 *Manitoba Law Journal* 202 (1987).

A Systems Perspective on the
Uniform Selection Guidelines

Introduction

The legal aspect of employment selection is becoming a dominant concern in human resource management today. Under Title VII of the Civil Rights Act of 1964, as amended, it is illegal for employers, employment agencies, and labor organizations of 15 or more members to discriminate on the basis of a person's race, color, sex, religion, or national origin. Presidential Executive Orders have also been issued with requirements similar to those of Title VII. Within the past few decades, various government agencies have issued guidelines designed to help employers interpret and comply with these federal laws regarding employment selection. A great deal of confusion among employers resulted, however, due to the ambiguities and conflicting standards of the different sets of guidelines. An employer could often be in compliance with one set of guidelines while violating another. The issuing agencies (EEOC, DOL, DOJ, CSC) eventually recognized the need for a common interpretation and adopted, effective September 25, 1978, the "Uniform Guidelines on Employee Selection Procedures."

Application

Under strict interpretation of the law, all employers are subject to the same selection mandate - to provide equal employment opportunity. However, in practice, the *size* of the organization dictates the degree to which selection procedures must be justified (validated). As a general rule, the larger a firm is, the greater the utility of rigorously applying the Uniform Selection Guidelines. For example, when a large company deviates statistically on selection rates across race, sex, or religion, the company runs a high risk of litigation. This principle (called adverse impact) is *prima facie* evidence of discrimination and will be the focus of the next section.

When considering the selection process, two important factors are involved, i.e., selection procedures and selection decisions. The Guidelines state that the full range of assessment techniques (also called "predictors") is covered. This includes traditional paper and pencil tests, work samples, weighted application blanks, interviews, and so forth. Similarly, virtually all employment selection decisions are covered. That is to say, procedures used to hire, place, promote, transfer, train, demote and terminate employees are all subject to review under the Guidelines.

Obviously, it is critical for the employer to understand both their rights and obligations under the law.

Basic Principle

The spirit of the Guidelines can be explained in one sentence. The use of any selection procedure which has an adverse impact on employment or membership opportunities for members of any race, sex, or ethnic group, will be considered to be discriminatory unless the procedure has been validated in accordance with the Uniform Guidelines. At this point, it is necessary to define several terms. *Adverse impact* is a differential rate of selection (for hire, promotion, etc.) which works to the disadvantage of a covered group (EEO-1 group). It is statistically derived by what is known as the "four-fifths rule of thumb." In other words, an adverse impact occurs when the *selection rate* for a covered minority group is less than 4/5 or 80% of the rate of the group of candidates with the highest selection rate (usually whites or males). However, as can be seen in Appendix I, the fact that an employer has complied with the 4/5 rule will not necessarily eliminate the possibility of adverse impact.

When making comparisons of selection rates, two figures are required: the number selected (hired, promoted, terminated) and the number of candidates. The formula for a selection ratio is simply:

$$\frac{\text{\# selected}}{\text{\# applied}}$$

For example, if in a particular organization one out of every three males that apply for a job are selected but only one out of every six females that apply are hired, then there is adverse impact (adversely affecting females).[1] At this point, the firm has a limited number of options. In general, the only practical solution to defending adverse impact is to conduct a validation study. Of course, the employer may always opt to eliminate the adverse impact by either abandoning or changing the procedure(s) causing the differential rate of selection. Unfortunately, the data gathered from a validation study is usually the best means by which intelligent modifications can be made to the selection system to eliminate the adverse impact. Thus, through the front door or through the back, validation is often a necessary expenditure.

At times, an employer may be able to prove that the adverse impact is necessary for the safe and efficient operation of the business (appropriately called "business necessity"). In this case, justification of the selection procedures is not needed. However, recent court decisions have narrowly defined this option.

For a detailed account of the adverse impact process and the realm of alternatives available to the employer, again see Appendix I.

Validation

The process of validation is part of the highly technical and complex field of psychometrics. The major portion of the Uniform Guidelines is devoted to explaining the three types of validity acceptable and their technical standards.

The average person often has difficulty understanding that there are many different types of validity. But, by analogy, there are many different types of transportation. Whether one rides a bicycle, drives a car, or flies a plane to some destination depends on practical considerations, e.g., the purpose and distance. The same is true for validation. The overall objective is to demonstrate the job-relatedness of a selection procedure (or procedures). In other words, validation is the effort to show exactly *what* a certain selection procedure (predictor) is in fact measuring and *how well* it is measuring it. To add even more confusion, validity can never really be measured but instead must be *inferred*. As an example, suppose we developed a test of leadership for presidential candidates. To validate this test, we would first have to show that this test really measures "leadership" and not something else. Next, we would need to demonstrate that leadership is a requisite ability for the job of President. Finally, it would be necessary to illustrate that this test can differentiate between "good" leaders and "poor" leaders. Hopefully, it is becoming clear why validity must be inferred. In the final analysis, validity is a value judgment (albeit, statistical techniques are often involved).

As there are many possible ways to travel from one place to another, so there are many methods of validation. The assumption is that they all achieve the same end result. The following three sections will briefly present the acceptable validation techniques under the Uniform Guidelines.

Criterion-Related Validity

This first type of validity is merely a correlational relationship between the scores on a selection device and the scores on a measure of on-the-job performance (called a criterion). The general framework is:

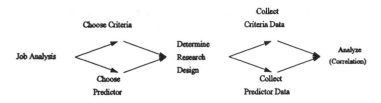

A job analysis is always required by the Uniform Guidelines, regardless of the validation method employed, with *one* exception: when using criterion-related validity with "objective" criteria measures. This sounds easy to implement, but choosing criteria is confounded by many problems. For example, "objective" data measure *outcomes* of behavior in lieu of behavior itself. This means that factors beyond one's control contaminate the relationship between job performance and the predictor. Further, objective measures have limited applicability. There are other complexities to be considered, such as temporal dimensionality, criterion contamination, and composite/multiple criteria problems.

Space limitations preclude the discussion of these issues here, yet the author strongly suggests that an employer research the literature before attempting a validity study. This will not only help to understand the problems involved but also assist in determining the research design, i.e., the type of criterion-related validity study necessary - synthetic, concurrent, or predictive. The assumptions, theoretical underpinnings, and objectives are somewhat different for each type. The most important thing to keep in mind about criterion-related validity is that it is a purely statistical technique. Validity is assumed when the correlation is significant.[2]

Before moving on to the two remaining validity techniques acceptable under the Uniform Guidelines, it should be mentioned that the overall validity correlation may covertly discriminate against a covered group. In other words, a predictor may yield different validity coefficients when groups of candidates are analyzed separately. Unfair discrimination cannot be said to exist when inferior test performance by some group is also associated with inferior job performance by the same group. But frequently, the validity coefficients obtained for two groups may differ significantly when job performance of the two groups is equal; in other words, the test may accurately measure one group, but not the other. The variable differentiating the two groups, be it sex, race, etc., is known as a "moderator variable."

For clarification, a few cases are graphed:

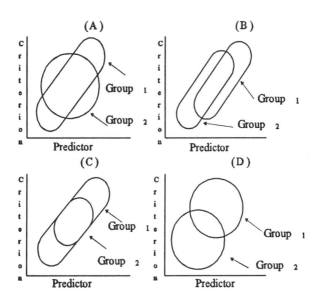

CASE A: This is called *differential validity*. It exists when the validity coefficients are significantly different for two groups, and at least one of these correlations significantly differs from zero. This particular case is often referred to as *single-group validity*, because the predictor is justified (valid) for only $Group_1$. $Group_2$ demonstrates a zero correlation, i.e., no relationship. For this group the predictor is unfair or discriminative.

CASE B: This is called *test unfairness*. There is a positive correlation for both groups, however, $Group_2$ underperforms on the predictor without exhibiting inferior performance on the job. The employer has two options: eliminate this test for $Group_2$ applicants or use a lower cut-off score for $Group_2$.

CASE C: This situation is both legal and appropriate, because the inferior test performance of Group$_2$ is tied to inferior job performance.

CASE D: This is the most clear-cut case of discrimination. The predictor here has absolutely no predictive value for either group (zero correlations). But when the data are analyzed in aggregate form, a positive correlation appears to result. The predictor should not be used for two reasons: it probably has adverse impact, and it is not helping the employer select individuals who can perform the job.

The Uniform Guidelines require this kind of analysis when it becomes technically feasible, that is, when the company has a sufficient amount of test-criteria data on minority members. The present status of minority employment in many companies is such that separate validity studies are either impossible or based on such small samples that results are quite tentative. The current government requirements appear to recognize this practical problem, but they still do not relieve the firm of the responsibility to eventually do the research.

Content Validity

This type of validity is most often simply a judgmental process. It involves making inferences about the adequacy of the predictor (test) in representing a sample of the significant parts of the job. In other words, given a certain job, calling for various activities to be performed in that job, content validity is concerned with whether or not the predictor contains a fair sample of those activities. The basic framework is:

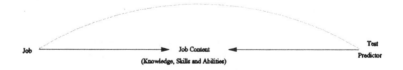

Job ————————————————▶ Job Content ◀———————————————— Test
                     (Knowledge, Skills and Abilities)   Predictor

This is strictly a behavioral approach. In a job analysis, the job is broken down into important tasks. These tasks are built into one or more predictors to simulate the actual job. For example, giving a typing test to applicants for the job of data entry clerk would be content valid. Still, it should be understood that most jobs require many different behaviors to be performed on the job. Therefore, in order to have content validity, it is necessary for the predictor(s) to adequately represent those different behaviors. This is most often accomplished by using a battery of selection procedures, e.g., an ability test, a role-playing exercise, an in-basket test and a management game. If the employer is confident that the selection procedures for a particular job are a reasonable behavioral duplication of the job, then content validity can be claimed - at which point complying with the Uniform Guideline's documentation requirements is all that remains.

Construct Validity

Construct validity studies attempt to answer two questions: what is the psychological construct being measured by the predictor, and how well does the predictor measure this construct? The focus is on a description of behavior that is broader and more abstract.

This is not accomplished by a single study. It requires an accumulation of evidence derived from many different sources to determine the meaning of the test scores. It is, therefore, both a logical and empirical process. The theoretical framework for construct validity is:

It is first necessary to show that the construct in question is, in fact, an important requirement for successful performance on the job. Then it has to be shown that the predictor measures this construct (e.g., leadership) and not something else (e.g., assertiveness, congeniality, personal power, etc.). Finally, it must be demonstrated that the test can differentiate between individuals possessing varying amounts of the construct. Overall, this is quite a difficult assignment!

For a short summary of these validity techniques, including descriptions, appropriate usage, and documentation requirements, see Appendix II.

Discussion

Validation is, at best, difficult to perform, expensive, time-consuming, uncertain in outcome, and often not even feasible due to a small sample size. Thus, both criterion-related validity and construct validity are not *practical* alternatives for many employers. The overwhelming trend is toward content validity for its cost effectiveness. However, a content strategy is not appropriate for demonstrating the validity of selection procedures which purport to measure traits or constructs such as intelligence, aptitude, personality, common sense, judgment, leadership, and spatial ability. This has led to litigation problems for many employers. Today it is much easier for a company to adopt a "numbers game" rather than the more burdensome task of validating and documenting the job relatedness of their employment decision making process. This means that with the increasing difficulty of validation, most employers will attempt to remove adverse impact by hiring and promoting in compliance with the "four-fifths" rule rather than struggle with the substantive technical standards of validation. This is unfortunate, because *without validation* the employer is naively assuming that adequately skilled people are being chosen for jobs in the organization. Once the emphasis moves from showing job relatedness to equating selection rates, the temptation is great to "fudge" the two figures composing the selection rate. For example, an employer may artificially increase a minority selection rate by throwing out some of the applicant data. There are quite a few other devious techniques, but this is not intended to be a discourse on how to beat the system. Rather, a more ethical and legal alternative is the focus here - a systems approach.

The Systems Approach

The systems approach discussed below has been successfully implemented by the author in numerous consulting contracts over the years. It involves building a selection/promotion system around a set of "dimensions" identified through a job analysis. The basic framework is:

Job ———————————————▶ Dimensions ◀——————————————— Predictor

The job analysis, the key element in the legal defense of the accuracy of an organization's selection procedures, is performed to isolate the dimensions. A dimension may be defined as a category under which *behavior* may be reliably classified. If the operational definitions are based on observable work behaviors, a selection procedure measuring those behaviors may be appropriately supported by a content validity strategy. In other words, the use of "dimensions" seems to move the effort from the realm of psychological constructs and places it squarely in the realm of content validity. This is extremely important to the company because of the cost and time savings of content validity methodology.

There are three essential steps in this procedure. First, the dimensions must be shown to be job-related and to describe all common and important parts of the job. Secondly, the predictors must be shown to be job-related and to represent the most common and significant job activities. They must also be shown to be comparable in complexity and difficulty level to that required on the job. Finally, the dimensions must be observable in the predictors. In sum, the predictors of the selection system are targeted to specific behavioral dimensions. There is some overlap where data is available from multiple sources and/or where additional information is needed. All the selection subsystems (e.g., hiring, promotion, termination, etc.) use the same dimensions, definitions, and rating scales.

The reader might well wonder how to choose a dimension. It is possible to choose dimensions through factor analytic techniques using incumbent questionnaire data, but a more practical approach for most organizations is a non-statistical, judgmental, cluster analysis process in which the job analyst groups and regroups behaviors until a logical grouping is attained.

Because rational judgments, rather than factor analysis (or other correlational techniques) are used, it is important to be able to substantiate the accuracy of the rational judgment. This can be accomplished by establishing a "paper trail" in the job analysis report which documents each decision made in the process. Examples of the behaviors that were classified under each dimension should be listed. This procedure stands or falls, therefore, on "expert judgment." For a visual outline of the systems approach applied to employment selection, see Appendix III.

There are many advantages to this type of approach. Communication, training, and administration time is reduced. Managers must learn only one set of dimensions and definitions. They are able to understand more quickly the interrelationships of the subsystems. Further, the selection subsystems deal with common elements (dimensions) and thus support and reinforce each other. This approach is designed to integrate smoothly with the other components of the organization's personnel system. But, most importantly, a content validity strategy is possible, thus greatly reducing costs.

Summary

The Uniform Selection Guidelines were prepared as a technical guide, not written as law. The courts have, in the past, not acted upon a uniform set of standards. In some instances, tests have been judged solely on the basis of face validity, while at other times extensive evidence is required. The determinant appears to be the sophistication of the judge with respect to personnel testing. This failure of the courts to act consistently or uniformly can be traced, in part, to the psychologists and their failure to develop specific and unambiguous guidelines on many issues in the establishment of content validity.

Naturally, an employer should make every effort to validate selection devices. In this regard, construction of a test in accordance with professionally developed standards helps ensure that the selection system is fulfilling its primary purpose, i.e., choosing the most qualified applicants. Often, however, employers are primarily interested in withstanding legal scrutiny and submit to a "numbers game." As a response to cost/time pressures, a systems approach has been developed by the author to provide for *both* equal employment opportunity in the workplace and a truly valid selection system.

Endnotes

[1] Comparisons of selection rates need not be made for subgroups, e.g., white males or black females.

[2] Or contributes *unique* variation in a multiple regression equation.

Appendix I

Uniform Guideline Procedures

1) Keep records on each covered group, including:
   # of applicants
   # hired
   # promoted
   # terminated

2) Review the selection system at least annually for evidence of adverse impact:

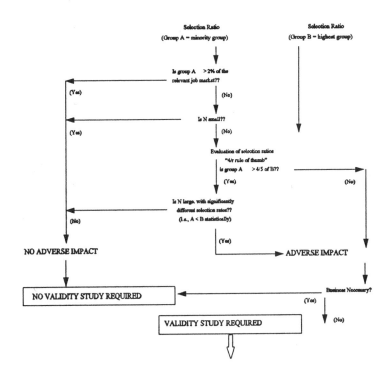

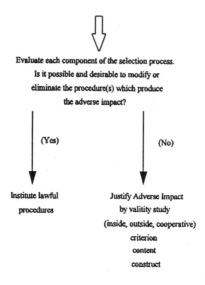

Evaluate each component of the selection process.
Is it possible and desirable to modify or
eliminate the procedure(s) which produce
the adverse impact?

(Yes)   (No)

Institute lawful   Justify Adverse Impact
procedures   by valitity study
                                   (inside, outside, cooperative)
                                           criterion
                                           content
                                           construct

1) Cease using predictors associated with adverse impact until validity study is completed, unless substantial evidence of validity already exists.

2) Use alternative selection procedures showing less adverse impact while the study takes place (i.e., using screening or grouping in lieu of ranking).

3) Investigate the validity and adverse impact of suitable alternative predictors.

4) Compare original and alternate predictors for validity and adverse impact. If validity is substantially the same, use the predictor with the lesser adverse impact.

5) After criterion-related validity study, continue to collect data until it is feasible to test for differential validity and differential prediction (test fairness).

6) If test is unfair to minority, revise or discontinue use.

Appendix II
Validation Techniques

Validity Technique	Description	When Appropriate	--- Required Documentation ---	
			For Each Technique	For All Techniques
Criterion	An empirical demonstration that the selection procedure is predictive or significantly correlated with performance on the job	When it is possible to obtain: • sufficient sample size • sufficient range of performance on both the predictor and the criterion • reliable and valid measures of performance on the job	A description of: • selection procedures • criteria measures • sample • statistical methodology • statistical results	• Location and date of study • Description of selection procedures (including why and how they were selected)
Content	A demonstration that the content of the selection procedure is a representative sampling of important elements of the job	When the job can be conceived as a meaningful, definable universe of behavioral response and when a sample can be drawn from the universe When it is feasible to develop work samples or measures of KSAs (which are necessary prerequisites to the job) *JOB ANALYSIS REQUIRED	A description of: • content of the job, identified from job analysis • content of selection procedures • evidence that the content of the selection procedure is a representative sample of the content of the job	• Description of how the job was analyzed • Description of which alternative selection procedures were examined and the results
Construct	An empirical *a priori* demonstration that the selection procedure is predictive of identifiable characteristics considered important for successful job performance	When it is necessary to relate mental processes, aptitude, or character traits to the job When the same selection procedure is used for a variety of jobs When expertise is available in the field of test validation *JOB ANALYSIS REQUIRED	A description of: • construct • how the construct relates to other constructs • evidence that the construct is related to the work • evidence that the selection procedure measures the construct	• Name of a contact person

Appendix III

SYSTEMS APPROACH

DIMENSIONS	Structured Interview	Biographical Data	Business Game	In-Basket Task	Leaderless Group Discussion	Fact-Finding	Role Play
Oral Communication Skill	☑		☑		☑		☑
Written Communication Skill			☑	☑		☑	
Reasoning Ability			☑	☑	☑		☑
Interpersonal Skill	☑		☑		☑		☑
Ability to Learn			☑	☑		☑	
Leadership Skill			☑		☑		☑
Planning & Organizing Skill			☑	☑	☑	☑	
Stress Tolerance			☑		☑		☑
Motivation to Work	☑		☑				
Energy	☑	☑	☑	☑	☑		
Management Control			☑				

** For <u>ONE</u> job

Appendix III

SYSTEMS APPROACH

DIMENSIONS	Selection	Training	Appraisal	Career Planning	Promotion
Oral Communication Skill	☑		☑	☑	☑
Written Communication Skill	☑	☑	☑	☑	☑
Reasoning Ability	☑		☑	☑	☑
Interpersonal Skill	☑	☑	☑	☑	☑
Ability to Learn	☑				☑
Leadership Skill	☑	☑	☑	☑	☑
Planning & Organizing Skill	☑	☑	☑	☑	☑
Stress Tolerance	☑	☑	☑	☑	☑
Motivation to Work	☑			☑	☑
Energy	☑		☑	☑	☑
Management Control	☑		☑	☑	☑

Subconscious Stereotyping in Business Decisions

By educating individuals about the legal aspects of employment discrimination, university courses, employer-sponsored training programs, various human relations seminars, and other sources are serving a valuable purpose - but they are addressing only half the problem. An individual may be extremely knowledgeable regarding the legal side of discrimination and yet, without consciously being aware of it, still discriminate in decisions involving such matters as selection, placement, promotion, training, and compensation. Based on evidence collected during numerous consulting experiences, the author is convinced that this continues today even among the most "enlightened" individuals, and that this implicit discrimination is most likely to be based on race or sex. In the following study, sex is the key variable:

The "Who" and The "How"

To test this contention, a sample of 512 graduating college seniors, 271 males and 241 females, were surveyed. All subjects were taking a Human Resource Management course that devoted considerable time to equal employment and fair employment practices. Thus, they had all been recently schooled in the legal aspects of employment discrimination and were more sensitized to this issue than might otherwise have been the case. Any implicit discrimination found in decisions made by this group might, therefore, underestimate the extent of the problem in the general business community.

Before being given the survey, the subjects were told that they would be evaluated on the quality of their responses to the various situations presented and that the evaluation would be a factor in the grade awarded in the course. In this way, it was hoped that commitment to the exercise would be increased with fewer subjects simply "going through the motions." Subjects were told to respond to the situations as if they were the Human Resource Manager of a large business organization.

They were then given eight incidents, each necessitating a typical human resource decision (e.g., hiring, firing), with forced-choice responses.[1] Each incident was presented in two forms - one with a female as the individual primarily involved in the incident (female version) and one with a male primarily involved (male version).

Of the 271 males in the subject group, 135 were given the male version of each incident and 136 were given the female version. Of the 241 female subjects, 120 were given the male version of each incident and 121 the female.[2] No subject was given both versions of any one incident since this (a) would not be realistic - having two identical applicants differing only by sex, and (b) would make fairly obvious the intent of the study, thus distorting the findings, since few people would respond in an overtly discriminating manner. It was, after all, subconscious discrimination that the author was interested in.

Responses to Eight Incidents

The first three incidents involved a conflict between responsibilities on the job and at home. It is the author's belief that when these conflicts arise most individuals expect the male to place job responsibilities first and the female to give first priority to the home.

Incident 1

Jack and Judy Garrison have been married three years. Jack is an aspiring business executive and Judy is a successful free-lance writer. This is part of a conversation they had after coming home from a cocktail party at the home of an executive in Jack's division.

Judy: Oh, boy, what a bunch of creeps. Do we have to go to these parties, honey?

Jack: Judy, you know we have to. These things mean a lot to me. Tonight I had a chance to talk to Mr. Wilson. On the job, it would take a week to get an appointment with him. I was able to get across two good ideas I had about our new sales campaign, and I think he was listening.

Judy: Is Wilson that fat slob who works in marketing, the one with the dull wife? I spent ten minutes with her and I nearly died! She's too much. Jack, the people there tonight were so dull I could have cried. I prefer to talk to people who know what is going on in the world, not a bunch of half-wits whose main interests are their new cars and spoiled kids. I tried to talk to one guy about Virginia Woolf and he didn't even know who she was. These people are incredible. Do we have to go to another cocktail party again next week? I'd like to see a play instead. What an uncouth bunch in the business world.

Jack: One of my main ambitions is to get ahead in the business world. You know that these parties are required for bright junior executives coming up in the organization. And I'm a bright junior executive. If we don't go, who knows which of the other junior executives will get to Wilson with their good ideas?

Judy: Can't you relax and work a 40-hour week? That's what they pay you for.

Jack: I guess I'm too ambitious to relax.

Judy: I'd still like to go to the play. At least we could think about real problems.

Jack: And I'd be a mediocre, lower-management nobody for the rest of my career.

Judy: I want you to be a success, Jack. But the idea of spending more evenings talking to idiots is too much!

The "female version" had Judy as the aspiring executive and Jack as the reluctant spouse with all other details being identical. Subjects were then asked to choose one of three responses.[3]

Incident 1

	Female Version	Male Version
a. The spouse should go to the parties and stop making such an issue of it.	30%	72%
b. The junior executive should attend the parties alone.	42%	18%
c. The junior executive should stop attending the parties.	28%	11%

It is obvious from these results that the subjects expected the female to suppress her personal desires and support the male in his work role to a much greater extent than they expect the male to support the female in a similar situation. Such expectations make it easier for a male to succeed in balancing career and home demands than a female. Obviously, the male will have more assistance and less resistance in doing so.

The second incident looked at these competing demands from another angle.

Incident 2

Ruth Brown, an accountant in the main office, has requested one month's leave beginning next week. She has already taken her vacation this year. She wants the leave to take care of her three young children. The day care arrangements the Browns had made for the period covered by her request suddenly fell through, and they have been unable to make other arrangements satisfying their high standards. Ruth's husband is principal of a junior high school, and he cannot possibly get off during the next month.

The problem is that Ruth is the only person experienced in handling the cost section in the accounting department. We would either have to transfer an accountant with the same experience from another section or train a replacement for only one month's work. I have urged Ruth to reconsider this request, but she insists on going ahead with it.

I have also checked with the legal department, and we do not have to hold the position open for Ruth if she insists on taking the whole month off.

I would appreciate it if you could give me your decision on this as soon as possible.

The male version was identical except it involved Ralph Brown whose wife was a principal. Subjects were then asked if this was an appropriate leave request and whether they would grant leave with pay or without pay.

Incident 2	Yes - Female Version	Yes - Male Version
a. Is this an appropriate leave request?	51%	31%
b. Would you grant leave with pay?	72%	56%
c. Would you grant leave without pay?	11%	3%

In this case, the results indicated that sex stereotyping benefits females. A leave request for child care was considered acceptable by more than one-half of the subjects when it was made by a female but by less than one-third of the subjects when it was made by a male. As in the first incident, the evidence suggests that when a job/home conflict arises, the male is expected to accommodate his work schedule, while it is more acceptable for the female to miss work and devote her energies to the home.

Such stereotyping creates increasing problems for both husbands and wives as more and more wives pursue careers. Women will find it hard to advance as long as most employers believe that their first allegiance is, or should be, to the home and not the job. At the same time, males are going to find themselves more often in situations where their absence from work is necessary because of a working spouse, yet where their employers view the reason for such absence as unacceptable.

Incident 3

Situation three presented a direct career conflict between husband and wife:

> As you know, Ronald Cooper is a computer operator in my section. He has played a key role in computerizing our inventory system. Recently Ronald's wife was offered a very attractive managerial position with a large retail organization on the West Coast. They are seriously considering the move. I told Ronald that he has a very bright future with our organization, and it would be a shame for him to pull out just as we are expanding our operations. I sure would hate to lose him now.
>
> What do you think we should do about the situation?

The alternate form had Rhonda as the computer operator and her husband offered the job on the West Coast. Subjects were asked to choose from among four alternative responses.

Incident 3

	Female Version	Male Version
a. Try to convince the operator that too much has been invested in his (or her) career to leave now.	41%	88%
b. Don't try to influence the operator.	60%	11%
c. Offer the operator a sizable raise as an incentive to stay.	22%	28%
d. Try to find an attractive position for the employee's spouse in the organization.	8%	8%

It is obvious from the response pattern that the subjects viewed male employees as more worthy of retaining than female employees even when the qualifications of each were the same.

When looking at responses to the first three situations, one gains some insight into why absenteeism and turnover rates are higher for females than males even when they are at the same organization and compensation level. If employers do not make as much effort to retain females as they do males and if, as seen in Incident 2, females are more readily granted unscheduled absences, is it any wonder that the government reports slightly higher absenteeism and turnover rates for females than for males? [4]

The fourth and fifth situations dealt with an employee's unacceptable conduct - the question being what disciplinary action, if any, should be taken.

Incident 4

I have a problem and I don't see how to solve it. It concerns one of the design engineers, Jill Diller, who has worked for me for the past 15 months. Jill persists in arriving late every morning. She is always 10 minutes late, more usually 15 minutes to one-half hour. I am at my wit's end. I have tried everything I can think of - private discussions, written reprimands, threats, sarcasm, and more. She is still late every morning.

When Jill walks into the office, the work stops and everyone watches. Some of the designers are even joking that Jill's coming in late has something to do with her recent engagement. I don't like to get too tough with a creative employee like Jill, but her behavior is bound to hurt morale in the department.

The male version involved Jack Diller. Subjects were asked to select from among three courses of action.

Incident 4

		Female Version	Male Version
a.	Suspend for one week for continued tardiness.	72%	64%
b.	Threaten to fire and follow through if necessary.	51%	42%
c.	Don't make an issue of tardiness.	8%	11%

In the case of both the female and male employee, the subjects considered the situation serious enough to warrant the more severe actions. Yet they were slightly more inclined to take such action when the employee involved was a female. This may be connected to the value the subjects attached to employees of different sexes, as exhibited by the responses to Incident 3. Both the willingness to risk losing an employee through more severe disciplinary actions and the lesser effort made to retain female employees seem to provide insight into the value the subjects placed on employees of different sexes. The response patterns indicated that, when all else is equal, males were viewed as more valued employees. More effort was put into retaining them and severe discipline was less likely to be used for fear of losing them.

Incident 5

Situation five involved unacceptable personal, rather than work, conduct:

I would like to get your advice on a matter of great sensitivity involving one of the junior executives in our organization. It has been brought to my attention by an unimpeachable source that Bill Holman, assistant comptroller in my division, is having an affair with a prominent young socialite. I understand it has reached the point where any day now Bill's wife will publicly denounce the socialite as a homewrecker. I have been reluctant to bring this up, but I know Bill's marital problems will hurt his work. I would appreciate any advice you could give me on this.

The female version involved Renee Holman having an affair with a young playboy.   Subjects were asked to select from among three responses:

Incident 5

		Female Version	Male Version
a.	Do nothing unless the junior executive raises the issue.	50%	52%
b.	Advise junior executive to see a marriage counselor.	40%	56%
c.	Confront employee and threaten termination unless affair stops.	3%	4%

The only real difference between male and female respondents in this situation seemed to be in response (b). Subjects were more likely to advise a male employee to see a marriage counselor than a female employee. The author would speculate that the almost identical results to response (a) may have to do with the equal number of male and female subjects given each version. It may be that members of one sex (regardless of which one) are less likely to approach members of the opposite sex on issues such as this. For response (a) then, it is not a question of the sex of the participant but of the sex of the subject relative to the participant.

Response (b) indicates that the subjects were more willing to correct the unacceptable behavior of male than female employees even when this behavior was of a personal rather than a work nature. When the unacceptable behavior was personal (Incident 5) rather than work-related (Incident 4), the subjects were willing to expend more effort on male than on female employees.

Incident 6

This situation is becoming all too common today. By playing a numbers game, the organization has hired enough females to comply with the law but through subtle forms of unintentional sex discrimination does not allow them to develop as managers to the same extent that equally qualified males do. The females' comparative lack of advancement in the organization is then used as evidence that they are not as well suited for the work. This failure to advance can also lead to higher rates of absenteeism and turnover and thus perpetuate the cycle.

The difficulty here is that the decisions as to who advances may be made on the grounds of legitimate individual qualifications and may not be discriminatory at all. The discrimination occurred earlier, however, when females (because of employers' subconscious discrimination) were not given the same opportunities to develop as males. Incident 6 addresses this type of situation.

I am pleased that we have the opportunity to send a representative to the Dunbar conference on production supervision. I know from personal experience that it is a high quality conference, and it has developed such a favorable reputation in this area that it is considered an important form of recognition for those who are selected to attend.

I have reviewed our supervisory staff quite carefully and have narrowed the choice down to two people, both of whom I feel are qualified to attend. Unfortunately, we can send only one person, and I will leave the final selection up to you, depending on what you feel we want to emphasize. The two candidates are Susan Adams and John Elms.

Susan Adams is supervisor of knitting unit A. She is 25, married, and has no children. She has been employed by our company for three years. She is a college graduate with a general business degree, and we consider her to have good potential for higher level positions.

John Elms is supervisor of knitting unit B. He is 43, married, and has two teenage children. He has been employed by our company for 20 years. He is a high school graduate. He has been a steady, conscientious employee, advancing gradually from a helper's job to his present position. This may be as high as he will be able to go judging from our assessment of the information in his file. Selection for this conference would mean a great deal to John.

In the alternate form, the two names were reversed. Subjects were asked to select one of the two to attend the conference. When all responses were considered collectively, without differentiation by sex of the individual involved, the following results emerged.

Incident 6

Send 25-year-old: 31%
Send 43-year-old: 69%

Hence, regardless of sex, the majority of subjects felt that the older employee should be sent. When the results were sorted by the sex of the individual, however, the following occurred:

Send 25-year-old female: 23%
Send 25-year-old male: 39%

These results indicated that the subjects, when selecting younger workers with career potential to participate in a developmental conference, were more likely to expend company resources if the employee were a male - even when all other qualifications were equal.

Incident 7

This situation dealt with a selection/promotion decision for a position requiring extensive traveling:

Pursuant to our recent discussion about the need to recruit a Purchasing Manager for the new operation, I have developed a set of brief job specifications and have located a candidate who may be suitable for the opening. Will you please review the attached resume and give me your evaluation?

Job requirements for Purchasing Manager:

The major responsibilities of the new Purchasing Manager will be to purchase fabrics, materials and clothing accessories (buttons, belts, buckles, zippers, etc.) for the production of finished goods.

For the most part, the Purchasing Manager will have to travel around the country visiting wholesalers and attending conventions and showings. The person hired for this position should have a knowledge of the quality of raw materials and have the ability to establish a fair price for goods purchased in large quantities. The person selected for this position will have to travel at least 20 days each month.

RESUME

Name:	Mr. Carl Wood
Position Applied For:	Purchasing Manager
Place of Birth:	Cleveland, Ohio
Marital Status:	Married; four children, ages 11, 8, 7, and 4
Education:	B.S. Business Administration, Ohio State University
Relevant Work Experience:	One year as purchasing trainee, Campbell Textiles, Inc. Ten years' experience in various retail clothing stores in sales, buying and general management.
Interviewer's Remarks:	Good personal appearance, seems earnest and convincing. Good recommendations from previous employers.

The female version had Mrs. Karen Wood as the candidate. Subjects were asked to answer three questions.

Incident 7

		Yes-Female Version	Yes-Male Version
a.	Would you select this candidate?	23%	33%
b.	Is the candidate favorably suited for the job?	33%	38%
c.	Does the candidate have the potential to remain on the job?	30%	35%

Subjects apparently felt that employees with this set of characteristics, regardless of sex, were not suited for the position in question. The author believes that the presence of four young children was the deciding variable for the subjects.

Yet in all three areas of inquiry, males were selected more often or rated more favorably than females. This response pattern seems to indicate that the subjects were exhibiting the same values evidenced in the responses to Incident 2. That is, the first allegiance of males belongs to the job and of females, to the home and/or family. This type of subconscious sex stereotyping makes it more acceptable for a male to be selected for a job involving extensive travel than a female - even when both have the same employment qualifications and the same situation at home.

Incident 8

The final incident addressed the family vs. work dilemma even more directly:

> We are at the point where we must make a decision on the promotion of Cathy Adams of our Human Resources staff. Cathy is one of the most competent employees in the corporate Human Resources office, and I am convinced that she is capable of handling even more responsibility as Bennett Division Human Resources Director. However, I am not altogether certain that she is willing to subordinate time with her family to time on the job to the extent that may be required with Bennett.

I have had the opportunity to explore with her the general problem of family versus job, and she strongly believes that she would rarely stay late at the office or participate in weekend meetings. She believes that her first duty is to her family and that she should manage her time accordingly. This viewpoint has not affected her performance in the past, but it could be a problem in the more demanding position as head of Human Resources with the Bennett Division.

The male version involved Gerald Adams. Subjects were given three possible courses of action.

Incident 8

		Female Version	Male Version
a.	Do not promote.	34%	10%
b.	Persuade the candidate to make a stronger job commitment prior to promotion.	29%	32%
c.	Base the promotion on past experience.	40%	58%

The responses to (a) and (c) indicated that identical family demands and/or commitments did not disqualify males to the same extent they disqualified females. Not only were females expected to yield to family demands in the work vs. home dilemma (as shown in the previous situations) but even if they set priorities identical to those of their male counterparts, the males were still given more consideration for the job. The effects of this type of sex stereotyping will be difficult, at best, to overcome.

Conclusion

The conclusions to be drawn from this study are obvious. If the subjects used here are any indication, there is a good deal of unintentional, subconscious sex stereotyping taking place in the business sector of our society. The author feels quite strongly that, if anything, these responses underestimate the extent of the problem. The subjects were younger than most people in business, were college educated, and were undergoing a learning experience (the Human Resource Management course) that sensitized them to the area of employment discrimination. It is reasonable to expect that responses from such a group would be different from those of a more general sample.

While we as a society can legislate against overt discrimination, equally important and necessary are efforts to eliminate the type of subconscious stereotyping evidenced in the present study. Even if all members of the business community fully comply with the written laws regarding equal/fair employment, the barriers erected by the underlying, unfair attitudes found in this study will still be imposing. This study has tapped some deep-seated, gender-based values - and found them to be resistant to change, despite education. Only after this more difficult type of prejudice is eliminated will real equal employment opportunity be attained. Making people aware of the pervasiveness of the problem is the first step.

Endnotes

[1] These incidents were taken from an earlier survey conducted by Benson Rosen and Thomas Jerdee published in 1974: "Sex Stereotyping in the Executive Suite," *Harvard Business Review*, March-April 1974.

[2] In the present study, responses were tabulated by the sex of the fictitious individual involved in the incident, not by the sex of the respondent - although the number of respondents by sex was the same for both the male and female version of each incident. In a follow-up study, the author intends to tabulate responses by the sex of the respondent.

[3] In this and certain subsequent situations, the responses do not total 100 percent since more than one response was possible.

[4] Bureau of National Affairs, Inc., *Bulletin to Management*, 1995. Information on absenteeism and turnover is published quarterly in the bulletin.

Management By Whom?

Trends In Participative Management

A subject of increasing controversy in the field of management is the application of participative techniques to non-managerial personnel. Such techniques have been widely used - and even more widely debated. The debate involves the philosophical question of whether it is proper for workers to be included in such traditional management areas as planning, operational decision making and performance evaluation. It also involves questions of capability and motivation which challenge the potential effectiveness of whatever participative strategies are utilized. While the philosophical question broadly embraces virtually all such strategies, the question of effectiveness more pragmatically addresses the results to be obtained by using worker participation in structuring jobs, defining management-labor relationships and managing the firm itself.

Of the two issues, pragmatic effectiveness is of more importance. A negative finding for effectiveness would surely render the philosophical question moot.

A wide variety of participative techniques have been used in many different job environments, but the range of such techniques is basically limited to those that are relatively traditional in concept, representing a "bottom-up" approach and a group of more recently developed techniques that involve "top-down" participation.

The bottom-up approaches embody the goal of providing the worker with managerial values through participation in operational decisions, communications or benefits. These programs include such well understood and popular techniques as job enlargement, job enrichment, management by objectives, team building, and profit sharing.

The top-down approach envisages the worker or groups of workers in an executive role, participating directly in decision making, e.g., long-range planning. This participation includes the worker in actions and responsibilities traditionally reserved for the Board of Directors or the Chief Executive Officer. The European experience in this area involves participation mandated by law, with detailed and explicit procedures developed over a long period of time. The American experience, on the other hand, is based on localized programs, usually initiated by management.

111

By examining the current status of bottom-up and top-down approaches to worker participation in the management of an organization, it is possible to draw some conclusions concerning the future application of these approaches in the United States.

Bottom-Up Approaches

Job enlargement, one bottom-up approach, is the process of providing more variety in the number of tasks contained in a given job. Moving from the specific, individual job description to an enlarged responsibility for a wider scope of activities is the primary objective of the job enlargement process. For example, a machine operator's job may be narrowly defined to machine a specific material. Alternatively, the job may be enlarged or broadened by also requiring the person to obtain materials, maintain the tools and equipment and inspect the work. This method of involving workers in a greater variety of activities is viewed by many theorists as the most basic participative strategy.

Over the years, researchers have found that worker participation in a wider range of physical activities reduces fatigue and boredom, thereby increasing expected productivity. Job enlargement, however, does not represent an attempt to increase significantly the worker's sense of personal achievement or share of responsibility for results.

Strategies for enhancing the employee's personal identification with a job are called job enrichment. This approach, successfully adopted by the Texas Instrument Corporation and other firms, attempts to build employee motivation by loading a person's job with components of responsibility and autonomy, so that the individual then identifies with important managerial goals. There is considerable evidence that job enrichment can exert a positive influence on workers' attitudes and productivity. Nevertheless, the potential for generalizing this approach is controversial since some critics claim that reported results are unrepresentative. In summarizing prevalent reservations about the validity of the many enthusiastic reports of job enrichment successes, the author would point to the following shortcomings of research in this area:

- Selective reporting of results, distorting any evaluation of the effectiveness of the programs;
- Too few empirical studies, representing a limited range of working environments; and

- Biased results, reflecting the views of managers who initiated the programs of job enrichment, not the views of workers or unions.

The last point suggests that part of the difficulty in implementing job enrichment is that it is management imposed rather than a product of workers' or unions' initiative.

Management By Objectives (MBO) is a strategy for involving lower-level managers and rank-and-file workers in the planning and evaluation process that directs employee efforts toward organizational objectives. The technique was first proposed by Peter Drucker in the 1950s. Since then, it has been elaborated and systematized for use in virtually every organization and has enjoyed widespread popularity.

MBO has been used extensively in industry during the last three decades, but observers have noted mixed results. While some firms have embraced MBO enthusiastically, others have found it more difficult to apply than anticipated. In particular, the benefits of joint manager-subordinate goal-setting and review have been questioned. While MBO has become a popular managerial tool in government as well as business, there have been questions about its efficacy in motivating public-sector employees.

Team building is a concept that assumes that group participation in work activities will develop positive job attitudes and motivate individual members of work groups. Much attention in training managers has been devoted to this method. Like MBO, team building approaches are oriented to managerial recognition of the value of contributions by subordinates. Despite a great deal of managerial enthusiasm for this method, it remains to be seen whether subordinates will prove to be as enthusiastic as their superiors, i.e., those individuals who initiate group decision making and problem solving and normally retain final authority.

Profit sharing approaches to employee participation vary considerably, but they do share a common assumption - a belief that workers will be motivated to excel in their jobs when their compensation depends on the organization's profits. There have been some notable successes in this area, such as the Lincoln Electric Plan. Many other attempts at profit sharing have been disappointing or, at best, have yielded mixed results.

In the author's opinion, this grab bag of approaches makes it difficult to praise or blame any of the participative strategies outlined above - even in those situations where there are clear-cut results shown to be beneficial or harmful to employee morale or productivity. This is not to say, however, that other individuals have found it similarly difficult to pass judgment on the value of these participative techniques. Labor leaders in particular, as we shall now see, have consistently been very outspoken in their criticism of them.

The Union Perspective

Generally, organized labor has looked with skepticism on the traditional approaches to participative management discussed above. Most of these techniques are viewed as the theoretical constructs of academics who lack practical experience in day-to-day contact with non-supervisory employees. One objection is the implicit assumption made in participative plans (e.g., job enlargement, job enrichment, MBO, etc.) that the job can become a major part of the individual's life - that it can be made challenging enough to produce an attitude change toward the job. In certain situations this is true. It is in those instances that the traditional participative programs work best.

When the skills and intellect of the individuals performing the job are at a level high enough to allow them to incorporate significant enlargement or enrichment features into their present job description, such programs are successful. If the job is at a high enough level in the organization to include meaningful and challenging objectives or if the responsibility increases from job enrichment are not simply a facade, then the program has a chance of leading to a desirable employee attitude change. But in some lower-level jobs, where employees' possession of intellectual abilities and skills is demonstrably poor, participative programs have had little success. Among urban blue-collar workers, for example, the track record of participative management programs has been nothing short of disastrous. So, in the area where changes envisioned by the introduction of such programs are most urgently needed - at the lowest levels where major motivation and identification problems arise and the potential for increased productivity is greatest - participative management programs have realized the least success.

The sector of the labor force where these programs are least successful is precisely that sector where unions have their strongest representation. It is not surprising, therefore, that unions generally look with disfavor on such programs. Labor organizations question the practicality of these programs. It is not simply because they see them blurring the traditional "us and them" labor-management relationship (as many have charged); rather, it is because the very people who belong to these labor organizations are the ones holding the lower-level jobs where the programs have realized the least success.

Is there a cause and effect relationship between the variables involved? Is it union opposition that causes these programs to fail at lower organizational levels, or do the programs fail for other reasons? To answer that question, it is necessary to examine employee attitudes.

Since the days of Frederick Taylor and Scientific Management, it has been an article of faith among the management of manufacturing concerns that, for production efficiency, jobs need to be broken down into small increments with a specific task assigned to each worker. This in turn has created hundreds of thousands of repetitive, unchallenging jobs. Naturally these are the jobs where the identification, motivation and increased productivity expected to be gained through participative management are most needed, but they are also the types of jobs that (if held by an individual for a number of years) can cause an employee to adopt a very negative mental attitude toward the work.

This mental attitude is manifested in attempts, usually through a union, to get more time away from the job. More holidays, vacations, sick leave, etc., are demanded, since the worker now seeks satisfaction not *at* the job, but *away* from it. This same attitude can also result in demands for more monetary compensation to tolerate the same job. If a worker likes the job, a given rate of pay may be enough to keep him or her in it. If the person hates the job, he or she will invariably insist on more reward for the same level of performance. After years of conditioning in this approach to their employment, is it any wonder that many of these employees who belong to unions by virtue of their position are not wholeheartedly embracing participative management?

The situation is made even worse by the changing educational, financial and social levels of the typical union member. The blue-collar sector of the union movement is becoming better educated and better paid, while a larger percentage of overall union membership is white-collar and professional. The better educated and more financially secure employees become, the more they resist superficial attempts at participation. Even profit-sharing plans will suffer in terms of the attitude changes they seek to foster. As employees become better educated, they begin to expect more than a paycheck from the job.

These forces indicate the need to introduce employer practices reflecting genuine participation by employees in the operation of the enterprise. Instead of techniques that emphasize employee input at the lowest organizational levels, "top-down" plans would give employees a collective voice in operating decisions traditionally made by upper-level management. The introduction of such plans is crucial to improve not only the mental health and attitude of the individual employee but also the performance of the firm and, if implemented on a wide enough scale, the economy as a whole. While not seen as a cure-all in and of itself, the emergence of a top-down approach to management is a beacon of hope on an economically bleak horizon.

Top-Down Participative Management

"Top-down management" is usually defined as management that makes decisions, sets the rules, enforces standards, and generally exercises all the traditional powers of the owner/entrepreneur. "Top-down participation," on the other hand, implies sharing by the employee/worker in this process. Major decisions concerning the direction of the firm, products and markets, plans and policies, and conditions of work and employment are set by, or with major input from, the worker/employee. The philosophy of a property right in the job underlies the concept of top-down participation and may explain in part the resistance of management to worker participation in the direction of the firm.

Such top-down participation has taken many forms in the industrialized nations, many of which have carried the concept much further than we have in the United States.

In Germany, *Mitbestimmung* (codetermination, an equal say in management) is required by law. In this mandated system, one-third of the supervisory board (comparable to a Board of Directors in U.S. corporations) is drawn from the workers. The board is responsible for the overall operation of the firm, including the development of plans and policies, the allocation of funds, and decisions on issues such as products, marketing areas, etc. It also appoints a management board to conduct the day-to-day business of the firm.

Work Councils, comparable in a very broad sense to union locals in the United States, must be formed in any German firm employing more than five workers. Blue-collar and white-collar workers are represented proportional to their numbers in the company. The Work Council does not bargain for wages, and working conditions are normally negotiated on a regional or national basis. The Council, however, has a right to codetermination in deciding such issues as job evaluation, piece rates and wage structures, working hours, overtime arrangements, breaks and holiday schedules, staffing policies including guidelines for recruiting, assigning and dismissing workers, measures to mitigate the effects of layoffs on workers facing dismissal, training, occupational safety and welfare schemes, allocation of company housing, and workers' conduct on the shop floor.

Hiring, discharge, work allocation, promotion, and demotion decisions require the consent of the Council. Unilateral action by the employer in these areas is not allowed.

In the actual conduct of the business of the firm, the powers of the Work Council are more limited. In firms with more than 100 employees, the Work Council appoints an economic committee. The committee has the right to obtain information on such major issues as manufacturing methods, automation, production programs, and the financial condition of the firm. Analysis of this information is the responsibility of the economic committee. The consent of the Work Council is required for major actions such as plant closings and staff cuts.

The author has done extensive research in this area over the last ten years and has concluded that there is little possibility of such a system gaining a significant foothold in the United States. Countries such as ours, where a traditionally adversarial role has existed between labor and management, will take at least a generation to embrace such a system. While economic factors are indeed moving us in this direction faster than many would like, it will still take a considerable amount of time to develop a model that fits within our capitalist frame of reference.

A review of our country's labor history reinforces the idea of the voluntary basis of our labor/management relations and reduces the likelihood of adoption of the European method of codetermination. Systems like codetermination are the result of national law (unlike the normal give-and-take between American management and labor), confirming that European industrial democracy was fought for and gained within the political arena. Codetermination's political origins in Germany have resulted in hundreds of pages of manifold, complex legislation, bearing little relation to laws in this country. In the author's opinion, American workers and their representatives have both the expectation and the desire for two things that codetermination restricts: the freedom to create/operate systems independent of governmental influence and the freedom to contest any ensuing labor/management system.

In contrast to the mandated system of workers contractual presence on joint committees, there are situations where the American worker actually can own all or part of the firm and have management rights by virtue of such ownership. The Employee Stock Option Plan (ESOP) and its management arm, the Employee Stock Option Trust (ESOT), are employment benefit plans in which a company (usually a small, closely-held corporation) sells its stock to its employees. These plans work in conjunction with, or as replacements for, the normal retirement plans. The author would hypothesize that an employee owned firm (either completely employee-owned or partially owned through an ESOP) should have (a) increased profitability, (b) a better growth record, (c) increased productivity, (d) more employment stability, and (e) fewer work stoppages.

Summary

What is happening in the United States is not the codetermination system mandated in Germany. Yet neither is it the level of employee ownership some envisioned after the successes of employee takeovers at Youngstown Sheet and Tube or Kaiser Steel. Instead, we see management reluctantly granting both bottom-up and top-down participation to workers in return for economic concessions. Boundaries, systems, and rules are being formulated every day in the American workplace in individualistic *ad hoc* ways. Both labor and management have resisted the intrusion of the legislative process into this area, and for this the author applauds them. In the long run, a more equitable and less burdensome system will evolve based on the uniquely American combination of cooperation and confrontation between labor and management.

Strategic Human Resource Mandates

Kenneth A. Kovach
John A. Pearce II

As we look ahead to the next ten years, it is evident that significant demographic shifts are taking place in U.S. society that will profoundly impact corporate Human Resource Management (HRM). While strategic managers are being alerted to the general nature of the changes, little progress has been made in identifying their HRM consequences. Since new demographics will dictate bold new initiatives for planners, it is imperative that they be aware of what the coming changes are and begin to formulate strategies to deal with them. From the perspective of HRM, this article looks at some of the best available information on the most imposing changes of the next decade and suggests coping and proactive strategies for succeeding in today's highly dynamic environment.

The Changes

Dramatic transformations are occurring in the U.S. labor force. Changes in participant age, sex, race, ethnic origin and geographic location must be understood and analyzed separately, for each will dictate a separate response by corporate human resource planners.

Age: Younger Workers

The segment of the labor force under 25 years of age will decrease by 3.4 percent during the next decade, a drastic reversal from what was experienced over the last twenty years. As a result, human resource managers will be faced with a two-pronged problem. On one hand, less pressure will come from employee ranks for those jobs with the characteristics typically favored most by younger workers, e.g., incentive pay systems tied to personal performance and task-related programs including job enlargement and job enrichment. This is not to say that these programs will cease to be influential in determining employee attitudes but rather that they will be less emphasized due to the decreasing percentage of employees in the age group most influenced by them.

On the other hand, the smaller pool of younger workers will experience increased attention from recruiters seeking to fill entry level positions. To attract these employees, human resource planners will be forced to place a greater emphasis on in-house training and development programs. The younger age group's opportunity for rapid advancement is going to be somewhat limited by the bulge in baby-boom, middle-age workers who are ahead of them in the corporate hierarchies. The availability of in-house training and development programs, which will enable younger employees to distinguish themselves from their peers when competing for the limited number of mid-level positions, will be a valuable recruiting tool in the coming decade.

Age: Middle-Aged Workers

The 25-54 age group will be the fastest growing age segment of the labor force over the next ten years, increasing 27 percent. When compared with the decrease in the percentage of younger workers and a slight increase in older workers, the 25-54 year olds will be 'where the action is' for human resource managers. The baby boomers of post-World War II are the subgroup most responsible for this increase, as evidenced by the fact that the 40-54 age group will soon comprise 25 percent of the U.S. population.

A major challenge for human resource managers will be to prepare for the probable job displacement of many of these workers as a result of automation. The 25-to-40 segment of this age group will not be covered by the provisions of the 1967 Age Discrimination in Employment Act and the 40-54 segment will have less seniority than the traditionally more job-stable 55-and-over sector. Therefore, 25-to-54 year old employees will be most susceptible to job displacement. Additionally, when automation impacts workers in this age group, they will be forced to continue employment, either with the same employer or elsewhere, whereas older workers may choose early retirement. As a result, job displacement due to automation will hit middle-aged workers harder than any other age group.

Human resource managers must thus be prepared to introduce policies in company programs and union contracts that address the issue of job displacement due to automation. Job security as a trade-off for wage increases has become an increasingly accepted idea. The "deals" in this regard between management and labor in the automobile, steel, airline, and general manufacturing sectors in the past decade are only a trickle compared to the flood of such arrangements one can expect to see due to technological advances in the future. Such arrangements will be born of economic necessity by both employees and employers. For example, one of the most popular forms of job security is likely to be a clause wherein employees above a certain seniority level will be retrained for another position within the company should their present job be automated.

Pension portability will also be a response to automation's impact on middle-aged workers over the next ten years. The older of the baby boomers are now of an age where they must begin long term retirement planning. Increased solvency problems with Social Security and ERISA restrictions on options for vesting of private pensions will make portability of seniority for pension rights a major issue in the near future. Inter-corporate and inter-industry agreements for pension portability will become commonplace, with combined employer funding of such plans expected to be a major concern of human resource experts.

"Attrition" arrangements whereby the employer reduces the labor force by agreeing not to replace employees who leave through normal attrition, rather than by layoffs, will likewise gain wide acceptance. Such arrangements will be palatable to middle-aged workers faced with the alternative of job loss, and will allow employers to address the issue of technology and displacement in a socially acceptable way.

For employees who are displaced due to automation, the employer is likely to have some type of supplemental unemployment coverage. Over 5 million employees now receive coverage under such plans, whereby the company finances a private unemployment plan to supplement state plans for workers above a certain seniority level. The middle-aged workers of the near future will be drawing from such plans since they will have a qualifying level of seniority to be eligible but (as opposed to older workers) will not have enough seniority to avoid the technologically induced layoffs. As a result, supplemental unemploy-ment costs will rise as the number of covered employees goes to an estimated 10 million during the next five years.

Age: Older Workers

The segment of the labor force aged 55 and older will increase by 3.4 percent during the next decade - exactly offsetting the decrease in the percentage of younger workers. While the increase in this age segment will be dwarfed by the growth of the middle-aged group, older workers will present unique and serious problems for human resource managers.

Nowhere will these problems be more acute than in the areas of retirement and health care costs.

By the turn of the century, a number of factors will have come together to drastically increase retirement costs for the typical U.S. employer. The increase in older workers eligible to receive retirement benefits does not begin to tell the story of the approaching problem with retirement financing. More and more employers will be forced to offer early retirement options as a result of 1986 changes in the Age Discrimination Act whereby the upper age of the protected group went from 70 to infinity. Such options will be offered in an attempt to replace older workers with younger ones as a means to save on wage costs (where seniority is a wage factor within jobs) and insurance costs (when age profiles influence company premiums). Moderating the widespread use of such policies will be increased retirement costs and rapidly rising starting wage rates for the undersized pool of younger workers. Additionally, the increasingly popular practice of using later employment years, as opposed to income averaging, when figuring income for pension purposes can be expected to continue and to further increase pension costs.

Cost containment managers should anticipate yet another major negative factor that will influence retirement costs. The introduction of cost-of-living adjustments (COLAs) to pension payments is presently done by only a small segment of employers and even there takes place on an *ad hoc* basis. Starting with the organized labor sector and gradually spreading to the rest of the labor force, COLA clauses in pension plans will become more prevalent during the next decade with regularly scheduled, rather than sporadic, adjustments. Such adjustments already take place in Social Security and federal and military pensions, but the federal government has found it possible to operate with huge deficit budgets. Such a luxury is not available to the private sector, and the financial implications of COLA clauses in the pension plans of major employers are staggering. Current estimates are that even a weak COLA clause - one that adjusts for only 50 percent of the inflation rate - will increase the cost of the average private-sector plan by 30-33 percent over the next decade. Yet a dramatic increase in the number of these clauses seems probable, meaning that human resource managers and cost containment specialists should prepare accordingly.

In addition to pension issues, the larger segment of older workers will cause problems in the area of health-care costs. In 1988, 10 percent of the U.S. Gross National Product (GNP) went to medical expenses. By the year 2000, the figure will rise to 18 percent. From the corporate perspective, this escalation raises serious questions about health-care cost containment. Since people typically incur 85 percent of their health care expenses during the last two years of life, it is easy to see why even a modest percentage increase in the older segment of the labor force foretells a drastic increase in health care costs. Also to be remembered is that, since 1967, health care has been the area of the U.S. economy hit hardest by inflation.

As a result of the aging labor force and the impact of inflation, budget analysts, corporate planners, and human resource managers will need to devise a corporate strategy for health care cost containment. They should be looking at policies to curb excessive use of hospitals through utilization reviews, outpatient and surgicenter care, insurance coverage of second and even third opinions on elective surgery, reimbursement for health services at home, greater use of pre-admission testing, and increased private use of professional standards review organizations. Health Maintenance Organizations (HMOs) also offer significant cost advantages when required as part of the employer's insurance package. Today, only 13 percent of employer-provided health coverage includes use of an HMO. By the year 2000, almost 60 percent of such plans will have use of a specified HMO as a component.

Finally, it can be expected that more of the cost for health care will be passed on to the employee. In 1990, 50 percent of employer health care plans were contributory. In 1994, the figure rose to 62 percent and by the year 2000, it may well approach 80 percent.

Obviously, containment of retirement and health care costs will be a major area of activity in the near future as a result of the increase in older employees.

Sex: Female Employees

There can be no doubt that one of the most striking recent changes experienced in the labor force has been the increasing participation of women in full-time jobs. By the year 2000, women will comprise 65 percent of the entering labor force. Their percentage of the labor force will have increased 27 points from 1989 levels - and they will comprise 47 percent of all U.S. workers.

The stereotypical family unit of a generation ago, with the male breadwinner, the female housewife, and one or more children, applies to less than 15 percent of U.S. households today. At present in the U.S., nearly 50 percent of married women with children under two-years old are working, with 62 percent of all mothers working outside the home. If the present trend of an annual three percent increase in working mothers continues, by the year 2000 we will have a situation in the U.S. where over 80 percent of all mothers with children at home will be working. Only part of this increase will come from women seeking self-fulfillment through careers. The rest will be the result of economic necessity.

As these trends continue through the next decade, they can be expected to elicit a different set of responses than those occasioned by the age shifts discussed earlier. While changes in labor force composition by age can be dealt with through internal company policies, the increasing number of women in the full-time labor force can be expected to draw a legislative response. The most important Congressional response thus far has been the Family and Medical Leave Act. This legislation requires all companies with 50 or more employees to provide unpaid leave of up to twelve weeks every year for parents of newborn or newly adopted children, up to twelve weeks to care for a seriously ill family member, and up to twelve weeks for the employee's own serious illness. Magnifying the cost impact of this legislation is the fact that as a result of the age trend discussed earlier, women entering the work force in the greatest number will be those of childbearing age who will disproportionately seek the benefits made available under the new law.

Another legislative response that seems likely is the Act for Better Child Care. Having already cleared the Senate Labor and Human Resource Committee and with a large number of congressional sponsors, this bill would set federal standards for child-care facilities, establish a referral system, provide financial assistance to low-income families who need such care, and help fund the expansion of existing facilities. When one considers that at present there are 36.2 million children with one or both parents working, yet only 2.5 million child-care slots in licensed facilities,[1] there is reason to believe that employers will be playing a major role in establishing such facilities during the next decade.

Thus, on the two big issues tied to female labor force participation, family and medical leave and child care, the human resource manager of the future should implement company policies similar to those just discussed rather than wait for legislative dictates and then assume a passive role of compliance. In addition, companies should address the needs of their female labor force through internal initiatives such as pooled sick leave, flex-time, summer working hours, four-day weeks, split days, job sharing, and telecommuting.

Race and Ethnic Origin: African-Americans, Hispanics

Although Caucasians will remain the major labor group in the U.S., their absolute numbers will increase only 15 percent over the next ten years, compared with a 20 percent increase for African-Americans and a 74 percent increase for Hispanics. The fertility rate among Hispanic women is presently 96 births per 1,000 compared with 83 for African-Americans and 69 for whites. These facts, coupled with heavy immigration, will make the Hispanic growth rate faster than that of any other race or ethnic group in this country.

Present projections indicate that Hispanics will soon comprise 10.5 percent of the work force and will surpass African-Americans as the largest racial minority sometime in the next fifteen to twenty years. Human resource planners and recruiters will have to adjust their mindset on minority employment from simply African-American to *Hispanic* and African-American. As the relative number of each of these groups increases in the next ten years, their skills and productivity are likely to be an increasingly important element in determining a corporation's future prosperity.

The problems to be faced when dealing with this growing segment of the work force stem from the deprived backgrounds and low education levels that characterize a disproportionate number of these employees. While 86 percent of white workers presently have at least a high school diploma, only 60 percent of Hispanics and 73 percent of African-Americans have this level of formal education. With the fastest-growing occupations requiring a college degree or extensive training beyond high school (e.g., computer analyst and processor projected to increase 75.6 percent in the next five years; medical assistant projected to increase 90.4 percent; paralegal personnel projected to increase 103 percent, etc.), the lack of highly educated and trained personnel among the fastest growing racial and ethnic groups dictates a greater emphasis on in-house training programs. Such programs will, by necessity, be job specific and targeted toward expediting the employment of the least educated personnel in entry-level, non-supervisory jobs.

Recall the earlier findings that the decrease in the number of younger workers and the bottleneck created by the baby boomers will increase the importance of training for the under 25 age group. Now we see that an increasing share of this young age group will consist of lesser educated African-American and Hispanic workers. The conclusion is that during the next decade such training programs should be job specific and aimed at entry-level positions.

Geographic Location: South and West

Since the late 1950s, the North's population growth has slowed while growth in the South and West has increased rapidly. Between now and the year 2000, the North's population will increase 4 percent; growth in the South and West will exceed 20 percent. Current trends indicate that by the year 2030 the population of the South will overtake that of the Northeast and Midwest combined. Of the 32.5 million new jobs created by the year 2000, 18 million will be in the South, 10 million in the West, and under 5 million in the North. Among the 50 fastest growing metropolitan areas over the next ten years, 20 will be in the South and 16 in the West with 11 in California, 6 in Florida, and 5 in Texas. Furthermore, the far West, especially California and Washington with their extensive production facilities, will dominate the production sector of the economy as more and more businesses relocate. The shift of industry follows the population movement which, in turn, attracts more industry. The cycle is already in motion and is irreversible in the foreseeable future. Plant closings and relocations from the North, Northeast and Midwest will become more common as a result of these population shifts.

The fact that industry is and will continue to relocate to the South and West seems indisputable. If one agrees that the shift will continue and then contemplates the number of citizens affected and the resultant political pressure for regulation of such an industrial movement, it is clear that this geographic shift of population and industry will occasion a legislative response.

Thus far, organized labor has forced the issue of plant closings in three arenas. At the bargaining table, they have been moderately successful in getting contract clauses that require management to deal with labor on the effects of plant closings (advance notice, retraining, relocation allowances, and reinstatement rights) though not on the closing decision itself. The second arena is the court system where the U.S. Supreme Court has recognized a management duty to bargain over the effects of plant closings[2] but has removed the actual decision to close from mandatory bargaining.[3] Finally, in the Congressional arena, bills have been introduced to eliminate or cushion the impact of employee dislocation. It is in Congress that the definitive word on plant closings and relocations can be expected to surface sometime in the next few years. Congress is presently awaiting a report on plant closing from the Task Force on Economic Adjustment and Worker Dislocation formed by the Secretary of Labor. The report is expected to recommend legislation that would require the following actions by companies contemplating closing and/or relocation:

- Employers will be required to give three months' advance notice of a plant closing.
- Closings will be prohibited unless and until the employer has met with representatives, if any, of employees and consulted in good faith for the purpose of reaching a mutually satisfactory alternative or modification to the plant closing plan.
- A 15-member National Commission on Plant Closings and Worker Dislocation will be established to study and report legislative recommendations concerning closings.

Thus, employers can be expected to continue the rush to the South and West but will be required to comply with soon-to-be passed legislation regulating conditions of such relocations.

Conclusion

The labor force trends discussed in this article will all have major implications for human resource managers during the next ten years. Only by being aware of such trends can responsible individuals begin to formulate intelligent corporate responses. The responses discussed can serve as a starting point for strategic human resource planning. In some cases, bold corporate initiatives are called for, while in others simple legislative compliance will suffice. In any event, the labor force changes over the next decade will have serious negative repercussions for those caught unaware. This article has been an attempt to help planners avoid such situations and to begin to think about their reactions to the coming demographic changes. The time to begin was yesterday.

Endnotes

[1] United States Congress, House Committee on Education and Labor, 1994.   Act for Better Child Care, Hearing, Washington, D.C., U.S.G.P.O.: 15-16.

[2] *First National Maintenance Corp. v. NLRB*, 1981. 452 U.S. 666.

[3] *NLRB v. Adams Dairy, Inc.*, 1965. 350E 2d, 108.

New Directions in Fringe Benefits

Economic supplements, or fringe benefits, are compensation other than wages or salaries. Such benefits comprise more than 35 percent of the compensation of the typical U.S. employee today, and the proportion is increasing annually. In recent years, fringe benefits have grown twice as fast as wages and salaries. During the early 1930s, however, benefits comprised less than 4 percent of typical payroll costs. Since World War II, fringe benefits have increased dramatically, and in the last ten years have nearly tripled in cost.

Clearly, today the term "fringe" is a misnomer. Fringes are no longer extras. The great majority of Americans rely on them as their first line of defense against illness, unemployment and old age. Currently, fringe benefits provide protection against the contingencies of life from the first day of employment to retirement and beyond. Many of these benefits are not new to the compensation package. Some were introduced unilaterally by employers as early as the turn of the century. Fringe benefits, however, now play a far more important role in labor relations than has been the case in the past. A great variety of fringe benefits can be found in industry today, with some labor agreements containing special (and often unique) benefits.

There appear to be several reasons for this growing emphasis on fringe benefits. As this country has grown richer and more self-assured, the desire to eliminate risk and increase personal security has grown stronger. Employees have shown a strong tendency to want to eliminate insecurity of every conceivable kind. While employees could buy some of these benefits directly, they seem generally to find it more convenient to have their contribution for these benefits deducted from their paychecks. In most cases, too, fringes provide important income tax savings. When the company pays for the benefits, the employee does not have to pay tax on the money spent to purchase them. Furthermore, employees often recognize that an organization's mass purchasing power can buy various insurance and benefit plans more inexpensively than they could individually.

Collective bargaining has also contributed to the growth of fringes. Unions do compete with each other, and there is considerable prestige attached to being the first union to win a new type of fringe. Union members may give their union more credit for a new benefit than for an equally costly increase in pay. When one union wins such a benefit, other unions will usually follow suit with nonunion firms then feeling compelled to join the parade to continue attracting good, new employees.

Employers provide fringe benefits partly to raise employee morale, partly to meet their social responsibilities, and partly to make more effective use of their work force. With the possible exception of profit-sharing plans, however, it would be unrealistic to expect benefit plans to motivate higher productivity. The idealistic belief that employees will be grateful for the organization's beneficence and will, in turn, express their appreciation by harder work has largely disappeared today. Fringe benefits may improve employee morale and make both unions and employers look good to employees, but they do not generally contribute to increased productivity.

New Influences on Fringe Benefits

Given that fringe benefits are important to employees, labor unions, and employers, why are they changing and in what direction? Many companies are concluding that they must offer a range of benefits to match the changed realities of the new lifestyles that abound today. Benefits have traditionally been designed to fit the needs of the breadwinner, dependent spouse and family. Several current trends have transformed this lifestyle.

- Fewer male employees are now the sole supporter of the family.
- More couples are remaining childless; those who do not are having fewer children.
- Marriage is not as prevalent as it once was.
- Work spans are more discontinuous, especially among women with children.
- Retirement is no longer expected at age 65.

The work force is thus characterized by a greater variety of family and behavior patterns than ever before. In fact, traditional families consisting of a working husband with a dependent wife and children now constitute less than 15 percent of the nation's work force. Roughly half of all workers belong to families that have two or more incomes and another 14 percent live alone. The number of unmarried couples living together is more than double what it was ten years ago. Most conventional benefit programs provide a single worker with some unwanted coverage, like life insurance. At the same time, the value of the total benefit package is generally far less than that for a married worker at the same salary and seniority level. Furthermore, members of two-income families may duplicate their spouse's benefits in areas such as health insurance, while unmarried couples who live together often cannot obtain coverage.

The general trend in fringe benefits for the future, then, is toward more flexibility in meeting the needs and wants of the employees. While most companies still maintain conventional benefit plans, the flexible plan is an idea whose time has come. Despite concerns over the difficulties and cost, corporate interest in the idea is growing. There are dissenters, however, with labor unions being one of the most vocal critics of flexible benefits. Union leaders have expressed the fear that employees, given a choice, may eliminate benefits they need. Unions, thus, generally favor a comprehensive plan that covers every contingency.

Even though most companies are not yet ready for sweeping changes, fringe benefits may be repackaged in several different mixes. Such packages may address needs of single workers, those who are married with no children, employees with young dependents, parents facing college expenses, and "empty-nesters" interested in retirement. Many companies may substitute defined contribution plans for defined benefit plans (called the *cafeteria approach*) thus providing the opportunity for a benefit package more tailored to a particular employee at the same cost to the employer.

Under the cafeteria approach, every employee receives a core of essential benefits. Then employees can "buy" other benefits with credits earned on the basis of wages and seniority. Few companies have these plans today, mainly because of the administrative costs involved and their pessimistic assessment of the employees' capability to make intelligent choices. Neither of these reasons should be roadblocks. After an initial investment to program the various choices available, the cost of administering the cafeteria plan is not prohibitive - particularly in light of its potential returns. The argument about employees not being capable of making intelligent choices is another example of management confusing education level with intelligence. Thus, one can expect that the cafeteria-style benefit plan will become more prevalent in the future as a way to satisfy the needs of an increasingly diverse work force.

New Directions

The typical benefits package today is made up of four main components:

1. **Pay for time not worked.** The demand for leisure is being met with more holidays, longer vacations, and shorter work weeks. The number of celebrated holidays keeps increasing with half the union contracts specifying ten or more paid holidays per year. The trend for the future is certain to include even more paid holidays, including such holidays as the employee's birthday, the date on which the employee joined the union, and personal days. It is also certain to include longer paid vacations. Employees in the future will get longer vacations than before, have them earlier in their careers, and be freer to choose when to take them. Although the two-week vacation after one year of service is still typical, workers are beginning to qualify for longer vacations sooner. The maximum amount of vacation time that a worker may receive has also been increasing and should continue to do so.

In comparison to most European countries, the American worker gets very little vacation. Many European countries set legal minimums on vacation time, and nowhere is the legal minimum as little as two weeks a year. Since many of the more generous vacation plans in this country result from pressure by organized labor and since many large labor unions are becoming international in scope, pressure for more vacation time can be expected to continue. Even today, many employers have adopted "floating" days off, and others have instituted vacation banking systems that allow workers to save and withdraw days off throughout their employment.

Another kind of pay for time not worked is dismissal pay. Such pay is now a common product of collective bargaining, but it is likely to become even more prevalent in the future as unemployment, due to both economic and technological causes, continues to be a problem. Supplementary unemployment benefit plans also address the problem of dismissal and subsequent unemployment, and over 5 million employees are now covered by such plans.

2. **Insurance.** Most organizations now provide several forms of protection against the loss of income and extra expense caused by sickness. Companies in more than a dozen different geographic areas have formed groups to plan and carry out cost-cutting strategies for health care benefits. These programs include efforts to curb excessive use of hospitals through utilization reviews, outpatient and surgicenter care, insurance coverage of second and even third opinions on elective surgery, reimbursement for health services at home, greater use of pre-admission testing, and increased private use of professional standards review organizations.

Trends in recent years involve an increase in the amount and duration of insurance benefits; extension of benefits to retired workers as well as to those dependents not yet covered; defrayal of costs for some medically related drugs; protection against catastrophic illness and accidents; dental, visual and mental health benefits; and preventive health care plans. The fact that the insurance package has increased in cost faster than other fringe benefits have over the last five years means that this area will be one of the troublespots for employers in the years ahead.

3. **Retirement.** The continuing trend toward early retirement has resulted in a heightened awareness within American corporations of the importance of retirement planning and education programs. Most pension plans relate benefits to past earnings, but there is a trend to weigh more heavily the income received in the last years of employment. Today, in the more liberal companies, pensions and Social Security benefits together may total as much as 80 percent of an employee's after tax pre-retirement income, whereas 25 percent was much more common a decade ago.

There has also been a marked increase in the vesting allowances for workers covered by pension plans. Under normal economic conditions these would be expected to continue in the future, but more and more employers have recently been trying to reverse this trend by shifting more of the burden of financing the program and keeping it actuarially sound back to the individual employee. Whether this is the start of a new long-term trend or simply a temporary concession depends on the performance of the U.S. economy over the next few years.

While most private pensions do not include a cost-of-living allowance, more and more companies are making *ad hoc* pension adjustments every two to three years, with the trend toward routine adjustments. Most companies compute pensions on final pay - with a trend toward a smaller number of years being the basis for the computation - thus increasing the pension amount. A few companies base the computation on career averaging rather than final pay thus softening the effects of changing jobs in mid-career. Some top executives are even able to negotiate a supplemental executive retirement plan when changing jobs so that they lose nothing in the switch - a practice that can be expected to continue in the next decade as employers compete for proven, upper-level human resources.

Another relatively new idea that is rapidly gaining popularity is for the company to provide retirement planning for each employee. Today many companies, well aware of the innumerable pitfalls awaiting the unprepared retiree, are making pre-retirement counseling a new and vital benefit for employees. The more responsible companies now offer corporate-wide, multi-hour seminars that in the aggregate involve thousands of employees and spouses. As recently as ten years ago, pre-retirement planning was largely looked on as the prerogative of top executives. In the last five years, retirement counseling in companies has doubled with great variation in the scope of the programs offered. A few give only the information that the law requires and call that pre-retirement planning but many voluntarily go much further.

The typical corporate program is less than four years old, was purchased outside the company, and was then tailored to its own needs. Participants spend a minimum of 15 hours in group sessions which make use of printed and audiovisual materials, lectures, and some seminar-type discussions. It is clear that in the future corporate America will take more responsibility than ever before for the retirement planning of its employees.

4. **Service and prerequisites.** A variety of other fringe benefits are also available to employees today. Some employers provide amenities such as recreation rooms, jogging tracks, saunas, and picnic facilities for use by employees. Because of land costs, most elaborate amenities of this type are confined to suburban locations. Tuition-aid plans are available to many workers, but only three to five percent of white-collar workers and a lower percentage of blue-collar workers take advantage of them. Younger workers use these plans more than older workers do, with men and women using them equally. Participation increases with previous educational attain-ment and with income. Professional and technical workers use them more than others, and people in the West participate more than those who live elsewhere.

Versatile tuition-aid programs are offered by some companies. Others provide adoption benefits. These generally range from $800 to $1,000 per adoption, but some companies pay the same amount that an employee would receive through a medical plan for a normal delivery.

Given the lifestyle trends discussed earlier regarding children, marriage, work spans, etc., these types of benefits can only increase in appeal in the next ten years. If profit and loss statements dictate a reduction in the number of dollars a company will give for fringe benefits, items in this miscellaneous category will be the first to go, for workers have not become as accustomed to the newer fringes as they have to the old standbys.

Other Developments

Some innovative benefits being explored by companies today have a high probability of being implemented on a large scale in the future. One such benefit is the Tax Reduction Act Stock Ownership Plan (TRASOP). Under this plan, the company establishes a tax-qualified trust for employees and contributes employer stock equal in value to 10 percent of the amount taken by the company as an investment tax credit. Such a plan can benefit both the employees and the company.

Another new idea is the Matching Charitable Contribution Plan. Under this plan, the company makes contributions up to a specified limit to qualifying charities of the employee's choice in an amount equal to that contributed by the employee. Advantages of this plan include social value and employee morale boosting.

Some firms have a sick leave pool. Under this arrangement a portion of the employee's sick leave is pooled, to be used by those who need it. Other companies are experimenting with varying work hours such as flex-time, summer working hours, four-day weeks, split days, job-sharing and a floating schedule. Each of these ideas is indicative of the innovative thinking that will lead fringe benefits in entirely new directions in the next ten years. Such innovative ideas do not necessarily have to increase the cost of the fringe benefit package to the employer.

The Cost of Coverage

Despite substantial concern over the increasing cost of providing employee benefits, a majority of top management indicated in a national underwriters' survey that they had no plans to scale back their benefit program in the future. Fifty-nine percent of those surveyed said they planned to expand their benefit programs in the future while 38 percent said they would maintain their programs at current levels.

Approximately half of those responding to the survey cited potential increased federal regulation of the pension system, the introduction of some form of national health plan, and increases in the Social Security tax rate as among the most pressing problems they face in the area of fringe benefits. Fifty-one percent indicated they would like to see benefits play an increasingly larger role in the total employee compensation picture. Half of the managers surveyed indicated that the major development they would like to see in pensions and employee benefits in the future is a relaxation of government regulation and interference with more emphasis placed on individual savings. Fifty-three percent said they planned to pass along to their employees some of the increased costs of providing benefits, and 51 percent plan to pass some of the costs along to the consumer. A quarter of the respondents said the fundamental change they would make in their employee benefit program would be to have employees share more of the costs.

Conclusion

In conclusion, factors affecting the direction of fringe benefits in the future can be summarized as follows:

- Benefits have risen as a direct result of union-won demands over the years. When companies consider basic pay demands too high, they move to the benefits area as an additional negotiating chip.
- Successful experimentation with "cafeteria plans" has shown that employees regard the option of picking and choosing benefit alternatives as an extremely attractive addition to traditional compensation programs.
- People do have different needs according to their age, financial and family position, attitudes, and lifestyle. Younger employees tend to favor benefits that can be of frequent or immediate use, such as vacation days, holidays and flexible working hours.   Older employees are usually security conscious, preferring life insurance and retirement-related benefits.
- For certain employees, extra vacation days or the opportunity to take a leave of absence is of enormous psychological value - far beyond its actual cost to the company.
- Increasingly, organizations with well-constructed benefit programs are gaining a competitive edge in the recruiting process. The swing elements, however, are not the traditional benefits but rather the additional special coverages.
- Whether the employer continues to pay the lion's share of the cost of these new packages (or shifts more responsibility to the employee) is directly related to the performance of the economy and its resultant influence on company profit and loss statements.
- Fringe-benefit packages are undergoing their most radical change since World War II, with emphasis placed on coming up with new ideas and tailoring the system to individual employees rather than increasing the level of existing benefits and offering one package to

all. This will, in turn, give fringe benefits more "bang for the buck" and increase their importance in the total compensation scheme beyond their already sizable, and constantly growing, 35 percent.

Fringe benefits will be one of the most important areas of employer-employee interface in the next ten years. A well-informed manager cannot afford not to keep current with new developments in this important, expensive, and rapidly changing area.

Health Care And Small Business:
A Potential Disaster

ABSTRACT

The American public recently became acutely aware of a problem that plagues American citizens and businesses alike - the rising cost of health care. While the debate over the Federal government's role in health care brought this problem to the top of the American policy agenda, the problem is hardly a new one.

This article begins with a discussion of the reasons why health care costs have skyrocketed and the problems that these rising costs present for small businesses. It takes the reader through a discussion of the most popular mechanisms for controlling health care costs in small businesses, includes an evaluation of these mechanisms, and concludes with suggestions for addressing the problem.

The Problem: Rising Health Care Costs

The relevant statistics on the state of the current health care system in this country are shocking. Every month two million people lose their health care coverage. During the next two years, one out of four Americans will be without coverage for a period of time. There are almost 39 million Americans without health insurance today and another 22 million who are underinsured.[1]

The consumer price index shows medical costs rising at nearly two and one-half times the rate of inflation. Health care costs will consume close to 13 percent of the gross national product this year - currently the largest share of any industrialized nation. This percentage is projected to grow to nearly 17 percent by the end of the decade.[2] These new health figures mean that by the year 2000 nearly one-sixth of total national output will be consumed by health care costs, compared with only one-sixteenth in 1965 (Exhibit 1). Annual health care spending is projected to grow from $671 billion in 1990 to $1.6 trillion at the turn of the century.[3]

To place these overwhelming statistics in context, consider that health benefits are the second most prevalent fringe benefit offered by employers, following paid vacations. It is this widespread offering of health benefits by employers that explains the feeling of entitlement that employees have concerning health coverage. A bitter conflict has erupted between employers and employees during the past decade as the cost of insuring workers has skyrocketed.

Health care costs have risen so fast that by 1991 many American corporations were spending an amount equal to one-fourth of their net earnings to provide medical coverage for their employees.[4] This figure is presently over one-third for the typical U.S. corporation. The problem underlying the surge in health insurance premiums is the inability of the nation to bring rising medical costs under control.

Three major reasons for the surge include:

1. the high cost of advances in medical technology and drug therapy;
2. the failure of proposed cost savings methods; and
3. the increased use and abuse of the system.

1. The nature of the health care system virtually assures that medical costs will continue to grow faster than the economy. Advances in medical science produce some cost-saving breakthroughs, but they also make possible more sophisticated and expensive treatments. One reason why U.S. health care costs are greater than those of other industrialized nations is the use of more high-technology health machinery and equipment.

The U.S. has far more magnetic resonance imaging machines, a greater rate of expensive organ transplants, and more open heart surgery centers than any other industrialized nation. It is the use of such equipment and procedures that has dramatically increased the dollar amount of health insurance claims. It is not uncommon for companies to file claims for millions of dollars for just a single employee. This was not possible ten years ago because much of this expensive medical technology had not yet been invented.[5]

It is our insatiable demand for ongoing research in new medical technologies which contributes to the relentless upward pressure on health care costs. The cost-benefit analysis of the use of this technology in particular cases poses a classic moral and theological dilemma. As yet, we as a society have been unwilling to come to grips with the issue of economics versus continuance or quality of life in the area of health care.

2. Another reason for rising health care costs is the failure of Health Maintenance Organizations (HMOs) and Preferred Provider Organizations (PPOs) to sustain their promises of achieving major cost-reduction breakthroughs. In the 1980s, cost increases spurred intense new competition in health care delivery. This competition resulted in the growth of HMOs, which provide all health services to members for a flat fee, and PPOs in which affiliated medical practitioners provide services at a discount. While HMOs and PPOs do offer cost savings of up to 20 percent when compared with traditional fee-for-service plans, the percentage savings offered by HMOs and PPOs has not grown appreciably in the last five years.[6] The reality is that fee increases in HMO and PPO plans over the last five years have kept pace with those of conventional plans. HMO premium increases have been slightly below those of conventional plans for most years, but PPO premium increases have equaled or exceeded those of conventional plans virtually every year.[7] These organizations served only to provide a false sense of optimism among employers and insurers that the explosive inflation in health care costs had been contained.

3. A third cause of the health care crisis is the increasing use and abuse of the system itself. A primary reason for the increasing use of the system is the aging of the population. The average life expectancy of a U.S. citizen has risen from 77.6 years in 1940 to 83 years today, and is expected to rise to 86 years by the year 2040.[8] A substantial increase in the elderly population will place additional strain on the health care system as the elderly are the most likely to incur heavy medical costs.

Based on current trends, spending on Medicare and Medicaid - the government health insurance programs for the elderly, poor, and disabled - will consume 26.4 percent of the federal budget in the year 2003, up from 16.5 percent in 1994.[9] Another instance of increasing use is the expanded coverage, in many cases state government mandated, in the areas of mental health and substance abuse. These treatments account for nearly ten percent of medical plan costs.[10]

Abuse of the health care system can be seen in two instances. First, many employees, fearing the loss of their jobs in bad economic times, will schedule elective surgery to ensure the cost will be covered by their employers. Second, the litigiousness of society has forced doctors to practice defensive medicine by performing more tests and services than might otherwise be necessary. Studies suggest that up to 25 percent of doctors' procedures are done for defensive reasons.[11]

The author would never contend that these are the only reasons for the escalating cost of health care. He would, however, argue that they are among the biggest factors.

The Impact On Small Business

The escalating cost of health care continues to have an enormous impact on business, particularly small businesses. There was a time when health insurance was an affordable benefit companies automatically offered to their employees. Today, health care costs are seen as the greatest threat to the survival and profitability of small businesses. Of the uninsured, the Small Business Administration has estimated that 8.2 million are private wage-and-salary workers and 1.6 million are business owners. Almost 75 percent of those 8.2 million uninsured workers are employed in firms with fewer than twenty-five employees.[12]

The health of the U.S. economy is closely tied to the health and growth of the small business sector, including small family firms. Small businesses have historically created a significant share of new jobs. In the last decade, small firms have been responsible for creating virtually all of the nation's job growth. Companies with nineteen or fewer employees created 78 percent of all new jobs over the last six years.[13] A growing number of small companies, struggling to maintain their profitability and unable to cope with rising health care costs, are being priced out of the health insurance market. Thus, the prime new job generators in the economy are also the firms with workers least likely to be covered by health insurance. The continued unavailability and high cost of health insurance for small businesses could adversely affect the future growth of the economy.

Any reform of the health care system should specifically address the factors that cause small businesses to be more severely affected than large businesses by the health care crisis. These factors include:

1. the inability to provide secure and comprehensive coverage;
2. cost shifting;
3. the discriminatory practices of insurers;
4. the tax deductibility of premiums; and
5. the administrative burden.

Small businesses, including the self-employed, face enormous disadvantages as purchasers of health insurance and suffer the most due to their lack of negotiating power. Many small companies have been hit with annual premium increases of 20 to 50 percent in recent years.[14] Many are no longer able to provide coverage for their employees due to reasons such as insufficient profits, high turnover rates, and unavailability of group coverage (Exhibit 2).

1. While some small businesses are no longer providing coverage, others have resorted to offering policies so full of exclusions and deductibles that only catastrophic coverage remains. This leads to employees having little choice of plans. In the smallest businesses, those with fewer than ten employees, fewer than one-fifth of the workers with health benefits were offered more than one plan.[15]

When employers limit workers' choices of health plans, mismatches can be the result. Employers' priorities are typically different from those of their employees. The employee wants all services covered, special services such as vision and dental coverage, low out-of-pocket costs, and a choice of doctors. The employer often simply wants to save money. By offering fewer choices, employers seek to maximize their buying power with individual plans.

2. For small businesses that are still able to afford health care coverage, comparable plans and benefits cost on average 35 percent more than for larger firms.[16] A major reason for this is the cost shifting caused by the uninsured population. Uncompensated care is provided to the uninsured at emergency rooms throughout the country. The cost of this care is four to five times the cost of similar care at a doctor's office.[17] Cost shifting occurs because when one group pays less (or nothing), the others must pay more to cover the cost.

Large, self-insured companies frequently have a great deal of leverage and can negotiate with providers to reduce the impact of the cost shift. Small employers, however, have virtually no ability to reduce this cost shift and must bear its full brunt. Unfortunately, the smaller the business the more disproportionate the burden. No part of the business community is hit harder by the high cost of the uninsured than small business.

3. The discriminatory practices of insurers are another factor causing small businesses to be hit hard by the health care crisis. Approximately 15 percent of small firms fall into industries that are routinely "redlined," meaning that insurance companies refuse to provide coverage to entire industries that are considered high-risk.[18] These industries include automobile dealerships, barber and beauty salons, construction companies, florist shops, and trucking firms.

Employee characteristics are also a contributing factor in lower small firm coverage. Small businesses employ a disproportionate share of young and old workers, women, low income, seasonal, and part-time employees. Insurers tend to charge high premiums for these groups, thus forcing small businesses to exclude them from coverage in an effort to keep down health insurance costs (Exhibit 3).

Additionally, some insurers engage in price baiting and gouging by offering discounted rates for the first year of coverage to be followed by much higher rates in the next year. For a small business, with fewer employees to pool the risk, large medical expenses from a single critically ill employee or dependent can trigger an explosive rise in firm rates or the firm being dropped by the insurance company altogether.

4. The differences in the way tax laws treat health insurance plans provided by firms with different corporate structures also places an undue burden on the small business. Self-employed individuals can deduct only 25 percent of the cost of health insurance expenses incurred on behalf of the taxpayer, taxpayer's spouse and dependents. However, most incorporated businesses are allowed to deduct 100 percent of their health insurance expenses.[19] This is clearly unfair to the self-employed and the owner-operators of unincorporated small businesses and by definition serves to increase the cost of their health insurance relative to larger companies.

5. A final factor that causes smaller businesses to pay higher health care costs compared to larger companies is the administrative burden. Small businesses pay up to 40 percent of their total health care expenditures in administrative costs, versus the five percent that large companies pay on average.[20]   Small businesses face an array of paperwork that severely taxes their limited administrative resources. Unlike larger firms, small business owners generally do not have a benefits department. As a result, the small business owner loses valuable time away from the business trying to effectively handle the legal and financial complexities of benefits administration. To further complicate matters, many small firms attempt to contain costs by changing insurance carriers every few years. Comparison shopping for health insurance plans is time consuming, and small business owners must frequently obtain expensive outside expert advice.

Clearly, small businesses have a large stake in solving the health care crisis in this country. The question now becomes, "What can be done?"

Suggestions For Containing Costs

The primary drawback to small business owners addressing the cost of their health care package is the potential loss of employees to companies with more attractive coverage. Health coverage can vary substantially across companies. Therefore, prior to making any drastic changes, a company should first take a very close look at the coverage they offer, paying particular attention to the relatively small components of their coverage that can potentially cost a great deal. These components include prescription cards, dental, and eye care plans. Employees are less likely to make career decisions based on what are considered to be minor benefits such as these. Cutting some or all of these minor programs, however, can result in relatively large cost savings.

If more drastic or sweeping measures are necessary in a particular instance, small businesses can consolidate their insurance plans. As mentioned earlier, health care providers reserve their best rates for large customers, so small businesses pay 20 to 35 percent more than large businesses for comparable health care.[21] If small businesses join in their insurance purchasing efforts, they can buy insurance in bulk and reduce their individual costs. When companies join forces, they develop the leverage with insurance companies that is necessary to obtain the lowest possible rates.

There are many organizations nationwide that can help small businesses find these insurance coalitions, called Multiple Employer Trusts (METs). Examples of this type of "joining forces" include the Small Business Service Bureau (SBSB) and Cleveland's Council of Smaller Enterprises. The SBSB pools the purchasing power of more than 2,000 members and can offer more plan options and obtain rates significantly lower than members could obtain individually. The Cleveland coalition covers 13,000 member companies with one to 150 employees and obtains premium costs for their members that are 35 percent below average for the market.[22] However, many fear the viability of these organizations. As a result, employees of small organizations dislike the risk associated with joining a large trust. Generally, insured METs - those backed by insurance companies - are less risky than those that are self insured. Therefore, opting for insured METs may assuage some of the concerns of employees regarding this option.

Another option for small businesses is to switch to managed-care plans. These plans include HMOs and PPOs. Managed-care has become the fastest growing trend in the health care industry. Seventy-two percent of

Americans who obtain health insurance through an employer are enrolled in a managed-care plan, compared with less than 20 percent in 1984.[23] These plans guarantee business for hospitals and doctors in exchange for lower health care prices and save consumers approximately 20 percent in health care costs.[24] The Group Health Association of America will help small businesses locate such plans.

Although these managed-care plans were supposed to be a grand revolution in the health care industry, they have not met expectations. Cost savings on individual office visits have been offset by more frequent visits. In addition, employees are limited to certain doctors and hospitals who may not be the best available for a particular patient, procedure, or illness. When major medical events occur, the authorization process and bureaucracy the patients have to endure can be overwhelming and extremely frustrating.

As mentioned earlier, over the last five years premiums for HMO and PPO plans rose at approximately the same rates as premiums for conventional plans.[25]   However, for smaller organizations, many consultants still view well run managed-care organizations as attractive options when compared to conventional insurance programs.

Regardless of the type of insurance employers provide for their employees, they can benefit from carrying out cost-containment strategies. These strategies have already been widely adopted by large employers. Smaller firms are far less likely to have implemented such strategies.[26] Four out of ten small and mid-size northeastern companies surveyed in 1993 had not tried any cost-containment strategies.[27]   These strategies include requiring:

- pre-admission certification to authorize medical services and predetermine the patient's length of hospital stay;
- second opinions for elective surgery;
- outpatient surgery, if it is possible;
- concurrent review, to monitor a patient's treatment and hospital stay;
- discharge planning to decide what additional treatment is necessary; and
- management of high-cost cases to determine the most economical treatment for patients with long term and terminal diseases.

Both the pre-admission certification and the second opinions require the employee/patient to go to a great deal of effort to get their treatment through the review and approval process. This situation may be exacerbated by the fact that the employee is suffering and is often not in a condition to "jump through the insurance company's hoops." Outpatient surgery can also be a negative as patients are sent home just hours after surgery. Complications can occur while the patient is not in a medical treatment facility. The remaining cost-saving measures of concurrent review, discharge planning, and high-cost case management, may at times work against the interest of the patient. The goal of these measures is cost containment, not the physical well-being of the individual.

Obviously, these cost-containment measures have potential negative effects on the employee/patient. There are also questions about the costs associated with executing these strategies. The additional involvement in the medical environment has inherent costs. This is especially true for the second opinion requirement as it appears that, in most cases, the second opinion only confirms the first. Therefore, the cost of the second opinion may simply add to the total treatment costs.

Small businesses can also save money just by shopping around for insurance. Premiums for essentially the same coverage can vary as much as 50 percent.[28] Insurance brokers may be able to help obtain lower prices and save time spent shopping, but their fees are paid by the insurance company. Therefore, the insurance brokers may not be impartial in their recommendations.

Another reason small businesses must be careful is that, as mentioned earlier, many insurance companies offer first year prices that are unbelievably low and then escalate costs substantially in the following year. One way to avoid such a problem is to enter into a two- to three-year contract so that the insurance company is obligated to offer the original price for a longer period.

In shopping around, small businesses must be careful to avoid insurance companies that are not viable entities even though they offer the lowest price. In the process of buying insurance, companies are buying the insurer's promise to make the future payments for medical costs. Companies need to investigate their potential insurer's financial status, which may include reviewing their annual financial statements and reports from ratings firms. Several financial publishing firms, such as the Standard & Poors Corporation, investigate and report on the financial standing of insurance companies.

If small businesses choose to keep the traditional fee-for-service type of insurance, there are ways to decrease costs other than simply changing providers. Many large businesses who continue to use traditional insurance engage a managed-care provider as a consultant. In the consulting capacity, the managed-care provider reviews medical service bills for compliance with state limitations and reasonableness. They also review claims to ensure that the cost-containment strategies discussed above are being properly implemented. Since a company's insurance premiums are based on the history of payments that the insurance company has had to make (the company's "experience rate"), the company has a vested interest in reducing the cost incurred by the insurance company. The fee charged by these managed-care companies is normally a percentage of the amount they save the employer. Thus, the reduction in health care costs more than offsets the consulting fee.

Another way to cut fees while maintaining traditional insurance coverage is to implement a wellness program. Many insurance carriers reduce premiums for companies that have such programs. As a result, a growing number of employers are setting up these wellness programs; however, not many small employers have joined in this trend.

A wellness program includes things like monitoring cholesterol and blood pressure, encouraging smokers to quit, and promoting fitness, stress management, and weight control. Very simple procedures, such as altering what is available in vending machines and adopting no-smoking policies, are part of these programs. These programs may also include a reward system for employees who succeed in achieving goals set by the program such as quitting smoking and losing weight. Bonuses may also be given for staying healthy and not requiring medical services.

The benefits of wellness programs can be monumental. Not only do companies get a discount up front for setting up the program, but they also get reduced premiums based on their experience rates. Obviously, people in good health tend to need less medical care. Therefore, as companies' employees get healthier and their experience rates decrease, their premiums decrease as well. Improved employee health can have tremendous additional benefits to companies such as increased productivity and decreased sick time. For example, smokers who have quit greatly increase their productivity by not venturing outside once an hour for a cigarette. Although costs to small businesses for these programs may be rather high, the reduction of health insurance costs and increased productivity make these programs a highly desirable option. Many hospitals will help companies sponsor such programs and provide training and classes to employees free of charge to the company.

Small businesses may also want to consider self-insuring for small claims, because with this option, businesses only have to insure themselves for losses that exceed a pre-determined threshold. This leads to lower premiums. There are, however, drawbacks with the self-insurance option. There is talk in Washington that this option may be abolished in the future for companies of less than 5,000 employees. Insurance companies charge between $6 and $12 per employee, per month, to administer these types of plans.[29] Most importantly, the discipline necessary to save for future health care expenditures, even when employees are healthy, may be a difficult task for small business owners. If companies are not disciplined in their saving efforts, employees, as well as employers, suffer when substantial health costs are incurred.

The least popular option among employees is the shifting of more of the health costs to the employees. Ways to shift these costs include requiring payroll deductions to cover part of the premiums and adding or increasing employee-paid deductibles or co-payments. Although small firms pay greater insurance premiums than larger companies, they are less likely to pass the costs on to employees. Traditionally, many small businesses have paid 100 percent of employee health care costs, as a great number of the employees are family members and close friends. A Small Business Administration survey found that 70 percent of all firms with fewer than 100 employees paid all of the employees' health premiums and, on average, paid 87 percent of the family premiums.[30]

The idea behind employee-paid deductibles is that employees should insure themselves for small claims, as they do with automobile insurance, and then depend on their employer-provided insurance only to cover substantial claims that might be beyond their ability to pay. Of course, raising deductibles could severely affect lower-paid employees. It has therefore been suggested that deductibles and co-payments should be altered based on employee compensation levels. While some contend that this will come to pass, the author would argue that this presents an inequity unless the cost and usage can be shown to increase for employees at higher income levels.

Although having employees pay some, or a larger portion of health care costs may be a last resort for small businesses, there appear to be substantial associated benefits. If employees know they will feel the negative financial effect of obtaining medical services, they will be more hesitant and may not seek unnecessary treatment. They have an economic stake in the decision. Conversely, an employee may neglect to obtain preventive care due to the cost of the deductible and subsequently develop a more serious problem that is then covered under the employer-provided insurance.

Finally, employers may want to consider flexible benefit plans and flexible spending accounts. Flexible benefit plans, otherwise known as cafeteria-style plans, let employees pick and pay for only those benefits they want. Twenty-two percent of small businesses have these types of plans and 17 percent intend to add them within the next five years.[31] Implementing a flexible spending account allows employees to save on taxes. These accounts allow employees to set aside pre-tax income to pay for health-related expenses. The author views this as the most likely option to be implemented in the immediate future.

Conclusion

It is evident that the cost of health care is growing far faster than the rate of inflation and that a disproportionate amount of this cost burden is being placed on small businesses. Relief needs to be provided to small employers whether it comes in the form of sweeping health care reform or through incremental changes. The measures adopted so far are fine for the short term; but if the U.S. economy is going to continue to grow, it must find a way to remove the health care burden from its greatest job generator, the small business. Some combination of the ideas put forth herein are a necessary first step. The time to begin their implementation was yesterday!

Endnotes

[1] Bowles, E.B., "The Effects of Health Care Reform on Small Business," Statement of the Administrator of the Small Business Administration before the *House Committee on Small Business*, January 26, 1994, pp. 1-8.

[2] Thompson, K.D. & Davis, E., "Wanted: An Agenda For Small Business," *Black Enterprise*, November, 1992, pp. 53-58.

[3] Rich, S., "Health Costs to Consume 16% of GNP by 2000, Agency Says," *The Washington Post*, September 24, 1994, p. A2.

[4] Swoboda, F., "Health Care Costs Climb 21.6% in '90," *The Washington Post*, January 29, 1991, p. D1.

[5] *Ibid.*

[6] Feldman, J. & Garrett, E.M., "Curb Your Health Costs," *Money*, 1994, 23: pp. 58-63.

[7] Schwartz, M., "Health Coverage By Small Employers Waning," *National Underwriter*, March, 1993, Vol 1, p. 55.

[8] Marmon, L., "Needed: A New War on the Deficit," *Fortune*, 1994, Vol. 130 (10), pp. 191-198.

[9] Hilzenrath, D.S., "Health Plan Choice Limited at Most Firms, Study Finds," *The Washington Post*, October 4, 1994, p. C1.

[10] Thompson, R., "Curbing the High Cost of Health Care," *Nation's Business*, September, 1989, pp. 18-20.

[11] *Ibid.*

[12] Lichtenstein, J.H., "Factors Affecting the Provision and Cost of Health Insurance in Small Family Businesses," *Family Business Review*, 1993, Vol. 6(2), pp. 173-178.

[13] Thompson, R., "Small Firms' Stake in Health Reform," *Nation's Business*, November, 1993, pp. 18-25.

[14] *Ibid.*

[15] Hilzenrath, D.S. & Morgan, D., "Health Care Costs Continue to Rise Faster Than The National Income," *The Washington Post*, September 27, 1994, p. A5.

[16] Thompson, R., *op. cit.,* 1993, pp.18-25.

[17] Bowles, *op. cit.*, pp.1-8.

[18] *Ibid.*

[19] Lichtenstein, *op. cit.*, pp.173-178.

[20] *Ibid.*

[21] Thompson, R., *op. cit.*, 1993, pp.18-25.

[22] Feldman & Garrett, *op. cit.*, pp. 58-63.

[23] Thompson, R., *op. cit.*, 1993, pp.18-25.

[24] Feldman & Garrett, *op. cit.*, pp. 58-63.

[25] Schwartz, *op. cit.*, p. 55.

[26] Thompson, R., *op. cit.*, 1989, pp.18-20.

[27] Feldman & Garrett, *op. cit.*, pp. 58-63.

[28] Lord, C., "Health Care: A Benefit You Can Afford," *Motor Age*, 1993, pp. 56-60.

[29] Feldman & Garrett, *op. cit.*, pp. 58-63.

[30] Thompson, R., *op. cit.*, 1993, pp.18-25.

[31] Feldman & Garrett, *op. cit.*, pp. 58-63.

Exhibit 1

<u>**Health Care Expenditures as a Percentage of GNP**</u>

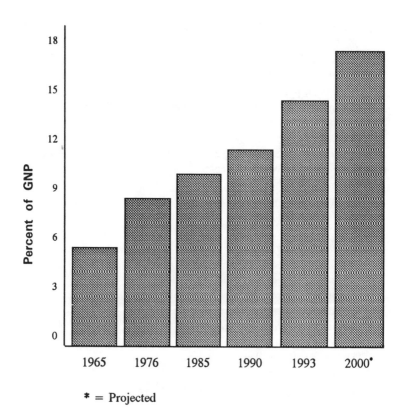

* = Projected

SOURCES: Rich, S., *The Washington Post*, September 24, 1994.

Bowles, E.B., Statement of the Administrator of the Small Business Administration before the *House Committee on Small Business*, January 26, 1994.

Exhibit 2

Reasons for Not Offering Coverage, by Firm Size

Reasons for Not Offering Coverage	Total	1-9	10-24	25-99	100	101-499
Insufficient Profit	67%	68%	62%	54%	36%	67%
Insurance Costs	62%	61%	70%	41%	68%	62%
Turnover	19%	17%	31%	36%	83%	18%
Group Coverage Not Available	16%	17%	3%	22%	0%	16%
Lack of Interest	13%	13%	5%	5%	0%	13%
Administrative Costs	9%	10%	2%	0%	51%	9%
State Minimums	1%	1%	0%	0%	0%	1%
Other	9%	3%	21%	5%	54%	9%

* Responses sum to more than 100 percent due to multiple answers.
SOURCE: ICF analysis of SBA, Office of Advocacy, Health Benefits Database, 1994.

Exhibit 3

Reasons for Offering Coverage Which Excludes Workers, By Firm Size

Reason / Type of Worker Excluded	Total	1-9	10-24	100	101-499
For Some Reason	73%	70%	80%	78%	88%
Part-Time	68%	65%	72%	71%	77%
Seasonal/Temporary	50%	50%	49%	45%	57%
Hourly Workers	8%	10%	5%	4%	8%
Over Some Age	3%	2%	4%	3%	1%
Under Some Age	2%	3%	1%	1%	1%

* Responses sum to more than 100 percent due to multiple answers.
SOURCE: ICF analysis of SBA, Office of Advocacy, Health Benefits Database, 1994.

Do We Still Need Labor Organizations?

In light of recent history,
the answer may surprise you.

It is common knowledge today that organized labor is losing strength in numerical and political terms as well as in the influence it exerts over the rest of the labor force. Numerically, labor unions have gone from 42% of the labor force in the 1950s to less than 16% today with every indication that this downward trend will continue. Were it not for the large number of newly organized public employees, the numbers would be even more ominous for labor unions. Further, the author contends that because of the restrictions on unions in the public sector (many cannot discuss wages and are prohibited from striking), the value to labor as a whole of a certain number of *public* employees organizing is not nearly as great as a like number of *privately* employed workers organizing. Thus, even the decreasing numbers may not tell the whole story of labor's deteriorating position.

Losing Clout

Politically, it should be clear to even the most casual observer that unions are losing their clout. The day when the powerful labor boss could "deliver" the labor vote, and hence was admitted to the inner circles of politics and politicians, is gone. It is hard to image a modern day John L. Lewis working closely with the President to draft key pieces of legislation or inviting members of Congress to his office to "discuss" their votes on upcoming issues - practices that were once a source of pride and status for powerful labor leaders. Labor's present political influence can best be gauged by its track record on such major issues as the Common Situs Picketing Bill, the Striker Replacement Bill, and Labor Law Reform - all defeats.

While organized labor has long been felt to be the trend-setter for wages and terms of employment with the rest of the labor force following with a certain time lag, even here we are witnessing the declining strength of unions. Except in a few big industries (steel, automobile, etc.) where unions enjoy a virtual monopoly, the increasing number of non-unionized firms has reintroduced the cost of labor as a comprehensive factor in market strategies. More and more frequently unions have had to consider the impact of their economic demands on the employer's ability to attract enough business to maintain employment levels. The construction industry is the most dramatic and widely known example of this phenomenon, but it is happening in an increasing number of less publicized instances. The "Southern Strategy" of the automobile employers, the move to the South of the big steel companies, and the inability of the mining unions to organize new mines are all indicators that even in industries long considered union strongholds, this factor will become increasingly important in the future.

A Look Backward

The question growing out of the above discussion is obvious: Do we still need labor organizations? Is it now possible that they have outlived their usefulness?

To answer questions such as these, it is important to take a brief look at labor history. Such a look back reaffirms one of the more important lessons to be learned from history in general: if people are pushed hard enough, are subjected to adverse enough conditions, they will take actions they would never have dreamed of had things been more equitable. It is only within the context of the time that today's labor student can understand why otherwise normal individuals would sit in unheated Michigan and Ohio automobile plants in the middle of winter for 44 days or why they would barricade themselves in steel mills and vow to fight to the death unless working conditions were improved. Read about what workers did to organize the first textile unions, the first mining unions, the first railroad unions, and then ask yourself if you would be willing or able to endure what they did. The author contends that you would probably be willing to if you were subjected to the treatment that those individuals were and if you realized that your children were destined to spend their lives in the same conditions.

The purpose here is not to discuss the historical plight of the American worker, yet it is crucial to understand what this plight was. For the first 150 years of this country's independence, the American worker was free politically but a virtual slave industrially. A look backward at management practices such as company-owned housing, water supplies, stores, etc., with their inflated prices, the payment of workers in company scrip, the unsafe and unhealthy working conditions, the unbelievably long workweek, the ridiculously low wages making it impossible for most families to live on the earnings of a single breadwinner, the completely arbitrary employment and personnel practices, and the company police forces, to mention only a few (in fact, the complete lack of consideration of the worker as a human being) puts the remarkable growth of labor unions in the early 1900s in a different light. Certainly at this point in U.S. history, workers were ready to support any type of organization that promised them relief from their miserable industrial existence. Thus, labor unions filled a real need: they brought humanitarianism to the workplace and a degree of dignity to the American worker.

Yet, ironically enough, because of their success unions have eradicated most of the conditions that led to their foundation. Thus, an often heard argument today is that while unions were necessary once, they are no longer necessary now. Proponents of this argument contend that the American worker today enjoys a higher standard of living than ever before and that we now have laws such as the Fair Labor Standards Act, the National Labor Relations Act, the Occupational Safety and Health Act, etc., which set a floor for wages, working conditions and general treatment of employees below which no employer is allowed to go. Thus unions are not needed to address conditions of exploitation; the law has stepped in.

The Deterrent Effect

While there is much support for this point of view, there are exceptions to it. While laws and subsequent conditions of employment may have changed, basic human nature has not. While it may be a pessimistic assessment of humanity and one with which the reader will likely disagree, a certain percentage of your fellow human beings will take advantage of you if the price is right. Through the ages, history has repeatedly proven this to be a truism, and anyone who does not realize it is either uninformed, extremely idealistic, or naive. While the laws provide deterrents in the form of minimum acceptable standards, it would certainly be unacceptable to the majority of our working population to exist at these minimum standards. For many, even a small retreat backward, be it in terms of compensation, working conditions or safety standards, would be completely unacceptable. Yet if the law were the only minimum, the only deterrent, there would be plenty of room for retreat in the standards enjoyed in the workplace by the majority of the U.S. labor force.

The biggest single deterrent, besides the law, to the reduction of standards in the workplace is the combined action of the workers - call it a "union" or any other name you wish. This action does not even have to come to pass to serve its purpose, for in many instances the mere possibility of such action is sufficient. There can be no doubt that the level of benefits received by many nonunion workers today is in part buttressed by their employers' desire to reward them at such a level that they remain unorganized.

Thus, while unions may have outlived their usefulness in terms of their original objectives, they are still needed because of what the author would refer to as their "deterrent" effect. Although the traditional browbeaten working conditions in which unions were formed has been replaced by today's more humanistic, less extreme conditions, unions continue to be the instrument inhibiting exploitation of the worker. The irony is that even those individuals in the blue-collar sector who would suffer first and most if unions were to disappear tomorrow do not realize the vital role labor organizations play in today's economy. It is not necessary for unions to be as strong as they once were, for the problems they are trying to correct are not as severe. The government has taken over part of their original purpose through various pieces of legislation. Yet it is still vital that labor organizations continue to exist, not only for those who benefit directly from them, but also for those who believe in the need to maintain the dignity of the worker. Unions find themselves in the same peculiar position as the military in that what they cause to happen may not be nearly as important as what they cause *not* to happen. This fact alone, in the author's opinion, continues to make unions what they have always been - an absolute necessity to the well-being of the work force.

Organized Labor's Deteriorating Condition

Any serious student of organized labor is aware that the American labor movement has experienced, and will continue to experience, hard times. Its membership is declining, the industries upon which its strength was built are in serious trouble, and unfavorable demographic, economic and political trends have seriously weakened its once unparalleled influence. Many who work in the field view this as a favorable trend, destined to mitigate problems from high inflation and unemployment to an unfavorable balance of payments, while others see it as a threat to the "checks and balances" necessary for reasonable labor management relations. Regardless of one's perspective, there can be no doubt that the deteriorating position of organized labor and its resultant effects in other sectors of the economy is one of the major socio-economic trends in the U.S. over the past twenty-five years.

The author proposes to examine this phenomenon by dissecting the problem itself and discussing its various components: exploring the major factors contributing to the problem; looking at the response to the problem by management, the government and independent consultants; and finally by assessing labor's potential for rectifying the situation.

The Problem

There are three equally important components of labor's present unenviable condition, one being numerical, one political and one jurisdictional. Numerically, the picture could not be worse for labor organizations. Despite the growth in the labor force over the last twenty-five years, unions now have fewer dues-paying members than they did in 1980. In the last seven years alone, total membership has dropped from twenty million to barely over sixteen million, and there is every indication that this trend will continue. Obviously, with the increasing number of jobs and the decreasing number of union members, the percentages present an even more ominous picture than the absolute numbers.

Organized labor's percentage share of the labor market has dropped from 42% in 1954, to 28% in 1965, to 18.8% today.[1] This numerical decrease (which translates into dues, which translates into economic clout) is the independent variable that drives all the other dependent variables discussed in this article. Organized labor has long dismissed this trend as attributable to demographic factors, but the validity of this claim is undermined when one considers the magnitude of the numbers. Any institution that loses ten percent of its membership while the universe from which it can draw increases twenty-five percent, is in serious trouble. The numbers, as they say, speak for themselves.

Politically, the loss of influence by organized labor is obvious. Every American who follows the news is aware that labor poured more than ten million dollars and deployed thousands upon thousands of volunteers to support the Democratic candidate in the latest presidential election. Their politically stated goal was to deliver sixty-five percent of the union households for Democrats while holding Republicans to thirty-five percent. Exit polls showed that nearly one-half the labor households voted Republican.[2] Yet one must look beyond this well-publicized failure to understand the severity of the political component of labor's deteriorating condition. The failure to wrestle a new Labor Law Reform Bill out of Congressional committee, the revision of the Davis-Bacon Act, the lifting of import quotas on Japanese automobiles despite labor opposition, the fact that two more states have Right-To-Work Laws than was the case five years ago, and the high probability that the Administration's sub-minimum wage for teenagers will weather the AFL-CIO's attack, all speak loudly and clearly to labor's political condition. Regardless of what advances it achieves at the bargaining table (an area to be discussed later), unless labor reverses its political direction, it may well "win a few battles but lose the war."

Jurisdictionally, the overwhelming percentage of organizing successes have appeared in the public sector. Over twenty percent of total union membership is now in this area. In the federal sector, sixty-one percent of the work force is now represented, while in the non-federal public sector, thirty percent are represented. Even in these sectors, however, the growth is slowing markedly since the big increase of ten years ago. More important is the fact that these new public members are being recruited to replace (not in addition to) private-sector members. With many in the public sector being prohibited from negotiating over wages and technology, from striking, and from covering their union with a security clause, one must question whether public sector employees give labor organizations as much clout as an equal number of their private sector counterparts. Thus, the numbers tell only part of the story regarding labor's deteriorating position. The jurisdictions covered by the numbers provide additional insight.

The Factors

There are five major factors contributing to the present condition of organized labor:

- the outcome of certification and decertification elections,
- the shift from blue to white-collar jobs in the economy,
- the increasing number and percentage of women in the work force,
- the generational and philosophical gap between union leaders and members, and
- the National Labor Relations Board.

Regarding union elections, even among the decreasing number of workers receptive enough to listen to labor's message, the numbers bode ill. Over six hundred bargaining units decertified their unions in each of the last three years. Unions have won less than one-half of the certification elections in each of the last ten years and have lost three-quarters of the increasing number of decertification elections during the same time period. When studied longitudinally, one sees that these trends are, in fact, accelerating and will probably continue into the foreseeable future.

Another contributing factor is the shift we have seen in this country away from blue-collar manufacturing jobs to white-collar, service-oriented jobs. While the blue-collar manufacturing worker has traditionally been the cornerstone of the movement, there was only a 0.4 percent growth in such jobs over the past five years. The blue-collar base of organized labor has been dependent upon industries that are shrinking, automating, closing, moving, or going international. The millions of new jobs created have been almost exclusively in the white-collar, service-oriented sector where union organizing success has been mediocre at best. While efforts to organize this sector have increased drastically in the last decade, the successes have not been of such a magnitude to offset the losses in the blue-collar sector. Thus, labor, while it is making progress in the white-collar area, is not advancing rapidly enough to keep pace with the industrial shift from blue to white-collar work.

Additionally, the increasing number and percentage of females in the work force is a factor that should not be underestimated when diagnosing labor's present condition. Over the last ten years, the percentage of women unionized has fluctuated between 11% and 13% compared with 25% for men. As women, who are organized at approximately one-half of the rate of men, constitute an increasing percentage of the labor force, unions have increased their efforts to organize this "pink-collar" sector. Effort should not be confused with results, however, since as stated above, the percentage of women organized has not increased noticeably over the last few years.

One big problem in this area has been unimaginative union leadership. Fortunately for organized labor, groups such as the Coalition of Labor Union Women, The National Education Association and the Service Employees International Union, with their female leadership and large female membership, are working hard from *within* the system to educate the traditional white male hierarchy to the importance of organizing drives aimed at women and to the issues essential to such drives (pay equity, health and safety issues, equitable job classifications, child care, etc.). Despite the best efforts of such groups, however, it does not appear that women will become full-fledged members of the labor community in the near future. They continue to be concentrated in the job fields where unions are not well entrenched: administrative, service, part-time, and high-technology industries with many small and union-resistant companies. For these reasons, the increasing number and percentage of females in the work force is a contributing factor to organized labor's deteriorating position.

The generational and philosophical gap between union leaders and members must also be recognized as a factor. The union work force, in addition to becoming smaller, is becoming younger and better educated. Many old-line union leaders have failed to recognize the fact that this change makes it impossible to conduct business as they did twenty years ago. The new generation of union members have become disenchanted with their ossified and lethargic leaders, and they see the traditional union structure as incapable of responding to their needs and desires because of the type of individuals who hold key hierarchical positions. Additionally, young workers (unlike their parents) take a living wage as a given, not a benefit to be earned. They see work as more than just a financial necessity, and the relative generosity of state and supplemental unemployment benefits exacerbates this feeling. The post-war baby boomers are - and will continue to be - labor's dominant age group until the second decade of the 21st century. The fact that they are confounding labor's establishment with values and needs different from their parents is even more threatening than the normal young-versus-old split. Their increasingly middle-class outlook, made possible by the struggles of the two preceding generations of union members, makes them less likely to devote themselves to the labor cause. Their present is no longer measured by fears of the past but by hopes for the future.[3] The changes within this generation gap are critical, because it is in the industries with the most union growth potential that the problem is most acute. Better educated workers in the high-technology industries may well come to regard the unions as bureaucratic entities and as much a damper on their aspirations as any unenlightened corporation. One of the most serious threats to future union growth may come from this generational schism.

The final contributing factor to labor's condition is the National Labor Relations Board. Labor leaders have been unable to protect their members from what they perceive to be (and what under previous administrations would have been) violations of the National Labor Relations Act, the Railway Labor Act, the Labor Management Relations Act, and the Labor Management Reporting and Disclosure Act.

The reasons for this are twofold. First, the number of enforcement personnel, as well as the budgets of the agencies administering these acts, has been cut drastically. This creates a backlog that discourages the filing of charges and it means that, among those filed, a smaller percentage can actually be heard and, if need be, prosecuted. Second, present appointees to political positions within the regulatory agencies have shown no reluctance to reverse previous and, in many cases, long-standing decisions.[4]

The Responses

Responses to the situation discussed in the first section of this article have come from three main sources: management, local governments, and independent consultants. Management's most direct response has been to relocate to the Southeast and Southwest. In the last twenty years, the number of manufacturing jobs grew by forty-five percent in the Southeast and sixty-seven percent in the Southwest. It is crucial for the reader to realize that the *jobs* moved first, then the well-documented population shift was pulled along. It is somewhat of a "chicken and egg" phenomenon, but large numbers of individuals cannot relocate unless there are jobs available at the new location. Certainly, their very presence will create some new jobs, particularly in the service sector, but with the sophisticated logistics system in this country today, it is not as imperative as it used to be that most jobs be performed within the immediate, geographic market they serve. Hence, in the classic economic push-pull situation, the jobs *pushed* first and the population was then *pulled*. As a result, for the first time since Reconstruction, the Northeast and Midwest (once our industrial heartlands and solid union strongholds) no longer hold the majority of the American population.

A response favored by other companies has been to transfer jobs overseas or to subcontract work to countries with lower wage scales. The average consumer would be hard-pressed to notice the difference in quality between the work of a unionized American seamstress and a Taiwanese seamstress, yet a company will surely notice the ten-to-one wage differential. The result is that management shifts union jobs not only to the American South but to foreign countries as well.

A final management response has been to seek "give-backs" at the bargaining table. Many times unions are faced with the alternatives of either granting these concessions or losing some or all of their jobs. Major contracts settled during the last year produced wage increases of 2.8 percent over the life of the contract versus 6.6 percent increases five years ago. In fact, non-union wage increases have been exceeding those of union workers during recent times.[5]

Local government has been another contributor to unions' deteriorating condition. While management's response is to relocate, many local governments have begun to compete to be the beneficiaries of this relocation. In an attempt to retain or attract private capital, state and local governments have begun to give present or prospective industrial citizens tax and labor law relief. The creation of a "pro-business climate" is one of the major marketing points local jurisdictions are using to attract industry. Conversely, jurisdictions presently housing these industries have been forced to grant similar relief in an attempt to hold onto what they have. One need only look at the tax base and resultant city services and physical plants in industrial centers across different geographic regions to realize the magnitude and implications of this phenomena.

Finally, a new breed of independent consultant has surfaced as a response to labor's plight. Use of these **union-avoidance** consultants has become fashionable, widespread and effective. Such consultants as Stephen Cabot, Anthony McKeown, Alfred DeMaria, and Scott Myers are making fortunes teaching management how to keep a company union-free. Their success is based on their ability to convince employers that treating employees properly makes good economic sense. Stephen Cabot states that employers should blame themselves if their workers unionize, because it may well be an indication that they have not been fair, even-handed, or open-minded.[6] Success rates approaching 90 percent in keeping unions out are an indication of the effectiveness of such consultants. In addition to the success rate, the high fees paid to such people are easily justified when one stops to consider the economic advantage to a large company of remaining union-free. Rational economic thought connects the economic benefits to the company, to the high fees they are willing to pay for this service, and to the high number of individuals attracted to this line of work. Hence, the final response is simply the end result of economic evolution.

Conclusion

The logical question to be addressed in light of all the above is: "What can labor do now?" Given the magnitude and diversity of the factors contributing to the problem, there are no simple answers. Addressing one or two particular aspects of the problem at a time will not be enough.

First, there must be a philosophical rapprochement between organized labor's leadership and the work force of the present day. These leaders must recognize that the nature of American business has changed and that things will never be as they were when they were young workers. The reality of a better educated, high-technology or white-collar, service-oriented work force must be dealt with. Extensive use of simple attitude surveys among present and potential union members would go a long way toward making decision-makers within the unions aware that the use of self-reference criteria is no longer appropriate. Unlike thirty years ago, when today's decision-makers were elected to their positions, today's workers and potential union members have a middle-class outlook that gives rise to different objectives, images, and behavior than their parents.

Until today's union leader realizes this and reacts accordingly, little will be done to improve the unions' position. Attitude surveys are a quick, inexpensive way to find out about respondents' desires, attitudes, etc., so that the labor organization can bring itself and its actions in line with those of the individuals it is trying to attract. The author believes that such surveys will show that today's worker expects more than wages from the job, regards demands for wage increases beyond a certain point as job-threatening, and sees incessant union bickering over trivial work rules as needless and unproductive. Health and safety, job enlargement and enrichment, quality of work life, and pay equity may well emerge as issues labor should be addressing more vigorously at the bargaining table. Progress in these areas may well be the key to enrolling the new, better educated and female members the unions need so desperately to attract.

Additionally, more emphasis must be placed on retraining programs for workers displaced by automation and less on the lock-step protectionist policies of the past. For example, labor spends money to lobby for import quotas on automobiles. If one-half the money were spent on retraining existing workers for the new jobs in that industry, not only the union, but the industry and the entire economy would be that much better off.

Another tactic labor should try is to play economic hardball through the use of the billions of dollars in union pension funds. Shifting, or threatening to shift, these monies to "encourage" companies or local governments to modify their thinking and actions in the area of labor relations holds tremendous potential. The dollar value of corporate stock and local government securities held by union pension funds makes this, like the use of attitude surveys, a direct and immediate response by labor to its present situation.

While attitude surveys, retraining programs and pension funds all offer hope for the unions, the author must close on a pessimistic note. These and many other policies that could be recommended must still be implemented through those at the top of the hierarchy. In a survey of seventy-nine top labor officials, several agreed that arrogance, inability to prepare successors, dogmatism, adherence to outdated ideas, and shortsightedness are problems with the leadership of organized labor today.[7] The movement has lost its role as a cause for many leaders and is now simply a job. Many are more interested in holding union office for money and power than they are in affecting significant change.

If this is truly the attitude of many union leaders, and the author feels it is, then to expect them to distribute attitude surveys and respond accordingly (shift bargaining emphasis toward retraining and enrichment and use the pension funds as suggested above) is to expect too much. The author has proposed what he feels are the best and most immediate solutions, but one must be realistic enough to realize that human beings must be willing and able to implement them. Given the current composition of labor leaders and their attitudes toward their jobs, one should not attach a high degree of probability to their trying these ideas on a large scale. Given the magnitude of the problem, piecemeal implementation by individual leaders will not suffice.

Thus, the "human" factor becomes the overriding one in this situation and causes the author to be pessimistic about any reversal in the condition of organized labor in the foreseeable future. Those species and institutions that do not adapt over time become *at worst* extinct or *at best* lose their position of dominance. Organized labor has not adequately adapted to economic, environmental or sociological changes. As a result, it has lost much of the strength it enjoyed thirty or forty years ago. The real problem for labor today is not that this has occurred (for these things go in cycles), but that there is no effective, coordinated attempt being made by the leadership to reverse the situation. The most ominous question for a labor leader today should be: "Given present trends and your inability to combat them, what in the world will you look like in ten or fifteen years?"

Endnotes

[1] Broder, David S., "A 'New Day' For Unions," *The Washington Post*, March 10, 1985.

[2] Erlick, Mark, "Hammer Out A Warning," *The Progressive*, October 1989, p. 18.

[3] Tyler, Gus, *The Political Imperative: The Corporate Character of Unions*, (MacMillan Publishing Company, 1968), p. 290.

[4] Silbergeld, Arthur F., "How Recent NLRB Decisions Have Tilted Toward Management on Critical Issues," *Management Review*, July 1989, pp. 14-15.

[5] English, Carey W., "Why Unions Are Running Scared," *U.S. News and World Report*, September 10, 1989, p. 62.

[6] English, Carey W., "Business is Booming for 'Union Busters'," *U.S. News and World Report*, May 16, 1988, pp. 61-64.

[7] Graham, Harry and Heshizer, Brian, "Are Unions Facing a Crisis? Labor Officials Are Divided," *Monthly Labor Review*, August 1989, pp. 24-25.

Manager, Political Activist, Labor Leader, Statesman:

The Remarkable Life of
ASA PHILIP RANDOLPH

ABSTRACT

Asa Philip Randolph was many things to many people. He was a tireless crusader for African-American rights, a strategic manager and planner, a political activist, and a labor leader. Many of the changes he brought about and many of the conditions he created continue to shape American culture today. This article traces the career of this remarkable individual and highlights the contributions he made to U.S. society.

Introduction

Asa Philip Randolph was born into a poor family on April 15, 1889 in Crescent City, Florida. His father, a country preacher, hoped his second son would follow in his footsteps and take up the religious life. While Asa never became interested in this vocation, he did learn many principles of public speaking from observing his father. He performed well in his segregated elementary school and graduated as valedictorian from Jacksonville's Cookman Institute, a college-preparatory school.

Having no money for college, Randolph moved to Harlem in 1911 to find work. There he married Lucille Campbell Green in 1914. During his early years in New York, Randolph attempted to organize his fellow employees to seek better working conditions and higher wages. He tried to organize a group of porters and a group of waiters but the employees were afraid to stand up to management for fear of being fired. Randolph was later successful in coordinating an effort among elevator and switchboard operators and established his first union in 1923, The Elevator and Switchboard Operators Union. His intelligence and public speaking abilities quickly moved him from organizing small, local labor unions to speaking at large union meetings. Thus, his career as a labor leader began.

It was during those early days in Harlem that Randolph first confronted the problem of managing and leading others over whom he had no institutional authority.   During these days Randolph relied on his charismatic style of leadership. He developed this style out of necessity, and it was to serve him well throughout his life.

Randolph enjoyed reading about African-American labor leaders and other leaders such as Bill Haywood, Ghandi, Karl Marx, Elizabeth Gurley Flynn, and Eugene Debs.   His philosophies were shaped by these individuals and he became an avid supporter of the socialist system, sometimes entertaining thoughts of communism. Socialism, he thought, was the way to salvation for African-Americans, and in his early years in unions he argued for this system. With time, however, he drifted away from socialism and advocated working within the democratic system, peacefully trying to strengthen the power of organized labor.[1]

In 1917, Randolph and his longtime friend, Chandler Owen, began the *Messenger*, a labor newspaper that claimed to be the only radical African-American paper in America. The *Messenger* was successful even though at first it only reached the middle class socialists. Since Randolph was a pacifist, he used the *Messenger* to urge African-American men not to join the war effort in the late 1910s. He could not understand why African-Americans would want to enlist and fight for democracy abroad when there was no democracy for them in the U.S.[2]

At the *Messenger* Randolph became proficient at delegating responsibility to staff while he concentrated on strategic planning in areas of editorial policy and financing. Even at this early stage of his career, and lacking formal management training, it was obvious that Randolph had an understanding of basic management principles.

The Brotherhood Movement

With all the publicity that Randolph received from the *Messenger*, he was in great demand to assist African-American groups. One of the groups that approached him was the Pullman porters. Ashley L. Totten, a Pullman Railroad sleeping car porter, asked Randolph to come and speak to other porters about forming a union. He accepted Totten's offer to lead the new union and in 1925, in an Elks Lodge in Harlem, the Brotherhood of Sleeping Car Porters (BSCP) was born. "Fight or be Slaves" was the motto the Brotherhood adopted.[3] This union became the single largest representative of African-American workers in America.

The porters saw Randolph as a dynamic speaker capable of leading their union. Since Randolph was not a porter, he was not threatened with being fired by the Pullman Company. One of the early problems with the formation of a union was that the porters were scattered all over the country and were constantly moving about. The new union had to devise a way to reach all of them even though there was no money to hire men to organize the workers. Randolph saw the porters as the ideal group to strengthen African-American unionism because they worked on railroads all over the country. He raised $10,000 and toured the entire country to form a solid union to fight the Pullman Company.

In 1925, while touring the country, Randolph met Milton Webster in Chicago. Webster was fired from his job as a Pullman porter after 20 years of service for "insubordination." His insubordination consisted of trying to organize a union of porters. The porters had a great deal of respect for Webster and would follow any man he endorsed to lead them. Webster heard Randolph speak of uniting the porters to force the Pullman Company to bargain with them and immediately let it be known that he would back Randolph. Randolph, in turn, appointed Webster assistant general organizer of the Chicago division of the BSCP.

Randolph moved from city to city gathering followers everywhere he went. By the end of 1926, groups of the Brotherhood had been set up in cities all over the country, from New York City on the East Coast to Portland, Oregon and Los Angeles, California on the West Coast.[4]

Randolph kept in touch with the porters through the *Messenger*. Every issue listed the porters' demands:

1. Recognition of the BSCP as the legitimate porter's union and abolition of the Plan of Employee Representation (the company union)
2. An end to tipping and a raise in salary to $150/month
3. A basic 240-hour work month
4. Fair pay for overtime and deadheading (spending time on   railway cars without pay)
5. Stop double heading (using two engines to pull more railway cars)
6. Conductor's pay for conductor's work
7. Establishment of a pension plan
8. 4 hours' sleep on the first night out and 6 hours on the following nights.[5]

The *Messenger* was the key to the success of the Brotherhood of Sleeping Car Porters, as it was a channel to reach the porters and their sympathizers throughout the country. Randolph wrote a series of articles describing the poor working conditions of the porters. Porters were overworked and the lowest paid members of the working class. Yet as poor as a porter's job was, it was considered good by the African-American community because African-American men could only find manual labor jobs. African-American males that had any education sought jobs as porters. The Pullman Company was well respected in the African-American community because it was the single largest employer of African-Americans in the U.S.

To prevent the porters from forming their own union, the Pullman Company formed a company union called the Plan of Employee Representation (PER). The company handpicked its leaders and told them how to vote. The BSCP knew that they, rather than the PER, represented the majority of the porters but they still needed to be recognized by the Pullman Company. The BSCP realized that would never happen if there was a company union, yet the members of the BSCP could not publicly denounce the PER or they would be fired (porters were fired even if they were suspected of associating with the BSCP). The Brotherhood, therefore, kept its membership list secret. Because of this secrecy, Randolph had to change his management style from an emphasis on charismatic leadership to an appeal to followers to work for the long range benefit of their organization and their race.

In May 1926, the Railway Labor Act was passed which allowed the railroad workers to organize. Randolph now believed that the Pullman Company had to meet with the Brotherhood. But this law did not apply to the railroad porters. They tried to peacefully and legally get recognition, to no avail. Their only option was to strike. Randolph realized that a strike might be deadly to the union, because the Pullman Company would hire strikebreakers of all races. William Green, President of the AFL, also warned Randolph against striking.

Randolph decided to hedge his bet by mobilizing for a strike but not actually striking. He hoped the threat of a strike would be enough to coerce the Pullman Company into an agreement. When the Pullman Company heard of the strike, it approached Randolph with a deal. If Randolph resigned from the union, the Pullman Company would meet with the Brotherhood. Randolph demanded that the Pullman Company recognize the union before he resigned. The Pullman Company would not agree to do this. Randolph then went ahead and ordered a strike vote. Six thousand Brotherhood members voted in favor of the strike and 17 against.[6] The Pullman Company called their bluff and, in effect, told the Brotherhood to proceed with the strike. The company was confident that the strike would have little effect on its operation of railway cars. Thinking that the strike would break the union, Randolph called it off. This was a humiliating defeat for the Brotherhood and for Randolph. The Pullman Company fired everyone that it believed had voted for the strike and hired replacements. Membership in the union dwindled from thousands to a few hundred, and union offices were closed all over the country.

Randolph realized that the Brotherhood needed help and turned to the AFL for assistance. The Brotherhood applied for AFL admission in the early months of 1929. The Brotherhood lacked the funds and the membership to obtain an international charter so William Green (AFL President) permitted each district to join independently (which was less expensive). With the support of the AFL, Randolph believed that the Brotherhood's position was now secure.

Throughout his career, Randolph sought such coalitions with groups within the existing power structure. As the manager of an "outside" group, he realized this gave him ties to what many recognized as "legitimate" power. Using this, he could work for change from both within and outside the system.

The Stock Market Crash of 1929 worsened the conditions faced by the Brotherhood. Many businesses closed and people lost their jobs. This was especially difficult for African-American workers because white workers were now desperate enough to take their lowly positions. Many porters lost their jobs and looked to the union for help. Most Brotherhood offices closed, and the leaders started to live from day to day. Even though the Brotherhood membership was at an all time low, the Pullman Company sent Randolph a $10,000 check to stop working for the Brotherhood. Randolph immediately returned the check and declared that he was not for sale. This incident gave the Brotherhood and Randolph a much needed boost. After this, everyone knew that Randolph was loyal and would not stop fighting until the Brotherhood was accepted by the Pullman Company.

The passage of the National Industrial Recovery Act (NIRA) and the Emergency Transportation Act (ETA) in 1933 helped almost every potential union or union member in the country except the porters. These two Acts did not cover porters. The ETA, designed for railway workers, did not include the porters because Pullman technically was not a railroad company. The porters were also excluded from the NIRA, designed for everyone but railway workers, because under the terms of this legislation, porters were defined as railway workers. Therefore, the porters were not covered under either piece of legislation.

Randolph went before Congress and insisted that the porters be included in future railroad legislation. At Randolph's insistence, President Roosevelt amended the Railway Labor Act in 1935 to include porters. This law required corporations to negotiate with unions that represented a majority of their employees. The Pullman Company also found a way around this law. The Company secretly founded the Pullman Porters Protection Association (PPPA) with a few porters loyal to the company. The Pullman Company said that they would not recognize the BSCP because the real union was the PPPA.

In 1935, using all the money in their treasury, the Brotherhood conducted an ambitious membership drive. This paid off as membership and dues increased significantly. William Green announced that the Brotherhood would be admitted into the AFL as a full member. In 1935, the Brotherhood proudly took its place among the 105 official AFL international unions and made history by being the first African-American union to become affiliated with the federation. Even though the AFL accepted the Brotherhood, the Pullman Company still asserted that the PPPA was the porters' true representative.

Randolph again went to Congress to protest the Pullman Company tactics. The federal government intervened and supervised a vote of the porters to determine which union they preferred. The overwhelming winner was the Brotherhood.

On July 29, 1935, the Pullman Company agreed to a meeting with the leaders of the Brotherhood. The union met with the Pullman Company's President, A. J. Curry. Pullman executives kept stalling on an agreement hoping that the amended Railway Labor Act of 1935, which included the porters, would be declared unconstitutional in court.

In the spring of 1936, the Supreme Court ruled that the amended Railway Labor Act was constitutional. On August 25, 1937, twelve years to the day since the first Brotherhood meeting in Harlem, the Pullman Company finally agreed to a contract. They signed the first labor contract between a large American corporation and a union of African-American workers. The porters gained higher salaries, shorter working hours, and job security.[7] Asa Philip Randolph was the chief union negotiator.

Other Labor Organizations

The Brotherhood continued to advance the civil rights cause by helping other African-American laborers. African-American women were unionized under the BSCP and were called the Ladies Auxiliary. In 1938, the Brotherhood also helped form the Joint Council of Dining Car Employees and the International Brotherhood of Red Caps on airlines. The Red Caps, known today as Sky Caps, worked in the same poor conditions as the porters on the railroads. The Brotherhood's reputation even spread to Canada, and in 1946 the Brotherhood organized the porters of the Canadian Pacific and the Northern Alberta Railways.

With the law on its side (Executive Order 8802), Randolph helped form the Provisional Committee for the Organization of Colored Locomotive Fireman in 1941. There was a shortage of firemen on the railroads, but railway companies were still not hiring trained African-American men. The Brotherhood sued the all-white Brotherhood of Locomotive Firemen and Engineers for colluding with the railway companies in preventing the hiring of such men. In 1944, the Supreme Court outlawed the collusion between the railway companies and the all-white union and forced them both to pay damages.[8]

In 1936, a group of young African-American intellectuals approached Randolph about forming an organization to unite the African-American community. Randolph helped form the National Negro Congress (NNC) to further African-American rights organizations and to help African-Americans cope with the depression. Unfortunately, the NNC was not successful in bringing African-American groups together because the NAACP never endorsed the NNC. These two organizations should have been allies, but the NAACP saw the NNC as a potential threat to its influence in the African-American community and as a competitor for funds. The main reason for the demise of the NNC was the infiltration of the organization by Communists. Randolph left the NNC when it overwhelmingly voted against U.S. participation in World War II. He realized that its views were vastly different from his own and were detrimental to the success of African-American organizations. The NNC did, however, give Randolph practical civil rights experience.

Early Civil Rights

In 1939 when World War II broke out in Europe, the U.S. needed to increase its defensive capabilities. The military build-up helped the domestic economy and created many new jobs.   By 1940, the U.S. economy had taken a healthy upturn, and defense-related firms had numerous job openings. African-Americans flocked from southern states to northern urban areas for these jobs, but most companies refused to hire them.

Randolph voiced his opposition to the companies' policies at a convention of the BSCP in September, 1940. He urged the President, Congress, and especially the African-American community to fight for equal opportunity in defense-related and government jobs. He also called for desegregation in the armed forces and the elimination of Jim Crow laws. Eleanor Roosevelt attended the convention and influenced the President to investigate.

President Roosevelt met with Randolph but only agreed to minor concessions concerning African-Americans in the Air Force. Randolph responded by beginning strategic planning for a march on Washington on July 1, 1941, to bring together over 10,000 marchers supporting his cause. He also established the March on Washington Committee which for decades after would remain a powerful force in coordinating civil rights activities. The response was overwhelming and two months before the planned march, over 100,000 people were scheduled to attend.

Roosevelt, desperate to avoid the bad publicity and possible violence, issued Executive Order 8802 which made it a crime for government funded companies to refuse to hire applicants based on race. It also established the Fair Employment Practices Committee to enforce the Order.[9] Randolph called off the march feeling that he had been victorious. Compliance with the Executive Order, however, was slow until the bombing of Pearl Harbor on December 7, 1941. When the U.S. entered the war, Randolph refrained from coordinating any marches or protests for fear of being labeled an anti-war activist.

After the war, Truman requested legislation for a draft which required African-American men to join a segregated army and navy. Randolph capitalized on this to launch an effort to fully desegregate every branch of the armed forces. After a fruitless meeting with President Truman, Randolph and his colleague, Grant Reynolds, met with the Senate Armed Services Committee and delivered their civil disobedience ultimatum. They declared that if the draft was implemented with the armed forces still segregated they would recommend to men of all races that they not sign up, but instead march peacefully against it. This received the attention of the Senate and the President but produced no concrete action. A poll conducted by the NAACP after Randolph's "ultimatum" revealed that 70%

of African-American draft-age men would refuse to sign up for a draft if segregation continued.

In 1947, Randolph established the Committee Against Jim Crow in Military Service and Training to fight against military segregation. This Committee was later named the League for Non-Violent Civil Disobedience Against Military Segregation. This organization coordinated pickets in front of the White House and Congress threatening widespread civil disobedience if Truman's draft became law. In June, 1948, the draft was signed into law without a desegregation clause.

Randolph immediately went into action organizing marches, pickets, and boycotts throughout the U.S.. Realizing that he might be imprisoned for coordinating such acts, Randolph said, "I am prepared to oppose a Jim Crow army until I rot in jail." Randolph's management expertise was now on display as he deliberately made himself the focal point of the struggle. This political pressure eventually forced Truman to sign Executive Order 9981 on July 26, 1948 which stated that African-Americans were to be treated exactly the same as whites in the army and the navy.

The Civil Rights Movement Matures

The beginning of the civil rights movement is marked by the refusal of an African-American woman, Rosa Parks, to give up her bus seat for a white person in Montgomery, Alabama in 1955. After Parks' arrest, E. D. Nixon, a disciple of Randolph's, began coordinating a boycott of Montgomery buses. Another of Randolph's colleagues, Bayard Rustin, was sent to help coordinate the bus boycott, which lasted until passage of the Civil Rights Act of 1957.

While still leader of the BSCP, Randolph took an active role in desegregating schools in the South. Even though the Supreme Court ruled in 1954 that segregating in public schools was unconstitutional (*Brown v. Board of Education of Topeka*), some southern states blatantly ignored the ruling, which sometimes led to violence.

On April 24, 1956, Randolph organized "The State of the Race" conference in Washington in which leaders of diverse African-American organizations representing over twelve million people concluded that the pace of the civil rights movement was too slow. Leaders at the conference issued a statement which called for the abolition of school segregation and new civil rights legislation to mandate fair employment practices.[10] This conference, however, failed to speed progress on civil rights and never convened again.

Disappointed in his effort to unify African-American leaders, Randolph joined forces with Martin Luther King, Jr. and the NAACP in coordinating and supporting a number of marches on Washington called Prayer Pilgrimage marches. The NAACP provided much of the financial support for the marches and, in turn, Randolph pledged "uncompromising support" for the association, warning white supremacists "to keep their evil hands off" the organization. The largest of these marches took place on May 17, 1957 and involved over 20,000 people at the steps of the Lincoln Memorial.   Dr. King attended many of the marches, but President Eisenhower conveniently was out of town for the events.

President Eisenhower finally focused his attention on school desegregation after sending troops to Little Rock, Arkansas to prevent mob violence at a local high school.   He called for a meeting of African-American leaders to discuss racial problems and invited Randolph "because he was a respected citizen in whom most Americans had complete faith."[11] Randolph presented Eisenhower with a nine-point program which would help fully integrate public schools in the U.S.

After Eisenhower showed little response, Randolph invited 100 African-American and white leaders to a New York conference where Dr. King recommended a march on Washington which would include thousands of school-age African-Americans.   The NAACP volunteered financial support for the event.   Randolph organized the march and on October 25, 1958, 9,500 African-American and white students converged on the Lincoln Memorial to show their discontent with segregated schools. Even though the President refused to meet with the leaders, Randolph called the march a success because of the pageantry and drama it supplied. After the Youth March of 1958, Randolph established a committee that would coordinate many other similar marches for the same cause.   Over the next two years, these marches brought thousands of children to the steps of the Capitol.   Though no major legislative victory was achieved, the marches enabled Randolph to forge alliances between African-Americans' rights organizations, churches, white liberals, and organized labor which would prove instrumental in carrying out the historic march on Washington in 1963.

Randolph with the AFL-CIO

After the AFL accepted the Brotherhood as a full member in 1935, Randolph began fighting against racial discrimination from within. When the CIO was formally expelled from the AFL in 1937, Randolph kept the

Brotherhood in the AFL to fight discrimination "where it's at." Randolph succeeded in persuading many AFL members to oppose discrimination, but the Federation's leadership would not cooperate.

Randolph financed most of the civil rights activities discussed thus far using funds from the BSCP. When membership in the Brotherhood waned in the 1950s due to a decline in railway transportation, Randolph turned to the AFL-CIO for financial support. Randolph had many friends there and persuaded the organization to support the civil rights movement.

After being elected vice president of the AFL-CIO in 1957, Randolph concentrated his efforts on purging the organization of member unions which practiced discrimination. The Federation's policy stated that unions could be expelled for corruption and communism but not for civil rights violations. In 1955, at an AFL-CIO convention, Randolph called for the ouster of unions that prohibited African-Americans from joining. This was the first time civil rights issues within the Federation were brought up at a convention.

These comments from the podium enraged George Meany (President of the AFL-CIO) because Randolph had not consulted him first. Tension between Randolph and labor leaders in the AFL-CIO ran high after this speech because many southern labor leaders opposed union integration. This is one of the few times Randolph violated one of his management practices of building an alliance with an established power base within an organization before pushing for internal change. Like any good leader, he did not make this same mistake twice.

Frustrated with the lack of support from the AFL-CIO, Randolph established the Negro American Labor Council (NALC) in 1960 to fight for first class citizenship for African-Americans and full equality of opportunity for all minority groups in every facet of employment. Randolph stated that the NALC was not a union but merely an organization to strive for equality. Randolph, however, kept his position in the AFL-CIO so he could make changes from within. In March 1961, he announced his "code of fair racial trade union practices" to the AFL-CIO leadership. This code denounced AFL-CIO policies and called for an end to racial segregation in the federation's unions within six months. It also called for establishment of a mechanism to enforce the new policy. The AFL-CIO leadership, especially Meany, strongly opposed this code and condemned Randolph for his slanderous accusations of the Federation. After the NALC and many white leaders pressured the Federation on Randolph's behalf, the AFL-CIO, in effect, apologized to Randolph and adopted a policy to "work harder to make sure all men in unions were treated equally."[12] By late 1961, the NALC was waning in membership but Randolph still used it as a base to launch his next big accomplishment: the 1963 march on Washington.

The March on Washington

In 1961, Randolph conceived a plan to coordinate a massive march on Washington to show his displeasure with the pace of the civil rights movement. He was appalled by statistics showing that more African-Americans attended segregated schools in 1961 than in 1952; that more African-Americans were unemployed in 1961 than in 1954; and that the median income of African-Americans had slipped from 57 to 54 percent of that of whites in the same time period.[13] He obtained immediate support from large African-American organizations like the NAACP, National Urban League, Congress On Racial Equality, and the Southern Christian Leadership Conference. Randolph's major objective was to obtain more jobs and better pay for African-Americans.

At the same time, Martin Luther King, Jr. was planning a march on Washington for the passage of a strong civil rights bill. Since Randolph felt two marches would diminish the strength of each, he joined forces with Dr. King and called the unified march, "The March on Washington for Jobs and Freedom." The leadership made two demands of the federal government: 1) promptly pass a civil rights bill enforcing school desegregation and ending police brutality; and 2) establish a federal Public Works program which would ensure an expanding economy, a $2 minimum wage, and the end of discriminatory practices in government offices, private businesses, and trade unions.

On August 28, 1963, Washington saw the largest protest in the nation's history attended by people of all races. Randolph gave the opening speech to the 250,000 attendees and later introduced Dr. King who delivered his famous, "I Have A Dream," speech. The march was entirely peaceful and a great success in Randolph's eyes. This event marked the first time that such a large number of white moderates showed their support for the cause. Partially as a result of Randolph's efforts, the 1964 Civil Rights Bill was passed by Congress and signed by President Lyndon Johnson. A. Philip Randolph took part in the signing ceremony.

Trophies in His Cabinet

Randolph had been widely recognized in many arenas for his contributions to the African-American labor movement and civil rights. Universities presented Randolph with honorary degrees, the NAACP awarded him the Springard Medal, New York honored him with an A. P. Randolph Day, and President Johnson presented him with the highest civilian medal, The Medal of Freedom. Today streets are named after him and his old high school bears his name. There is no doubt that he deserves these honors, for perhaps no man contributed more to the cause of African-American labor and civil rights.

Asa Philip Randolph died on May 16, 1979 at the age of 90. During his lifetime Randolph helped many African-American unions achieve not only better pay and better working conditions but also equality in major labor organizations. His efforts drove discrimination from not only the AFL-CIO but also from the U.S. Armed Forces, companies receiving government funding, and some schools in the South. Randolph united people with his vision and determination, creating solidarity and strength in the labor movement. His non-violent methods proved to be effective in furthering the African-American cause. Asa Philip Randolph was the first to give vision, organization, and dignity to the African-American labor force. For this, he deserves a special place in labor history. It is unfortunate that his contributions are largely unknown and unnoticed by students of labor and management history today. This article is written in tribute to Asa Philip Randolph.

Endnotes

[1] Wright, Sarah, *A. Philip Randolph: Integration in the Workplace*, New York, Silver Burdett Press, 1990, p. 32.

[2] *Ibid.*, p. 51.

[3] Santino, Jack, *Miles of Smiles, Years of Struggle: Stories of Black Pullman Porters*, Urbana, Ill., University of Illinois Press, 1989, p. 37.

[4] *Ibid.*, p. 71.

[5] McKissack, Patricia and Frederick A., *A Long Hard Journey: The Story of the Pullman Porters*, New York, Walker and Company, 1989, pp. 60-61.

[6] *Ibid.*, p. 93.

[7] Wright, *op. cit.*, pp. 86-89.

[8] Pfeffer, Paula F., *A. Philip Randolph, Pioneer of the Civil Rights Movement*, Baton Rouge, La., Louisiana State University Press, 1990, p. 92.

[9] Wright, *op. cit.*, p. 97.

[10] Pfeiffer, *op. cit.*, p. 175.

[11] *Ibid.*, p. 179.

[12] Wright, *op. cit.*, p. 111.

[13] Pfeiffer, *op. cit.*, p. 240.

The *Beck* and *Lehnert* Decisions and Their Impact on Union Security Agreements

Kenneth A. Kovach
Peter E. Millspaugh

Introduction

The relationship between employers and employees - labor/ management relations - has evolved substantially in the United States over the course of the past 100 years. The agent of change has varied as the times have changed, but each and every time there has been change of any magnitude - either pro-labor or pro-management - one or more agents of change have been present molding the outcome of events and shaping the evolution of labor history. These agents of change can assume many forms and may not be recognized for what they are until enough time has passed to look back at events with an objective, critical eye. They may be extraordinary individuals or the confluence of unique events. They may be violent or peaceful. In the pages that follow, we will consider how the determination of two individuals unknown to one another, Harry E. Beck, Jr. and James P. Lehnert, caused them to become late 20th-century agents of change in the ongoing evolution of labor/management relations in the United States.

Harry Beck and Jim Lehnert will be remembered - with respect or disdain, depending on one's point of view - for years to come because of their determination to stand up and challenge the legitimacy of clauses in union security agreements that permit unions to collect agency fees from non-union members working at agency shops. The validity of the underlying union security agreement was not an issue, since Section 8(a)(3) of the National Labor Relations Act (NLRA) explicitly authorizes an employer and a union to enter into an agreement requiring all employees in the bargaining unit to pay union dues as a condition of continued employment whether or not the employees become union members.[1] What was at issue in both the *Beck* and the *Lehnert* cases was whether agency fees collected under such union security agreements could legitimately be used by the unions for purposes other than "collective bargaining, contract administration, or grievance adjustment."[2]

Harry Beck, who lived in Maryland, knew labor unions and had at one time served as shop steward for the Communications Workers of America.[3] Jim Lehnert, on the other hand, was an academic on the teaching faculty of Michigan's Ferris State College.[4] What Beck and Lehnert shared in common was a recognition that agency fees they were paying to their unions - the Communications Workers of America in the case of Beck and the Ferris Faculty Association (an affiliate of the Michigan Education Association which is an affiliate of the National Education Association) in the case of Lehnert - were frequently being used to support political causes and other purposes to which they were opposed. Accordingly, each went to court to challenge the practice.

Union Security Agreements:
A Definition and Brief Legislative History

The concept of an agency shop - in which everyone within a bargaining unit is required to pay the equivalent of union dues whether a member of the union or not - first developed at the Ford Motor Company plant in Ontario, Canada in 1946.[5] The underlying principles of union security agreements were codified in American labor law in Section 8(a)(3) of the National Labor Relations Act. That provision, which is permissive and not mandatory, allows a union which is the certified exclusive bargaining agent for a group of workers to enter into collective bargaining agreements with the employers of those workers stipulating that all workers represented by the bargaining agent must pay representation or agency fees to the union.

Congress authorized the establishment of agency shops out of a sense of fair play. Such shops were intended to benefit workers by correcting abuses of compulsory union membership that had developed under "closed shop" agreements. Simultaneously, they were intended to provide unions with security against free riders or non-union workers who could reap the benefits of a union's representation services without paying for them.[6] The underlying theory is that, under the principle of exclusive representation, a certified union must represent all the workers in a bargaining unit; therefore, it is only fair that all such workers pay their fair share of the union's costs in doing so.

The legislative history of this provision is very explicit and warrants review. As Senator Taft, one of the authors of the 1947 legislation that bears his name, explained on the floor of the United States Senate:

...the argument...against abolishing the closed shop...is that if there is not a closed shop those not in the union will get a free ride, that the union does the work, gets the wages raised, then the man who does not pay dues rides along freely without any expense to himself.[7]

Members of the House echoed that view. For example, Representative Jennings pointed out that because members of the minority:

...would get the benefit of the contract made between the majority of their fellow workmen and the management...it is not unreasonable that they should go along and contribute dues like the others.[8]

Similarly, Representative Robinson noted that:

...If [union-negotiated] benefits come to the workers all alike, is it not only fair that the beneficiaries, whether the majority or the minority, contribute their equal share in securing these benefits?[9]

However, out of deference to "states' rights" advocates, the federal statute authorizing agency shops and hence union security agreements does not supersede or preempt state laws in this regard. According to Section 14(b) of the National Labor Relations Act, the individual states are free to prohibit agency shops and other union security clauses in collective bargaining agreements. The state legislatures in twenty-one "right-to-work" states have, in fact, enacted state laws prohibiting agency shops and other union security agreements.[10]

Nevertheless, the impact of union security agreements on the American work force and in the American political arena should not be underestimated. In order to appreciate the magnitude of the reach of union security agreements the reader should consider the following:

- an estimated 2 to 3 million non-union workers are subject to union security agreements;
- 15.4 million Americans are employed under compulsory union contracts;
- this system generates $10 million per day ($3.8 billion per year) in union staff payroll expenses; and the value of in-kind services for

political candidates generated by this system has been estimated at between $100 million and $350 million in an election year.[11]

Against this backdrop, we will now turn to consider the specific cases of Harry Beck and Jim Lehnert; how these two cases, while similar in many respects, can nevertheless be distinguished from one another in some important ways; and how the United States Supreme Court disposed of each.

The *Beck* Case

Harry Beck, and others who shared his view, was tired of seeing union payments going to support political candidates and causes to which he was personally opposed. They claimed that the expenditure of union funds on activities such as organizing the employees of other employers, lobbying for labor legislation, and participating in social, charitable and political events violated the Communications Workers' duty of fair representation. Organized labor's support of Democrat Hubert H. Humphrey in his unsuccessful bid for the presidency of the United States in 1968 prompted Harry Beck to take action.[12] In order to bring this practice to an end, Beck and 20 of his co-workers - financed by the National Right-to-Work Committee - brought suit against the Communications Workers of America in 1976 challenging the union's use of agency fees for purposes other than "collective bargaining, contract administration or grievance adjustment." After a twelve-year odyssey through the federal court system, the case was finally argued before the United States Supreme Court on January 11, 1988.

The issue was settled six months later when, on June 29, 1988, a divided Supreme Court, in an opinion authored by Justice William Brennan, held that:

> ...fees beyond those necessary to finance collective bargaining activities violated the judicially created duty of fair representation and non-union members' First Amendment rights...

and

> ...The National Labor Relations Act does not...permit a union, over objections of dues-paying nonmember employees, to expend funds so collected on activities

unrelated to collective bargaining activities ...[13]

In essence, the Supreme Court concurred with the lower court's conclusion that the union had failed to show that more than 21% of the funds were used in support of collective-bargaining efforts. It further agreed that the Communications Workers of America should: 1) reimburse all excess fees Beck and his 20 colleagues had paid since January 1976; and 2) institute a record-keeping system to segregate accounts for representational and noncollective-bargaining activities.[14]

The *Lehnert* Case

The *Lehnert* case is distinguishable from the *Beck* case in three very significant ways: 1) while Harry Beck was an employee in the private sector, Jim Lehnert was a state government employee serving as a faculty member at Ferris State College in Big Rapids, Michigan; 2) while Harry Beck was challenging the use of agency fees by a single union (i.e., the Communications Workers of America), Jim Lehnert was challenging the utilization of agency fees by a tiered triumvirate (i.e., the Ferris Faculty Association which is an affiliate of the Michigan Education Association which is an affiliate of the National Education Association); and 3) in the manner in which the *Lehnert* court resolved the issue of the use of agency fees for political purposes, specifically, to influence the outcome of pending legislation.

The total agency fee assessed against Jim Lehnert by the Ferris Faculty Association for the 1981-1982 year was $284.00. Of that amount, only $24.80 (or 9%) stayed with the local bargaining unit. The bulk of the funds - the remaining $259.20 - was divided between the state and national affiliates. Of the $284.00 collected under the union security agreement, $211.10 (74%) went to the Michigan Education Association and $48.00 (17%) was forwarded to the National Education Association in Washington, D.C.[15]

In deciding the *Lehnert* case, the Court held that:

> ...the considerations that justify the union shop in the private context - the desirability of labor peace and eliminating "free riders" - are equally important in the public-sector workplace...[16]

However, the Court rejected Lehnert's contention that he should be charged only for those collective-bargaining activities undertaken directly by the Ferris Faculty Association and not costs associated with the Michigan Education Association or the National Education Association. Specifically, the Court decided that in this case:

> ...membership in the local union constitutes membership in the state and national parent organizations ...Consequently, that part of a local's affiliation fee which contributes to the pool of resources potentially available to the local is assessed for the bargaining unit's protection...We therefore conclude that a local bargaining representative may charge objecting employees for their *pro rata* share of the costs associated with otherwise chargeable activities of its state and national affiliates, even if those activities were not performed for the direct benefit of the objecting employee's bargaining unit ...[17]

Prior to the *Lehnert* case, there was a clear and consistent judicial view that use of agency fees for political purposes - specifically, to lobby lawmakers - should be proscribed. The underlying rationale was that since unions traditionally have aligned themselves with a wide range of social, political and ideological viewpoints, any number of which might bring vigorous disapproval from individual employees, to force employees to contribute - albeit indirectly - to the promotion of such positions implicates core First Amendment concerns. As the Court noted:

> ...The right of freedom of thought protected by the First Amendment against state action includes both the right to speak freely and the right to refrain from speaking at all ...[18]

However, in the *Lehnert* case the Court continued to recognize a small exception to the general prohibition of the use of agency fees for political purposes. The reasoning enunciated by the Court took into consideration the inherently political nature of salary and other workplace decisions affecting government employees since the legislature and the employer are effectively one and the same entity. The *Lehnert* court concurred with a New Jersey case decided in 1985 which concluded that:

...To represent their members effectively, public sector unions must necessarily concern themselves not only with negotiations at the bargaining table but also with advancing their members' interests in legislative and other 'political' arenas...[19]

The *Lehnert* court then concluded that:

...the State constitutionally may not compel its employees to subsidize legislative lobbying or other political union activities outside the limited context of contract ratification or implementation.[20]

Implementation of the
Beck and *Lehnert* Decisions

While it took twelve years for the *Beck* case to reach its final resolution before the United States Supreme Court and ten years for the *Lehnert* case to be fully adjudicated, those decisions hardly brought the controversy to a close. In neither *Beck* nor *Lehnert* are the Court's decisions "self-enforcing." For the principles enunciated by the justices in these cases to become integrated into the workplace, a method of segregating covered expenditures from excludable expenditures would have to be established; a manageable framework for monitoring and policing union expenditures would have to be implemented; and a mechanism to expeditiously resolve controversies would have to be created. Since the use of agency fees for political purposes inspired both Harry Beck and Jim Lehnert to take the unions to court initially, it seems oddly appropriate that politics should haunt the process during the implementation stage as well.

In the pages that follow, this article will review the National Labor Relations Board's (NLRB) efforts to implement the *Beck* decision; the line of *Beck* administrative proceedings filed with the NLRB subsequent to the Supreme Court's *Beck* decision; and actions taken by the executive and legislative branches of government designed to shape labor/management relations in the post-*Beck* era.

NLRB's *Beck* Guidelines

Following the *Beck* decision, the National Labor Relations Board issued guidelines to all its regional directors advising them on a broad range of what came to be known as *Beck* issues. These guidelines specified that the threshold test that must be met before any *Beck* rights may be invoked is that the employee must be a "nonmember" of the union. An employee who had never become a full union member or an employee who had resigned full membership in the union would be able to invoke *Beck* rights, as would an employee who attempted to resign from the union but was unlawfully prevented from doing so.

In addition to being a "nonmember," the worker must object to the expenditure of funds for nonrepresentational purposes. The NLRB guidelines were very clear on this point, quoting from a Supreme Court decision rendered more than a quarter century before *Beck*:

> ...[D]issent is not to be presumed - it must affirmatively be made known to the union by dissenting employees. The union receiving money exacted from an employee under a union shop agreement should not in fairness be subjected to sanctions in favor of an employee who makes no complaint of the use of his money for such activities...[21]

In the absence of some objection on the part of the worker, the union is permitted to collect full dues under the union security clause.

Under the NLRB guidelines, if a union spends any portion of funds collected from nonunion members on activities other than "representational" activities, the union has an affirmative obligation to notify all nonunion workers at least once a year:

- that a stated percentage of funds was spent in the last accounting year for nonrepresentational activities;
- that nonmembers can object to having their union security payments spent on such activities; and
- that those who object will be charged only for representational activities.[22]

According to the NLRB guidelines if a nonmember should object, the union must provide the objector with information setting forth the union's major expenditures during the previous accounting year, distinguishing between representational and nonrepresentational functions. In addition, if the union is a local of an international and a portion of union security money is sent to the international, both the local and the international must provide the relevant information.[23]   The guidelines expand on this requirement noting that while "absolute precision" cannot "be expected or required,"[24] the information must reveal the major categories of expenses (e.g., "national convention," "organizing," etc.); whether the union considers the expenses to be representational or nonrepresentational; the total sum of expenditures; and the percentage of expenditures that were representational and nonrepresentational. If the objecting employee disagrees with the union's percentage allocation, the employee may challenge the union's determination either by invoking arbitration or by filing a charge with the NLRB. Unions are required to place disputed amounts in an interest-bearing escrow account until the matter is resolved.

The NLRB guidelines conclude with a list of "chargeable" and "nonchargeable" activities. Among the representational activities that are "chargeable" to nonmembers are:

- Collective bargaining, contract administration, and grievance arbitration
- Expenses of litigation incident to negotiating and administering the contract, settling grievances and disputes arising within the bargaining unit, fulfilling the duty of fair representation to the unit, handling jurisdictional disputes with other unions, and conducting other litigation before administrative agencies or courts concerning bargaining unit employees
- National conventions
- Union business meetings and social activities open to member and nonmember employees
- Union publications to the extent that they report on the union's representational activities
- Costs of union benefits available to members and nonmembers alike.

Nonrepresentational, and therefore nonchargeable, activities include:

- Union organizing activities, either in the represented unit or outside of it
- Expenses of litigation that do not "directly concern" the bargaining unit
- Union publications to the extent that they report on nonrepresentational activities
- Costs of union benefits that are not available to nonmembers
- Costs of a union building fund

- Lobbying
- Promotion or defeat of legislation
- Political campaigns
- Advertising related to nonchargeable matters[25]

While some may find the above lists of "chargeable" and "nonchargeable" activities a handy point of reference, others view them with skepticism either because they see them as a backing away from the black-letter law laid down by the Court in *Beck* or because they realize that the promulgation of guidelines provides no assurance that the guidelines will be followed.

NLRB's Enforcement Mechanism

The National Labor Relations Board processes all employee complaints through its Office of General Counsel, which decides whether or not to pursue the complaint. If the general counsel decides to proceed, the complaint is heard by an administrative law judge (ALJ). Decisions rendered by ALJs may be appealed to the five-member NLRB. As of this year, there are approximately 300 cases pending before the NLRB ALJs,[26] many of them *Beck* cases. In fact, at the time of this writing there are 21 cases pending before the NLRB that involve *Beck* issues.

The backlog of cases - particularly *Beck* cases - at the NLRB is due in no small measure to politics. This is ironic (although not surprising) since the use of agency fees to further political causes was an underlying issue at the very heart of both the *Beck* and *Lehnert* cases. Two Executive Orders - one issued by President Bush in the heat of his unsuccessful bid for re-election, the other issued by President Clinton less than two weeks after he was sworn into office - had a role to play in the off-again, on-again, off-again approach to enforcement of *Beck* rights by the NLRB and the Department of Labor (DOL).

President Bush's Executive Order

In a White House Rose Garden ceremony held on April 13, 1992, President George Bush, with Harry Beck looking on, signed Executive Order 12800. This Executive Order directed the Secretary of Labor to require all companies performing federal contract work to post notices in their plants and offices during the term of their contract informing workers of their *Beck* rights. President Bush also announced at the Executive Order signing ceremony that Secretary of Labor Lynn Martin would be proposing a rule clarifying and bringing up to date requirements for labor organizations to account for how workers' dues are spent. For *Beck* purposes, the most noteworthy proposed revision to forms LM-2 and LM-3 was the inclusion of a new schedule entitled "Statement C - Expenses." This schedule would be used by unions to allocate all expenses among eight new functional categories: contract negotiation and administration; organizing; safety and health; strike activities; political activities; lobbying; promotional activities; and "other."

The promulgation of Executive Order 12800 was characterized by Democrats as "an election year move that Bush bypassed during his first three years in office." Conservatives applauded Bush's move, describing the executive order as "championing individual freedom for American workers," while labor leaders condemned it as a "political gesture" that would ultimately have little impact upon their operations and activities. The reach of this presidential order was hotly contested, with the White House claiming that as many as 3 million workers could be impacted while union leaders said the number was closer to one million.[27]

Four days after promulgation of Executive Order 12800, the Department of Labor published twenty-eight pages of proposed rules revising the manner in which labor unions report their financial condition to the DOL, NLRB, and their members.[28] Fifty-one written comments, filling twelve binders, were received in reply. The rule was soundly criticized by representatives of both labor and management, with many singling out for criticism a proposed union security clause which the Management Association of Illinois said would require "a 17th-grade-level education" to understand. They went on:

> ...The practical impact will be that no employee or applicant for employment will be able to read this union security language and understand his or her rights - a real denial of workplace due process ...[29]

Also deemed highly controversial was the proposed requirement that each bargaining unit independently account for its expenditures in order to measure its compliance with *Beck* requirements. Internationals in particular, and labor organizations in general, took the approach that unit-by-unit accounting would be extremely costly and burdensome. The AFL-CIO estimated that it would incur annual bookkeeping and accounting costs of $192 million (or about $10 per member) if required to implement the proposed reporting requirements.[30]   Organized labor also challenged the appropriateness of such reporting, noting that Courts had, in the past, rejected the unit-by-unit accounting theory.   Claiming that it is "normal and reasonable" for a union to use its dues from all represented bargaining units to create a pool of resources, the AFL-CIO argued that:

> ...Many national union activities simultaneously benefit
> more than one bargaining unit...[31]

The AFL-CIO added that requiring unit-by-unit accounting would impose enormous burdens on any multi-unit union and overwhelming ones on any national or international union.[32]

W. James Young, an attorney for the National Right-to-Work Legal Defense Foundation, labelled the AFL-CIO's position as "the rankest form of hypocrisy."[33]   Irving Ross, a certified public accountant, said that labor organizations had created a "mystique" about the difficulty of accounting noting that "it's not as burdensome as some would have you believe."[34]

The circumstances under which President Bush issued his executive order - particularly the timing - certainly called into question his political motivations.   Invoking the memory of Thomas Jefferson, on whose 249th birthday the order was released, Bush quoted Jefferson's declaration that:

> ...To compel a man to furnish contributions of money for
> the propagation of opinions which he disbelieves and abhors
> is sinful and tyrannical...[35]

In addition, the President's action to inform workers of a right they had won four years earlier - an action the President could have taken at any point since he was sworn in as President - happened to occur on the very same day that the executive committee of the AFL-CIO recommended to its membership that they endorse Arkansas Governor Bill Clinton for the Presidency.

President Clinton's Executive Order

In one of his first official acts after being sworn into office, President Clinton issued Executive Order 12836, rescinding President Bush's Executive Order 12800, and "any orders, rules or regulations implementing...Executive Order No. 12800."[36]   Claiming that by revoking Executive Order 12800 he was ending the "government's role in promoting this one-sided version of workplace rights," Clinton characterized the Bush order as:

> ...distinctly anti-union as it did not require contractors to notify workers of any of their other rights protected by the National Labor Relations Act, such as the right to organize and bargain collectively...[37]

As one would expect, organized labor praised Clinton's action, while "right-to-work" advocates condemned it.   AFL-CIO President Lane Kirkland welcomed Clinton's action as:

> ... the first symbol of renewed commitment to the national labor policy set out in the federal labor laws and to the fair and vigorous enforcement of those laws...

while Rex H. Reed, executive vice president of the National Right-to-Work Legal Defense Foundation declared:

> ... By ordering his labor department to tear down notices of employees' rights against compulsory unionism, Clinton has turned back the clock and thrown the cloak of secrecy over federal contract workers...And with exit polls showing that 45% of unionized workers didn't vote for Clinton, that means nearly four million private sector workers will continue to walk with blinders on, courtesy of the union bosses and Clinton...[38]

Congressional Efforts To Codify *Beck* Rights

Numerous efforts have been made to codify the *Beck* decision since it was handed down by the Supreme Court.   The approach generally advocated by the proponents of *Beck* codification would amend the Federal Election Campaign Act of 1971 to include what has been labelled the Workers' Political Rights Act.

The Workers' Political Rights Act would impose more stringent reporting requirements on labor unions regarding their political expenditures.   Specifically, it would require labor unions engaged in political activities to provide written annual notification to their members, advising them:

- that members cannot be compelled to pay for the political activities of the union;
- that no employee can actually be compelled to join a union and that (in the case of a union shop) the employees may elect instead to pay an agency fee;
- that the amount of the agency fee shall be limited to the employee's *pro rata* share of the cost of the union's exclusive representation services to the employee's collective bargaining unit, including collective bargaining, contract administration, and grievance adjustment;
- that an employee who elects to be a full member of the union is entitled to a reduction in dues by the employee's *pro rata* share of the total spending devoted to political activities;
- that the cost of exclusive representation services and the amount of spending on political activities will be computed based on the immediately preceding fiscal year; and,
- on the union's full dues, reduced dues, and agency fees for the current year.[39]

Principal proponents of the codification of *Beck* rights in the Senate have been Senators Orrin Hatch (R-UT) and Mitch McConnell (R-KY). The opposition to their efforts has been led by Senators Howard Metzenbaum (D-OH) and David Boren (D-OK). When on July 31, 1992, the measure was debated and voted upon in the United States Senate, it was defeated by a vote of 59 to 41.

More recently, on May 27, 1994, Texas Republican Tom DeLay introduced in the U.S. House of Representatives the aforementioned Workers' Political Rights Act (H.R. 2307). Noting his concern that "no one is required to tell workers that they have the right not to contribute" to political causes they do not support, DeLay wrote to his colleagues in the House:

> ...What's worse, President Clinton has decided that workers should not be informed of this right...Clearly this is not right. Every member of the Congress who supports our nation's free and democratic heritage should speak out and oppose this abuse of our political process...[40]

Despite the fact that his bill has attracted 71 co-sponsors since its introduction, Representative Charlie Rose (D-NC), who is a member of the

House Oversight Committee to which DeLay's bill has been referred, has yet to schedule so much as a single Congressional hearing to consider the merits of H.R. 2307. An analysis of campaign contributions by political action committees (PACs) associated with labor organizations proves enlightening on this point.

Labor's PAC Contributions

Let us analyze the Federal Election Commission reports filed by the ten largest labor PACs. These ten PACs are those of the: International Brotherhood of Teamsters, American Federation of State, County and Municipal Employees, Service Workers International Union, United Food and Commercial Workers, United Autoworkers, United Steelworkers, International Association of Machinists, International Brotherhood of Electrical Workers, Communications Workers of America, and the National Education Association. Further, let our analysis include six election cycles covering the twelve-year period extending from 1983 to 1994.

The findings confirm what many would surmise - labor PACs are major players in the game of electoral politics, and the volume and amount of labor's campaign contributions have increased substantially over the past decade. By overwhelming margins, organized labor's PAC dollars are used to support Democratic candidates for office. Advocates of organized labor would, or course, be quick to point out that it is misleading to imply that PAC giving to incumbents is synonymous with "labor" giving to incumbents. An analysis of FEC reports filed in conjunction with the 1994 Congressional elections indicate that business PACs - those sponsored by corporations, trade associations and cooperative associations - gave candidates an amount three times as large as the amount given by labor PACs. Labor proponents would also note the bipartisan nature of PAC giving, pointing out that $24.9 million went to Senate Republicans.[41]

While all PAC giving may reflect a bipartisan balance, that is hardly the case with the PACs that represent organized labor. The political action committees for organized labor have a clear and unmistakable bias in support of Democratic candidates for office. For the twelve-year period studied, it can be determined that, with the exception of the Teamsters, in no case did a labor PAC give more than 5% of its dollars to support Republican candidates for office. Furthermore, the one exception to the rule - the Teamsters - saw their contributions to Republican candidates consistently decline over the period studied, from 15% in the 1983-1984 election cycle to merely 3% in the 1993-1994 cycle. Meanwhile, with the exception of the Teamsters, none of the labor PACs studied gave less then 93% of their contributions to Democratic candidates during that same period.

Whether or not it is legitimate to do so, numbers such as these provide great ammunition to opponents of organized labor such as Rex H. Reed, executive director of the National Right-to-Work Legal Defense Fund, who claim that President Clinton's action rescinding President Bush's executive order regarding implementation of the *Beck* decision is not the last action President Clinton will take on behalf of organized labor but rather "the first installation of his debt to Big Labor."[42]

Conclusion

The history of America's labor movement provides abundant examples of abuse of worker's rights by parties on both sides of the bargaining table. Our constitutional form of government, which emphasizes individualism, vision, and the entrepreneurial spirit while simultaneously maintaining a commitment to the equality of all, is admittedly vulnerable to abuse. Yet the system of checks and balances present in our form of government also provides workers and management with an appropriate means of redress.

Harry Beck and Jim Lehnert were, in many ways, trapped or caught in a system that had become top-heavy, if not unbalanced, in favor of organized labor - a system that some claim placed higher value on the organization than on the laborer. Common sense and notions of fundamental justice tell us that individuals should not be compelled to support political agendas which they themselves find repugnant. Both Beck and Lehnert challenged the status quo and, over time, affected broad-reaching reforms which impact all who work in union or agency shops. In the post-*Beck* era, support of the union is still required in areas directly related to issues of collective bargaining - the concept of "free-riders" remains anathema - but workers should not be compelled to support the union in areas going beyond collective bargaining.

The *Beck* and *Lehnert* decisions are good decisions, and good decisions make good law and sound public policy. In both cases, the Court refused to stake out an extreme position but rather sought that compromise which would result in a truly equitable decision for all the parties involved.

Political issues were at the heart of *Beck* and *Lehnert* cases, and it is politics that have muddied the waters since these decisions were rendered. Elected politicians, as well as the political appointees of the executive branch of government charged with enforcing these decisions, have interpreted them so as best to conform with their party's political agenda *vis-à-vis* the business community and organized labor. That is something we can expect to see continue, despite the fact that it brings about some generally undesirable yet nevertheless tolerable results, such as the situation where successive executive orders are promulgated, with the second nullifying the first.

As a result of the *Beck* and *Lehnert* decisions, organized labor will find its clout somewhat restricted. Union leaders will be held more accountable to their members as far as the expenditure of funds is concerned. Full and fair disclosure of expenditures should become the norm rather than the exception. While these results will at least marginally diminish the role of union leaders, the status and dignity of the rank-and-file union member will be enhanced.

Organized labor will continue to do battle with "right-to-work" advocates. Each side will doubtlessly claim that they are upholding fundamental American values, and the fact of the matter is that both are doing just that!

We can be certain that politics (which is oftentimes described as "the art of compromise") will continue to dominate this debate. Accordingly, we should expect the dialectical process to continue, which - like our partisan form of government - avoids extreme positions and by and large results in the establishment of norms which do not satisfy the hard-core, extreme partisans on either side, but are tolerable or acceptable to moderates on both sides. This is exactly what has transpired in the *Beck* and *Lehnert* situations. The beat goes on.

Endnotes

[1] 29 U.S.C. §§ 141-187 (1982 & Supp. V, 1987).

[2] *Communications Workers of America v. Beck*, 108 S.Ct. 2641 (1988).

[3] *Harvard Journal of Law and Public Policy*, Vol. 13, No. 2, Spring 1990.

[4] *Lehnert v. Ferris Faculty Association*, 111 S.Ct. 1950 (1991).

[5] Masse, Benjamin L., "Is the Agency Shop Legal?" *America*, Vol. 107, December 15, 1962, p. 1244.

[6] *Ibid.*

[7] 93 *Congressional Record* (1947), p. 4887.

[8] *Ibid.*, p. 3557.

[9] *Ibid.*, p. 3558.

[10] Bairn, Charles W., *The Permissible Uses of Forced Union Dues: From Hanson to Beck*, the CATO Institute, Washington, D.C., July 24, 1992, p. 10.

[11] Larson, John, "Harry Beck's Earthquake," *Policy Review*, 74 (Summer 1989), pp. 74-75.

[12] Devroy, Ann, "Bush Moves to Enforce Union Curb: New Order Covering Political Use of Dues Pleases Conservatives," *The Washington Post*, April 14, 1992, p A-1.

[13] *Communications Workers of America v. Beck*, 108 S.Ct. 2642 (1988).

[14] *Ibid.*

[15] *Lehnert v. Ferris Faculty Association*, 111 S.Ct. 1956 (1991).

[16] *Lehnert v. Ferris Faculty Association*, 111 S.Ct. 1958 (1991).

[17] *Ibid.*, 1961.

[18] *Wolley v. Maynard*, 430 U.S. 705 at 714; 97 S.Ct. 1428 at 1435; 51 L.Ed. 2d 752 (1977).

[19] *Robinson v. New Jersey*, 741 F.2d 598 at 609 (CA3 1984); cert. denied, 469 U.S. 1228; 105 S.Ct. 1228; 84 L.Ed.2d 366 (1985).

[20] *Lehnert v. Ferris Faculty Association*, 111 S.Ct. 1960-1961 (1991).

[21] *Machinists v. Street*, 367 U.S. 740, at 774 (1960).

[22] Collyer, Rosemary M., (NLRB General Counsel), Memorandum GC 88-14, *Guidelines Concerning CWA v. Beck*, November 15, 1988 p. 3.

[23] *Ibid.*

[24] *Chicago Teachers Union, Local No.1 v. Hudson*, 475 U.S. 292 (1986) p. 307.

[25] Collyer, *op. cit.*, pp. 6-7.

[26] Bureau of National Affairs, Daily Labor Report, 139 (April 20, 1994) p. 469.

[27] Devroy, *op. cit.*

[28] *Federal Register*, Volume 57, Number 75, Friday, April 17, 1992, p. 14244.

[29] Bureau of National Affairs, *Daily Labor Report*, 47 (March 12, 1993), p. A-6.

[30] Bureau of National Affairs, *Daily Labor Report*, 8 (January 13, 1993), p. C-1.

[31] *AFL-CIO News*, March 30, 1992, p. 2.

[32] *Ibid.*

[33] Bureau of National Affairs, *Daily Labor Report*, 47 (March 12, 1993), p. A-7.

[34] Bureau of National Affairs, *Daily Labor Report*, Special Report #60, March 31, 1993, p. CC-2.

[35] Bush, George, *Remarks of the President In Signing Ceremony For Beck Executive Order*, Office of the Press Secretary, The White House, Washington, D.C., April 13, 1992, p. 1.

[36] Clinton, William Jefferson, *Executive Order No. 12836*, The White House, Washington, D.C., February 1, 1993, p.1.

[37] Bureau of National Affairs, *Daily Labor Report*, 21 (February 3, 1993), p. AA-1.

[38] Bureau of National Affairs, *Daily Labor Report*, 21 (February 3, 1993), p. AA-2.

[39] DeLay, Rep. Tom, *Worker's Political Rights Act* (H.R. 2307), 103rd Congress at §2(b).

[40] Bureau of National Affairs, *Daily Labor Report*, 106 (June 4, 1993), p. A-9.

[41] *AFL-CIO News*, December 8, 1994, p. 1.

[42] Bureau of National Affairs, *Daily Labor Report*, 21 (February 3, 1993), p. AA-2.

Cases

Recruiting Techniques to Achieve
Affirmative Action Goals

The Resdex Laboratories of Cleveland, Ohio, have for many years relied on college recruiting and executive search teams as their only methods of attracting applicants. The company presently needs to recruit 197 highly-skilled technical personnel. This will require a concerted recruiting effort by the human resource department. The recruiting program was planned along with the company's newly organized affirmative action program. At the introduction of the program to key executives of this new program the company president stated, "We will meet and exceed the recommendations of the Human Resource Manager to insure equal employment throughout this company."

The Human Resource Manager plans a college search in the numerous universities throughout northern Ohio. Going over this strategy in his mind, he realizes that since it is the fall of the year, he will only be able to attract a few professors and a very limited number of graduating students. Additionally, he realizes that the university placement services will not be as receptive to his appeal as they would be to one of their regular college recruiting companies. Despite the obstacles, he estimates that he must fill at least 50% of his positions through this means.

In discussing how to fill the remaining positions, the president suggested the use of newspaper advertisements. He realized there would be a large number of resumes received and that the company's personnel department would have to sort through these resumes and develop an application form that could facilitate the interview process. The company began to advertise in the Cleveland, Columbus, Toledo and Akron/Canton newspapers.

In addition, the Human Resource Manager made several recommendations to the president. The first of these was the use of private employment agencies as a beneficial means of searching for qualified applicants. The president ruled out this source as the company could not afford to pay the fees involved. The second recommendation was more favorably received. It involved the promotion and intended promotion of those present employees who had either completed or would soon complete their advanced degrees. This progression of employees allowed the company's recruiters to devote greater attention to undergraduate degrees.

Additionally, the company's executive search team was sent to various other laboratories to recruit personnel. It was felt that the recent receipt of a long-term government contract would allow the company to attract applicants from their competitors.

A final recruiting method used was to provide a notice to all the company's present employees, providing them with a breakdown of those positions that were available. It was felt that since highly-skilled personnel normally associate with other skilled personnel, these present employees would be a valuable resource for attracting applicants.

Questions

1. Can the Human Resource Manager expect such a high percentage of technically-skilled applicants from college recruiting?
2. Did the Human Resource Manager consider a geographic area wide enough for recruiting such highly technical personnel? Should it have been statewide or nationwide?
3. Is the newspaper campaign wide enough to attract the highly skilled minorities and women necessary to meet affirmative action goals?
4. What other recruiting sources or strategies would you suggest?

"Word-of-Mouth" Hiring Referrals

TRA, Inc., has been providing restaurant services to buildings housing large corporations for the past 26 years. What initially began as a single contract to provide luncheon facilities for the central office of GMG Corporation has now expanded into a nationwide service employing over 100,000 people. Each unit is tailored to the needs and specifications of the building it serves. All of the TRA units are equipped to provide cafeteria services, executive dining rooms and banquets for conferences. Each pays rent to the company it is affiliated with and, in turn, takes pride in providing good, yet relatively inexpensive food served in an efficient and tasteful manner. TRA must be prepared to effectively handle a heavy influx of customers between the hours of 11 a.m. and 2 p.m. and to provide service to their customers within the limitations of their lunch breaks. Their customers include only employees of the affiliated corporations and their guests. None of the TRA services are open to the general public.

Each TRA unit is individually managed, and personnel policies are left to the general manager of the unit. Recently, problems have developed in the Morristown, New Jersey unit. Most of the employees, including the waitresses, bus people, kitchen help and general maintenance crews work between the hours of 9 a.m. and 3 p.m. This time period is ideal for mothers with school-aged children and others who desire part-time work. As a result, TRA consistently has a surplus of applications. All applications are accepted and kept on file, but are seldom used, as it has become a practice at this location to hire referrals from present employees. It is felt that this relationship between employees will facilitate a higher degree of cooperation than could otherwise be expected. Most of the lower-level positions are filled in this manner, and TRA has found that their employees tend to have a significantly lower turnover and absenteeism rate than the industry as a whole.

A year ago, the top management position for the unit became vacant and was filled by a recent MBA graduate. One of the first things that she noticed was the unit's hiring practices. She did not feel that they were in compliance with EEOC regulations, especially when she discovered that not even one employee who dealt directly with the customers was African American. Furthermore, when she referred to the personnel files, she found that 12% of the applicants were African American. As a result, she instituted a selection program designed to hire minorities. She considered applicants connected with present personnel last in an attempt to fill the payroll with a better representation from the general public.

After a period of several months, the turnover and absenteeism rate began to increase noticeably. The quality of the services dropped and the new manager has just been presented with a memorandum from the president stating his concern.

Questions

1. Was the method of selection used previously by this TRA unit effective? Was it legal?
2. What mistakes, if any, did the new manager make in her selection procedure?
3. What policies should have been instituted at the central headquarters of TRA concerning selection for these positions? Discuss various methods of selection that could have been implemented, and their advantages and their disadvantages.

Application Blanks and Job Relatedness

P. Everready was a Director of Human Resources at a medium-sized department store. He had been in this position for a number of years and had lived through many changes in the composition of the firm's application blanks. Because of recent interpretations of Title VII of the Civil Rights Act, it was getting harder and harder to get the information he wanted.

Everready liked to hire healthy people if he could, figuring they would be on the job more often and thus contribute to better company performance. Over the years as Human Resource Director, Everready knew from an analysis of employee evaluations that older, married women whose children had left home had higher annual evaluations than any other group at the store.

In addition to questions about gender, age, the number and ages of dependent children at home, and marital status, the application blank had a section concerning physical and mental health conditions. Applicants were required to complete a checklist stating whether or not they had now, or in the past, any of the conditions listed.

The department store P. Everready works for is located near a college, and many of the students apply for jobs at the store. Lately, the initial screeners in the Human Resource Department have been telling Everready that several applicants, mostly male, have been complaining that, "all this store hires is old ladies," and "what business is it of the store's if I ever had the chicken pox?"

Everready asked his people to prepare an analysis of application blank questions using the "Horizontal Percentage Method." He hoped to prove that even though he was asking non-neutral questions they were, in fact, job-related. After this was done, he wanted an expert on the legal aspects of Title VII to review the data and tell him where he stood in case he had to defend his position.

This is a summary of some of the absenteeism data gathered from the application blanks:

		High	Low	Total	%High
Gender	male	180	120	300	60
	female	240	60	300	80
(female)	age				
	18-25	25	75	100	25
	26-40	40	60	100	40
	41-65	75	25	100	75
(male)	age				
	18-25	20	80	100	20
	26-40	50	50	100	50
	41-65	30	70	100	30

The data on absenteeism showed that out of a possible 363 working days per year, females missed an average of 81 days, and males missed an average of 83 days.

The Title VII consultant looked at the department store's weighted application blank and their figures on absenteeism. He also looked at the geographic area from which Everready could reasonably recruit and select his work force. He found the area to be white-dominated (93%) with a median age of 23. The population was equally divided by gender. Everready's work force was 85% white and 15% male, with an average age of 30.

Question

1. Based on the information above, what advice and recommendations would you offer P. Everready in regard to how he is using the application blank? Explain. Would you suggest any changes? Explain.

Weighted Application Blanks

The Ajax Power Company has for many years relied on a single application blank for their selection process. It has come to the attention of the Equal Employment Opportunity Commission that the company has been hiring African Americans in a disproportionately low number relative to their availability in the surrounding labor market. The EEOC office also knows that the power company uses several questions on its application blank that are not neutral in nature and figure prominently in the selection process. With this information in hand, the EEOC has brought the Ajax Power Company to court on charges of discrimination in selection, in violation of Title VII of the 1964 Civil Rights Act.

Realizing the potential danger of their situation, Ajax Power Company called in a consultant to weight their application blank and to show that the three questions under consideration were not discriminatory but were, in reality, related to job performance. The main emphasis in the court hearing was placed on the question concerning the applicant's possession of a high school diploma. The EEOC contends that this question was placed on the application blank because a disproportionate number of African Americans in the geographic regions where Ajax hired did not finish high school. Ajax contends, however, that a high school education is necessary to run the complicated machinery in the power plant and that the question is job related. The other two questions are also believed by the EEOC to be creating adverse impact, yet they are felt to be job related by the employer.

The consultant took the 1,000 application blanks the power company had on hand, and the periodic supervisory evaluation of past and present employee performance and came up with the following:

	Answer	Total	High	Low	% High	Weight
High	yes	800	424	376	53	
School	no	200	94	106	47	
Education						
Question 2	A	275	198	77	72	
	B	340	224	116	66	
	C	385	266	119	69	
Question 3	A	407	155	252	38	
	B	314	132	182	42	
	C	279	126	153	45	

Questions

1. Weight the questions above using a 2, 5 and 10 percent spread.
2. Which set of weights would the power company use before the court to show that the questions are related to job performance? Why?
3. Which set of weights would the EEOC use to show that the questions are discriminatory? Why?
4. Do you believe the questions are related to job performance or do you believe they are discriminatory? Explain.

Introducing the Polygraph as a
Requirement for Employment

The Jarhead Company is a medium-sized department store chain operating in a major metropolitan area. It has eight branch stores within a 50-mile radius. The Company has approximately 950 employees and a payroll and accounting department of 15 people. In addition, each store has two employees who consolidate the store's monetary intake and forward it to the central office. All of the employees involved in handling funds have been working for the company for at least five years. There has not been a reassignment to the fiscal positions for over two years and all personnel are considered very experienced.

Approximately one year ago, an employee who had worked in the payroll and accounting department for eight years was caught embezzling funds from the company. As a result, the company has been reviewing security measures for control of funds and has made several changes. One of the changes is to require polygraph examinations, on an annual basis, of all personnel who handle large amounts of company funds.

Mr. Robert Delly has been a member of the payroll and accounting department for 15 years. He has held numerous supervisory positions within the department and has always been a trusted and valued employee. Never has a shortage of funds occurred in his area, and he is diligent in assuring his subordinates are trustworthy and thoroughly perform their duties.

When recently asked to take his first yearly polygraph examination, Mr. Delly objected and has filed a complaint with the Grievance Committee. He asserts that he has never given the company any reason to distrust him and that after 15 years of faithful service the company has committed a breach of trust by now asking him to take a polygraph. He has been informed by the Human Resource Department that he faces dismissal if he does not submit to the test.

Questions

1. Should Mr. Delly be required to take the polygraph examination as a condition of continued employment? Why or why not?
2. How would you handle this case if you were the Director of Human Resources?

The Privacy Act's Relationship to
Applicants and Employers

Juanita Walpole just moved to the Washington, D.C. area from Atlanta, Georgia. The recent move forced Juanita to quit her old job. She requested that her employee file be made available to her, but her employer refused.

After Juanita arrived in Washington, D.C., she searched the newspaper job advertisements in *The Washington Post*. A bank manager position interested her, but the job advertisement listed a masters degree as a requirement. Unfortunately, Juanita only had a bachelor's degree. Desperate to start work, Juanita applied for the job anyway and was told by the receptionist who gave her the application blank that the advertisement was supposed to specify a masters *candidate*. She was also shown a copy of the job description which stated that the position required "a college graduate."

Juanita proceeded to fill out the job application and found that one question asked about arrests. Juanita answered this and all other questions on the application blank but after returning home began to reflect on some of the things that had happened to her.

Questions

1. Was Juanita legally denied the right to see her file by her former employer?
2. Was the newspaper advertisement that Juanita responded to legal?
3. Does the application question dealing with arrests violate any law or set of guidelines and if so, which one?
4. If the answer to number 3 above is "yes," might the question have been worded differently to obtain the same information and, yet, clearly not violate the law?

Individual Rights and
Equal Employment Opportunity

Mr. I. Ben Hadd has been an employee of a large chain of hardware and lumber stores for the last three years. He began as a clerk in one of their major departments, Home Building and Lumber Supplies. After the first three months, and every six months thereafter, he received wage increases as called for in his union contract. Mr. Hadd had shown great managerial potential and began to advance rapidly. Within six months, he was placed in charge of the department's scheduling of employee hours and was given the title of Assistant Manager of the Home Building and Lumber Supply Department.

After eight months in this position, he was enrolled, at the company's own expense, in a two-week seminar where he was taught how to maintain the books and how to run an automated inventory system. Two months later, he was named manager of the department. After one year in this position, Mr. Hadd was offered the position of Assistant Management Trainee for an entire store. Although the new position did not offer an immediate increase in salary, the opportunity for later advancement and salary increases was apparent. However, the new position entailed moving to another state, 400 miles away, and working with all new personnel. Mr. Hadd weighed the pros and cons of the offer and decided to accept it.

At the new store, Mr. Hadd experienced problems during his first two weeks working under Mr. Large. Most of these problems were the result of personality differences between the two. During his third week at the new store, Mr. Large stated that within the two and one-half weeks since Mr. Hadd had moved to the store, an affirmative action plan had been approved, and goals had been established that had to be met. Mr. Hadd was informed that he would be back in the Building and Lumber Supply Department of Mr. Large's store and that his salary would remain the same. Mr. Hadd requested a transfer back to his position at his previous store but was informed that his position had already been filled and that there were no other vacancies at that store.

For the next two weeks, Mr. Hadd worked in the Building and Lumber Supply Department at the level of responsibility that he had when he first joined the company. He felt that the store manager was belligerent toward him and that he had been denied an opportunity for advancement through no fault of his own. He therefore decided to terminate his employment and

217

inform the union of his unjust situation, in hopes of being rehired at another store at an assistant manager level.

Questions

1. Can the company be forced to rehire him?
2. If the answer to #1 is "no," would he be eligible for state unemployment using the defense that he quit with cause?
3. How would you handle the situation at this point if you were the Human Resource Manager for the hardware chain?

Subjective Choices
Based on Employment Interviews

Illinois Central College is an open-admission school which operates on the quarter system. The admission, registration, and registrar functions are all performed by the Records Office, necessitating the use of various skills and abilities in the successful performance of the jobs. The Human Resource Office of the school collects all employment applications and sends them out to the various departmental offices when there is an opening. It is the responsibility of each office to review the applications for interviewing and selections. The state requires that three people be interviewed for each vacant position before a selection can be finalized.

In August, an opening for a full-time file clerk position occurred in the Records Office. This job required that the person hold a high-school diploma and have the ability to organize material for the students' academic records. The individual had to learn the responsibilities of record keeping and understand the confidentiality of records as set down by the Family Educational Rights and Privacy Acts. The job also required considerable overtime during registration periods.

Joni Jones, a young African American, applied for a job and her application was routed to the Records Office. During her interview, it was discovered that she was presently employed by another firm in a nearby town. It was learned that she had worked with the other company for three months as a telephone receptionist. General philosophies and policies of the Records Office were discussed by the interviewer. The candidate did not ask any detailed questions about the job she was seeking. She stated that if she were hired she would need to give the company where she was currently employed a two week notice.

The second interviewee was a middle-aged woman who was returning to the work force after eighteen years spent raising children. After the description of the office and a discussion of the overtime, she voluntarily withdrew herself from consideration for the position.

Priscilla Mudd was the third candidate interviewed. She had just graduated from high school and had no prior office experience. She had worked at a fast-food restaurant during the summer between her junior and senior years of school. Priscilla asked several questions and seemed very eager to find a full-time position. During the interview, the possibility of temporary registration work was explored. Priscilla was made aware that this temporary employment did not guarantee that she would have a full-time job with the college in the future.

Priscilla accepted the temporary position and worked during the two week fall registration period. During that time she proved to be very energetic and patient with the students. She also recognized and corrected errors. Since she demonstrated her ability to handle a varied work load, she was hired for the file-clerk position.

Questions

1. Discuss what the college is doing wrong in its selection process in general, and what it did wrong in this case in particular.
2. How would you change the process in general?
3. Would you have handled this particular case differently? If so, how?

Discrimination in Selection

Director of Health and Public Welfare for the Commonwealth of Virginia, Mr. John Brown had received only two applications for the position of Environmental Protection Officer. One applicant, Dr. Harold Schmidt, had a chemistry degree but had very little training in environmental impact. Schmidt, who was white, did not appear to be the most qualified candidate since he had no relevant employment experience other than his teaching and research position at Johnston University. The cut-off date of August 1st had to be extended even to consider his application.

The second applicant, Susan Dixon, an African American female, seemed to be fully qualified on paper. She had five years of experience within the department, had taken several courses that the Commonwealth recommended for its "Personal Growth" program and had demonstrated good, conscientious work habits. However, a colleague of John Brown had met with Susan at a workshop in the past month. According to him, Susan lacked interpersonal skills and easily became sarcastic when frustrated. After some informal inquiries by Brown, several of Susan's coworkers confirmed this. Mr. Brown suspected, though, that the reason they objected to her possible appointment was that there had never been a minority or female supervisor in that department.

So much dissension was being voiced over the possible appointment of Susan that Mr. Brown decided to select Dr. Schmidt (even though he would have to change the job specifications and extend the application deadline). Mr. Brown felt that the Department of Environmental Protection's effectiveness was dependent upon its staff's cohesiveness.

Questions

1. Do you think Susan Dixon could claim discrimination on the basis of sex and/or race?
2. How would you handle this situation if you were in Mr. Brown's position?

Job Performance and Discrimination
in Selection Decisions

The Liberty Plastics Corporation is located within a city with a population of 300,000. Liberty employs 425 injection-mold operators. For the past ten years, its Human Resource Department has been using a delayed selection procedure to maintain an adequate number of injection-mold operators.

The top-level management of the company became dissatisfied with the delayed selection procedure which, with a growing work force, had become an increasingly expensive selection method. With a view to simplifying the selection process and stabilizing the work force, the Human Resource Office was tasked with developing a more cost-effective selection procedure. Part of the directive given to the Human Resource Officer by the company's President was that the new selection procedures should reduce absenteeism.

A survey over the past 6 years involving 880 employees who held injection-mold operator jobs was used in the search for selection tools. Four of the questions being considered for use in the new process appear on the attached chart (see chart, next page).

All applicants were also required to take the psycho-motor portion of the General Aptitude Test Battery and score 80 or more to be considered for employment as an injection-mold operator. Results of the test can be seen on the chart.

This new selection procedure came to the attention of the Equal Employment Opportunity Commission after an African American unwed mother charged that she was not selected for an injection-mold operator's job because of her status as a single parent, declaring that this discriminated unfairly against African Americans who had a higher proportion of illegitimate births than whites.

	Productivity				Absenteeism			
	High	Low	% High	Weight	High	Low	% High	Weight
1. Sex								
a) Male	155	215	42%	4	205	165	55%	5
b) Female	285	255	53%	5	235	275	46%	4
2. Married								
a) Yes	308	242	56%	5	253	297	46%	4
b) No	132	198	40%	4	187	143	57%	5
3. Have Children (Married)								
a) None	184	156	54%	5	188	152	55%	5
b) 1 or More	107	103	51%	5	86	124	41%	4
Have Children (Single)								
c) None	134	146	48%	4	154	126	55%	5
d) 1 or More	21	29	42%	4	12	38	24%	2
4. Race								
a) White	255	235	52%	5	265	225	54%	5
b) Nonwhite	185	205	47%	4	175	215	45%	4
5. General Aptitude Test (Psycho-motor)								
a) 0-79	86	134	39%	3	112	108	51%	5
b) 80-110	192	208	48%	4	201	199	50%	5
c) 111-150	162	98	62%	6	127	133	49%	4

Questions

1. In the light of the figures shown in the chart, is the Liberty Plastics Corporation in violation of Fair Employment Practices by selecting on the basis of parenthood and marital status?
2. Discuss the use of the other questions in the selection process.

Racial Composition of the Geographic Area in Hiring Decisions

The Capitol Grand Food Company is a supermarket chain with 100 food stores in the Washington, D.C. metropolitan area, all located in Maryland and Virginia. The chain does not operate any stores within the District of Columbia's city limits. The retail work force of Capitol Grand Food Company consists of 3,000 workers, 53% male and 47% female. By race, 12% of the work force is African American while 88% is white. The management positions are department heads of produce and meat, etc., and are held by women 15% of the time and by African Americans 5% of the time.

Since the retail food industry in the Washington area is heavily unionized and the pay scale is very high, Capitol Grand Food Company has five times as many applicants on file as jobs available at any one time. The high pay and low turnover of the industry have resulted in a situation where Capitol Grand Food Company has no need to advertise job openings. With a ready supply of workers, they rely entirely upon word-of-mouth advertising.

The interview process consists of a math test and a standard questionnaire about past experience, schooling and general information. If there are no blatant reasons why an applicant is undesirable, such as having been convicted of theft, or questions which require further research, such as having been fired from their last job, the application is filed with the others. As an opening occurs in the general vicinity of an applicant, the person is called and informed of the job. This is done by going through the file arranged by application date, and calling the first applicant in the vicinity of the job. If an applicant turns down the offer, that application is taken out of the file.

The gender and racial makeup of the area where the Capitol Grand Food Company operates is relatively close to the makeup of the work force. The gender makeup of the suburban areas of Virginia and Maryland where Capitol Grand Food Company operates is approximately 52% female and 48% male, and the racial mix is approximately 85% white and 15% African American. However, if the District of Columbia were included in the operating area, the racial mixture would be 70% white and 30% African American.

Questions

1. If Capitol Grand Food Company were accused of unfair hiring practices, would the EEOC be likely to prosecute under their guidelines? If yes, for what specific reasons?
2. What do you think Capitol Grand Food Company would contend is their operating area? What do you think the EEOC would contend is their operating area? What do you think their operating area should be defined as?
3. Should the promotion practices of Capitol Grand Food Company be examined? Why, or why not?

Relevant Factors in Findings
of Sex Discrimination

The ABC Chemical Company sought to fill a sales trainee position. ABC placed an advertisement in a local newspaper which read, "Sales Trainee, male or female, no experience required. We are looking for an aggressive, career-minded individual." Jane Smith applied for the position. During her employment interview, she was asked several questions which she felt were prejudicial toward women. Some of the questions included: "What are your plans for marriage?" and "Are you really intent on making a career with ABC Chemical?" The interviewer also made a statement that, "You know, there aren't too many women in the chemical field."

After the interview, Jane was informed that the company would give preference to someone with a background in chemicals, which she did not have, and would notify her within the next few days about the status of her application. Two days later, Jane was notified by letter that she was not selected for the job. She charged ABC Chemical with sex discrimination in their failure to hire her.

When questioned by an investigator from the Equal Employment Opportunity Commission, ABC Chemical's Human Resource Director stated that the company had a firm policy against discrimination and had an affirmative action program to recruit minorities and women. He stated that the sex discrimination charge had no merit since the individual selected was more qualified due to his having taken a chemistry course in high school. He further indicated that Jane had shown a negative attitude during her interview by refusing to answer questions about her personal plans for the future. He stated that such questions are asked of all applicants, because the company is interested in their attitude toward a career. Lastly, he contended that the statement relating to the number of women in the chemical field was not made to discourage Jane but merely to inform her of factual information relative to the industry.

During the EEOC's subsequent investigation it was learned that, at present, no women were employed by ABC Chemical as sales trainees or sales representatives. There are presently ten trainees and 35 representatives. Although the individual hired had taken chemistry courses in high school, seven currently employed trainees and 24 representatives did not have a background in the chemical field. It was for this reason, as a matter of fact, that ABC's in-house training program was very extensive, lasting in excess of six months. In conversations with other applicants for the same position, it was learned that all were men and none had been asked questions concerning their marital status or future plans.

Questions

1. Was Jane Smith unlawfully denied employment because of her sex?
2. What factors would contribute to a finding of sex discrimination?
3. What remedy is available to Jane Smith in this situation?

Compliance with Title VII:
Numbers are Not Enough

Stalo, Inc., is a large manufacturing company with headquarters in New York City and plants located in fifteen states. Stalo also has six wholly-owned subsidiaries located in the southern part of the country. The company carries brand name electronic equipment and also manufactures its own line of electronic toys, household items and desk-top calculators.

For many years, Stalo has provided its employees with excellent benefits, working conditions and wages. The company has always cooperated with its unions and has never had a strike close any of its plants. In all its union shops, Stalo only hires people from union apprentice programs and union hiring halls, in accordance with their contracts. The high level of compensation has kept turnover to a minimum. With the low turnover rate, Stalo has generally filled job vacancies with people recommended by current employees. Employees who bring in qualified replacements are given a one hundred dollar bonus for each person hired who satisfactorily completes company training programs.

Stalo uses a decentralized Human Resource Department structure, and the main office personnel staff is small because hiring and recruiting is done at each individual plant. The Vice President for Human Resources is John Bowers, who possesses a general business degree from a small Midwestern college and has very limited knowledge in the area of fair employment legislation.

A year ago, Stalo was investigated by the EEOC after the Commission received numerous complaints against the company and its hiring practices. The company had never been in this position, and they knew very little about the existing laws regarding hiring practices. John Bowers decided to hire more women and minorities in entry-level positions that opened in the next year to comply with the laws as he understood them. He instructed the Human Resource Offices at each plant to make an effort to hire these two classes of people.

At the end of the year, the EEOC representative returned to Stalo to conduct a follow-up investigation. Mr. Bowers explained that the company had every intention of obeying the law and proceeded to show the investigator the results of his new selection emphasis. The company had hired thirty-two women in the various production lines throughout the company and seventeen minority males to work on the loading docks and to drive the company trucks. The investigator stated that Stalo was still violating Title VII of the Civil Rights Act.

Questions

1. What must Stalo do, in addition to the steps it has already undertaken, to comply with Title VII?
2. What statistical information determines compliance?
3. Should Mr. Bowers investigate the union apprenticeship programs and hiring halls? If so, why?

Sex Discrimination and Universities

When Cemaron University, a small college in Tupelo, Oklahoma, hired its women's resident supervisor from among 100 female applicants, little did they realize the trouble that was to follow.

The chosen applicant, a college graduate and school teacher, had two years of work experience in student counseling. After an extensive interview and a thorough reference check of previous employers, the applicant was selected as the women's resident supervisor to oversee approximately 150 female students in the college dormitory. Immediately thereafter, a male was interviewed and hired to supervise the men in the same dormitory complex.

The position required a college degree and a live-in status as part of the conditions for employment. The men's supervisor did not have a college degree but was, in fact, attending classes to complete his degree in elementary education at the university. The men's supervisor was paid a higher salary due to two facts: (1) he was responsible for 50 additional students and (2) male students caused greater disciplinary problems than female students.

In the spring of the school year, the men's supervisor started doing his practice teaching, which meant he was not available during the day for student counseling and other responsibilities. Consequently, the women's supervisor assumed some of his responsibilities. When the women's supervisor was asked to substitute teach at one of the local high schools from 10:00 a.m. until 2:00 p.m. each day for eight weeks, she assumed there would be no problem since the men's supervisor was being allowed to do his practice teaching all day. However, the Director of Housing, their immediate supervisor, flatly denied her the opportunity to substitute teach, justifying the action by saying that both supervisors could not be away from their duties at the same time.

Questions

1. Was the university discriminating against the women's resident supervisor?
2. Assuming that identical job descriptions existed, does the BFOQ requirement have any effect on the type of applicant who is hired for these positions?
3. Would the women's supervisor be entitled to the same amount of compensation under the Equal Pay Act?
4. If you were the Director of Housing, how would you handle this situation?

Nonprofit Organizations and Title VII

Camp Olympia is owned and operated by the Mountain Area Council of the Boy Scouts of America. The purpose of the camp is to provide a summer program of camping and educational recreation activities and to fulfill the objectives of scouting in general. In addition, the camp is a facility that can be utilized by individual troops throughout the year on a first-come, first-served basis.

The land and the buildings of the camp were purchased over a period of years. From 1984 to present, the funds for the property and buildings and their maintenance have been raised by the scouts of the area. The additional revenues come from many sources. For the ten month period of August 22 to June 2, the camp is for rent to any organization other than BSA, assuming it is not being used by a troop. Presently there is a boxing club operating in the camp. Local industry and the United Way also provide income to the facility. Finally, there is a fee charged to each scout who attends the camp during its summer session, primarily to pay for food, utilities and supplies.

Up until 1984, all of the staff, except the Ranger and Camp Director, were volunteers. In the fall of 1984, an extremely wealthy individual left a vast sum of money in trust to the camp to pay the wages of the summer staff. The trust provided that any person 15 years of age or older, white, and a member of the BSA, could be compensated out of the budgeted fund. Today, the camp operates in the red and this fund is a source of financial relief.

Up until last year, the camp was able to maintain its policy of an all-white staff without too much difficulty. During the summer of the past year, the camp enrolled in an international staff-exchange program which was organized by the BSA. The staff member sent to the camp was from India. The only compensation other than his room and board was to be his fare to and from India. When the camp director applied to the local bank where the trust fund was set up, the request was denied because this staff member was dark-skinned. Other measures were provided for the payment of the fare.

In the last year, some qualified minorities applied for summer employment, and because the payroll for the summer staff was budgeted based on the trust fund, they were denied jobs. Two of these individuals have now filed suit against Camp Olympia and the Boy Scouts of America.

Questions

1. Can the camp be forced to hire minorities and provide for their compensation from other sources?
2. Does the fact that the BSA is a private organization have any bearing on this case?

Sex Discrimination And Federal Employees

Erin Patrick, an African American employee of the ABC Agency in the United States government, rapidly rose from a GS-6 to a GS-11. She transferred to the MTK Agency in April of 1990 as a GS-11. In June of 1991, she was promoted to a GS-12, and in October of 1993, she became eligible for a GS-13 position in the Economics Department.

Erin's educational background consisted of a B.S. degree in Economics. She had taken several university-level courses in a variety of subjects from 1986 to 1991 as well as completing many courses offered in-house by her employer.

At the MTK Agency, Erin applied for promotion to a GS-13 in March of 1995 and again in July of that same year. In November of 1996, Erin applied for a GS-13 position as a Computer Systems Analyst. Although Erin was qualified for each of these positions, she was not selected. On each occasion, the officials making the selection were white males.

When Erin was turned down for the Computer Systems Analyst position, she filed an EEO complaint claiming discrimination on the basis of sex and race. She alleged that she had not been selected because she was a minority and a female.

A white male, Terrence Klein, was chosen for the Analyst position. He had only a high-school diploma and had completed three computer courses. Terrence received a promotion to GS-9 in 1992; Erin was promoted to a GS-12 in 1991. Both employees were rated high in the technical skills area.

Since 1994, the MTK Agency had promoted only one Spanish female, and no African American females, to GS-13 positions. During the same period, ten white females, 103 white males, and three African American males were hired or promoted to GS-13.

After Erin's complaint was received, the agency responded by stating that opportunities for advancement were uniformly available to all employees and that Erin was not discriminated against because of sex and/or race. The agency also maintained that Terrence was better qualified for the Computer Systems Analyst position, because he was rated slightly higher than Erin in technical competence.

Question

1. The court ruled in favor of Erin Patrick. Based on your knowledge of federal guidelines, list three reasons why the MTK Agency was found guilty of discrimination.

Weight to be Lifted as a BFOQ

Marsha Thompson was recently discharged from the United States Army. Upon discharge, Marsha returned to her hometown of Springfield, Virginia. During her four years in the Army, Marsha was a truck driver. Hoping to use her skills in trucking operations, Marsha applied to Ben-Hurst Trucking Company after arriving home.

It was a well known fact in town that Ben-Hurst was expanding operations considerably and had a need for fifteen new truck drivers. Since Marsha had four years of related military experience, she thought her chances of employment were excellent.

Ben-Hurst was an excellent company for which to work. They paid their truck drivers excellent wages and had a good benefits package. As a result of this, many applicants turned up for the fifteen new jobs. Of the thirty-five applicants for the jobs, all were men except Marsha. This did not discourage Marsha, however, because as she talked to the various men, few seemed to have as much experience as her. When some of the men complained to her that this was not women's work, she told them to mind their own business.

Marsha and the others were given a written test on Friday afternoon and told their results would be given to them Monday morning. On Monday, Marsha was informed that she passed the written test with an excellent score and was told to report to the trucking area for a driver's test. Upon arriving at the trucking area, Marsha noticed that there were now only about twenty applicants left. As far as Marsha could tell, she drove the trucks as well as any of the men.

After the driving test, all applicants were told to report to the docks for a weight-lifting test. The test required each applicant to lift one hundred pounds. Although Marsha was a fairly large woman, she was not able to lift the required one hundred pounds. All of the applicants were told that they would be informed by Wednesday if they were to be hired.

When Wednesday came, Marsha did not receive any notification. Upset over this, she called Ben-Hurst to find out why. Ben-Hurst told her that she qualified in all other aspects, but since she could not pass the weight-lifting test they would not hire her. They told her that this was a "*bona fide occupational qualification,*" and they therefore had the right to reject her. Marsha did not think that the company should be able to discriminate against her simply because she could not lift the weight.

Question

1. What factor or factors will determine whether the one hundred pound weight lifting requirement is, in fact, a BFOQ in this situation?

Physical Appearance as a BFOQ

Sally Jones is a college student looking for a job as a sales clerk in a dress shop. On March 19th, she was in Washington, D.C., filling out applications, but all positions seemed to be filled for the summer. However, her day brightened when she applied for a job in a tiny dress shop in Georgetown which actually had a sign in the window reading, "Help wanted. Experienced sales girl. Good looking only." Sally had sales experience and felt herself to be attractive, although she didn't understand why it was necessary to be good looking to be a sales clerk.

Sally applied for the position in question and heard nothing for a few weeks. As she expected, there were no openings available in the other shops she had investigated. However, three weeks after she had applied at the dress shop in Georgetown, she received a call requesting her to come in for an interview. Sally was thrilled, since she badly needed a job.

Based on the interview, Sally felt sure she would get the job. The manager of the shop seemed to like her qualifications and was very friendly. He told her he would let her know in a day or two. When he didn't call, Sally became angry and called the shop herself asking to talk to the manager. The manager seemed evasive to her questions on why she hadn't been contacted. Finally, the manager told her she hadn't been selected because she was not attractive enough. Sally was outraged and demanded to know how it was decided who was or was not attractive enough to work in a tiny dress shop. The manager gave no answer and hung up the phone.

Questions

1. Is this a case of discrimination or does the dress shop have the right to choose only "attractive" sales clerks?
2. Can physical appearance be classified as a BFOQ in this case?
3. What advice would you give to the manager of the dress shop?

Title VII and Job-Related Educational Requirements

The Brett Consulting Company, a growing consulting firm specializing in government contracts in the Washington, D.C. area, is facing a numbers problem in fulfilling its minority hiring goals. Its staff at the present time has a very high ratio of Ph.D.s, and it is having difficulty recruiting qualified racial minorities with doctoral degrees in electrical engineering or physics, its two main areas of consulting.

The Brett Consulting Company has eleven white male professionals, seven white female professionals, and three white female clerical staffers. They have doubled their number of employees in the last four years.

The benefits program with Brett consists of a profit-sharing retirement program, extensive health and dental insurance coverage, liberal salary increases and bonuses for overachievers. Through excellent employee selection and good business practices, Brett is on sound financial footing.

The company is too small to have its own human resource staff, and recruitment is done by two mid-level managers using personal referrals from their alma maters and word-of-mouth sources. The cost of campus recruitment is too high and has not been successful. The area universities have not been too successful referring candidates that fulfill the strict requirements for the open positions, and there is not a pool of minority graduates with a solid background in electrical engineering or physics in the geographic area.

The problem that exists is one of getting a more racially balanced firm without actually reducing the high educational requirements presently in place. James Conrad, one of two individuals making selection decisions, has been working for months trying to come up with a solution to this problem. He has decided that the only logical solution is to hire a private employment agency to recruit candidates. Based on previous recruiting attempts, he is afraid he may have to lower the educational requirement to a master's or even a bachelor's degree in order to attract racial minorities.

Questions

1. Can James Conrad specify a preference for minority candidates to the private agency?
2. Can the employment agency specify the preference for minority candidates in its recruiting?
3. Must the Brett Company lower their educational standards for applicants, to achieve a racially balanced staff?
4. What would the EEOC tell Brett if it were asked to investigate the company's recruiting and selection procedures?

A High School Diploma as a Job Requirement

Mike Jones was a young Puerto Rican who had dropped out of high school to help support his family after his father died. Despite this, he did manage to attend night school for two years and completed a program to become a computer programmer. At his first interview, it seemed that the interviewer, Mr. Clark, was impressed with Mr. Jones.

"Mr. Jones, I am impressed with your performance at computer school and your work record at your present job," Clark said. "I know that you applied for the programming job, but I can give you one other vacant position as a keypunch operator."

"I am anxious to get my career started," Jones said, "but I was applying for the programming job."

"Well, I'm afraid that the programming position requires that you have a high school diploma," Clark said, "and you did not finish high school."

"I know that I don't have a high school diploma, but I was near the top of my class in computer school and was highly recommended by my instructor."

"That may be true," Clark said, "but we have always required a high school diploma for that position. Perhaps you should have finished high school and then entered computer school."

"That doesn't seem fair," Jones said. "You seem to be saying that I am qualified for the programming job but cannot be hired because I don't have a high school diploma."

"I don't make the rules, Mr. Jones," Clark said. "I can't make exceptions to company rules. After all, you can advance to the programming position once you get a high school diploma."

Questions

1. Comment on the legality of the educational requirement, both in general and in this particular case.
2. What data must be gathered and analyzed by the employer in a case such as this to determine if the educational requirement is justified?

National Origin as a BFOQ

The Bali Hai Corporation started as a small Chinese restaurant in Boston, Massachusetts. The restaurant was an exact replica of a Chinese pagoda. Over the years, the restaurant owned and managed by Arnold Sing became known for its food and atmosphere. Customers were made to feel as if they were actually in China.

In the last few years, Sing has incorporated and opened other similar restaurants throughout the country. Sing continued his policy of hiring only waiters of Asian descent. He felt this added to his customers' dining pleasure and made for a more authentic environment. For kitchen purposes, though, Sing hired any applicants who were qualified.

About a year ago in Sing's Bali Hai of Washington, D.C., there was a shortage of waiters. An advertisement was placed in the paper for waiters, and the manager of the restaurant was instructed by Sing to hire only Asians. The manager was also reminded of Bali Hai's reputation of good food and authentic atmosphere.

Two young men, one African American and one white, both with considerable restaurant experience, applied for the jobs. The manager explained the policy of hiring only Asians to the young men and told them he could get them work in his kitchen.

The two men declined the position and instead went directly to the Equal Employment Opportunity Commission and filed a complaint. Sing's defense was that the policy was only intended to preserve the atmosphere of the restaurant. He said the Asian waiters were needed to make it more authentic.

Question

1. Is Sing's defense a good one under the law? Why or why not?

Job Qualifications and Task Performance

Giant Airline advertised for four flight officer positions. The requirements were a college degree and 500 flight hours. Five persons with the following qualifications applied for the four positions:

Candidate A: White male, degree in chemical engineering with 500 flight hours in a standard aircraft.

Candidate B: White male, degree in biology with 350 hours in a jet aircraft.

Candidate C: White male, Master's degree in mathematics with 200 hours in a jet rotary-wing helicopter and 250 hours in a standard aircraft.

Candidate D: White male, degree in astronomy with 600 flight hours in a standard aircraft.

Candidate E: Black male, junior college degree in English with 500 hours in a standard aircraft (Mr. Johnson).

Mr. Johnson was turned down for one of the available positions with the explanation that he was not as well qualified as the other four candidates due to his degree and flight time.

Mr. Johnson sued Giant Airlines on the basis of racial discrimination. He stated a college degree was not related to the type of position he had applied for and, in addition, he had the required flight hours, while some of the other applicants had not.

To establish that Giant's flight officer qualifications resulted in discrimination against minorities, Mr. Johnson showed that out of the approximately 590 flight officers in Giant's employ at the time of the trial, only nine were minorities. He contended that these statistics established a *prima facie* case of racial discrimination. Giant claimed that these bare statistics established nothing unless accompanied by similar information on the number of qualified minority applicants for the flight officer position.

The two job qualifications that Mr. Johnson challenged were the requirements of a college degree and a minimum of 500 flight hours. The evidence at the trial showed that Giant did not train applicants to be pilots, but instead required that their applicants be pilots at the time of their application. It could not seriously be contended that such a requirement was not job-related. Giant also showed that applicants who had flight hours were more likely to succeed in the rigorous training which Giant flight officers went through after they were hired.

The statistics showed that 500 hours was a reasonable minimum applicant requirement to insure their passing Giant's training program. The evidence also showed that because of the high cost of the training program it was important to Giant that those who began the training eventually became flight officers.

With regard to the college degree requirement, Giant officials testified that it was a requirement which could be waived if the applicant's other qualifications were superior, especially if the person had a lot of flight time in high-speed jet aircraft. The evidence showed that Giant flight officers went through a rigorous training course upon being hired and then were required to attend intensive refresher courses at six-month intervals. Company officials testified that the possession of a college degree indicated that the applicant had the ability to understand and retain concepts and information given in the atmosphere of a classroom or training program. Thus, a person with a college degree, particularly in the "hard" sciences, was more able to succeed in the initial training program and the unending series of refresher courses.

Question

1. Do you agree with the company's defense? Why or why not?

Age Discrimination in Employment

Johnnie Walker has worked for General Cement Company for eighteen years. He joined General Cement as an engineer and subsequently was promoted to Operations Manager for the northeastern region. He has served in this capacity for the past ten years. Recently, the General Cement Company was acquired by the Red River Corporation. Mr. Walker and several other upper-level management personnel have been notified that they will be replaced by Red River employees.

In light of his present situation, Mr. Walker is in the process of seeking employment elsewhere. Upon the advice of a close friend who works at the Harbour Cement Company, a newly established, up-and-coming cement company in the area, Mr. Walker applied for a managerial position with that firm. He filed an application and was interviewed by the Human Resource Director the following day. Mr. Walker was informed that he would be notified of the company's decision pending the completion of interviews with the remaining applicants.

The following week, he was notified by letter that he had not been selected for the job. In talking with his friend a few days later, Mr. Walker was told that the person who was hired to fill the position at the Harbour Cement Company was not as qualified as he was. The new employee had only ten years' experience as opposed to eighteen years for Mr. Walker. His friend also related that he felt the primary reason for Mr. Walker's not being selected was his **age**. It was his friend's opinion that the Human Resource Director felt the other applicant's age (fifteen years younger than Mr. Walker) better qualified him for the job.

Encouraged by his colleagues, Mr. Walker sought legal advice as to the possibility of filing suit against Harbour Cement Company under the 1967 Age Discrimination in Employment Act. In discussions with his lawyer pertaining to the application and interview, Mr. Walker recalled on the application form an inquiry as to his specific age. His lawyer advised him that he had legal grounds for filing suit against Harbour Cement Company on the basis of age discrimination.

Questions

1. Was it legal for the application to contain a question regarding the specific age of the applicant?
2. Is age a *bona fide occupational qualification* in this situation?
3. What advice would you give Harbour Cement Company at this point concerning their selection process in general and Mr. Walker's case in particular?

Age Discrimination and Physical Job Requirements

G. M. Enterprises, a small company employing 22 persons, had a vacant position after a recent resignation. Bob Blake, 43 years old, and Tom Boswell, 53, applied for this position. Both men had worked for the company for an equal number of years, but Tom had experience which was similar to that required for the new job. Both Tom and Bob had been to a company-sponsored training course at a nearby school. Completion of the course was considered important for the job in question. Tom had much better course scores, but Bob had passed with a score acceptable by company standards.

The new job required operating a rather complex piece of equipment and, at times, involved some heavy lifting. The younger man was given the job. The supervisor called Tom into his office to inform him of the decision.

"Well, Tom," said Duncan, the supervisor, "I'm sorry we could not promote you to the position, but Bob just seemed the best choice under the circumstances."

"I don't understand," Tom said. "I have had some related experience and had excellent scores in the training course."

"What you say is true, Tom," Duncan said, "but Bob is younger and you may not be able to do the heavy lifting a few years from now. Besides, you only have a few years until you are eligible for retirement. It just makes sense to promote Bob. He's younger and will be around for a longer time. It is a better decision from an economic perspective."

Questions

1. Is this situation covered by the Age Discrimination In Employment Act?
2. What data would you collect if you were hired to defend the company?

Reverse Discrimination

The Millers, Brad and Mary, moved to Tallahassee, Florida, for Mary to attend law school at Florida State University. Brad graduated from Georgetown University with a degree in business administration and worked in retail management for five years. He had graduated with top honors and had excellent recommendations from his former employers.

Tallahassee, Florida, is basically a college town, centering around two universities and the Florida State Legislature. The two universities are Florida State University and Florida A & M University. There is only one large shopping mall and a few department stores in Tallahassee, and as such, jobs in retail management are quite scarce.

Upon arriving in Tallahassee, Mary started classes at the law school and Brad began looking for a job. There were absolutely no openings anywhere in town for a retail manager, and Brad eventually had to settle for a teller position at a local bank. Brad kept abreast of the retail job market in Tallahassee, and finally an opportunity arose.

T. H. Sandy, a women's discount sportswear retailer advertised in the local newspaper for a store manager. Brad immediately made an appointment for an interview and sent in a resume as requested in the advertisement. Brad arrived early for his interview and was given an application form to complete. The application form was a long one and included a question concerning gender of applicant.

While completing the application form, Brad noticed that all of the employees of T. H. Sandy were female and all of the other applicants waiting to be interviewed were also female. Brad was finally called in for his interview, which he thought went very well. The interviewer told Brad that they had two more days of interviewing before a decision would be made, and that he would be hearing from them in about a week.

The next week Brad received a letter from T. H. Sandy informing him that he had not been chosen for the position and thanking him for his interest in the company. The letter gave no reason for the decision. Since this job was so important to Brad, he decided to visit the store and talk with the lady who had interviewed him.

In his meeting with the interviewer, Brad found out that the company had been very impressed with his experience and credentials but had decided against hiring him because he was a male. The interviewer showed Brad a job description for the manager's position and pointed out that one of the duties of the manager was to supervise all areas of the store, including the dressing room. Because of this particular duty, the company felt that the position called for a female. Brad left the store upset and discouraged.

After discussing the situation with his wife, who was now studying Fair Employment Legislation, Brad considered filing suit against T. H. Sandy for discrimination based on sex, under Title VII of the Civil Rights Act of 1964.

Questions

1. Was T. H. Sandy's decision concerning Brad Miller in conflict with Title VII of the Civil Rights Act of 1964?
2. Was it legal for T. H. Sandy's application form to include a question concerning gender?
3. Is sex a *bona fide occupational qualification* in this situation?
4. Legally, would it have made a difference if there had been no job description for the position of store manager?

Selection for a Position Without a Specific Job Description

The president of the Itty Bitty Machine Company approached Kirk Johnson, the Human Resource Officer, about the need to fill a soon-to-be-vacant position as the president's Administrative Assistant. Discussion between the president and Kirk indicated that the position was to be used as a stepping-stone for higher executive positions and, as such, would require a higher degree of education and experience than what would normally be required for an Administrative Assistant.

The position was then advertised within the company via the company newspaper. Three applicants submitted applications to the Human Resource Office for the position.

Frieda Spiher had worked for Itty Bitty for fifteen years. She had a degree in secretarial science and had been an Administrative Assistant to the Vice President for Production for the last five years.

John Moscella joined the company five years ago right out of college with a degree in Business Administration. He has been attending night school working on his MBA with about one year to go. He has been the Assistant Human Resource Officer for the last two years.

Richard D'Aleo is in charge of the computer room and has been with the company since it was founded twenty years ago. Richard is five years from retirement. He has a bachelor's degree in engineering, but has not pursued any further education.

In addition to working with John for the last two years, Kirk has been good friends with both Richard and Frieda since he came to Itty Bitty ten years ago.

Question

1. What recommendations should Kirk make to the president regarding selection for the position? Explain.

Married vs. Maiden Surnames and Title VII

June Garcia, 28 years old and married, worked for Goliath Electric as a line worker, testing and inspecting electrical semi-conductors. She had a very favorable record and had worked her way up from packing clerk to being a valued employee, one of the most consistent and best on the line. She also worked her way through college at night.

Mr. Bollin, Human Resource Director, was considering either June or Tom Henly, a 32-year-old white male, for the position of line supervisor. Mr. Bollin wanted to promote a minority, especially an Hispanic and felt Garcia would be excellent for the job.

Occasionally, Goliath received contracts that required their supervisors to have a security clearance. Mr. Bollin checked out both candidates' backgrounds to determine if either had anything that would preclude them from obtaining a security clearance from the government. Mr. Bollin discovered that June had been arrested three times while in high school for being with someone caught stealing (her old boyfriend). Mr. Bollin knew from past experience that an arrest record would keep Garcia from obtaining the required clearance.

Even though the company did not currently have a government contract, Mr. Bollin felt that Tom Henly should be promoted, since he had a perfect record. There was another supervisory position opening up soon in another department that June would qualify for.

One month after Tom Henly was promoted to the job, June filed an EEOC complaint stating that she should have been promoted and should be given back pay for the period that Tom Henly had been in the position.

Questions

1. Should June have been promoted? Why or why not?
2. Should June be promoted now? Why or why not?
3. Can a security clearance be denied due to an arrest record?

Employment Rights of Single Parents

Major Jim Jones is a career Army officer who has spent 17 years in the service. Last year, Major Jones' wife died leaving him to care for their two daughters, ages 7 and 10. The nature of Major Jones' job requires him to work shifts ranging from 4:00 p.m. to 12:00 a.m., 12:00 a.m. to 8:00 a.m. and 8:00 a.m. to 4:00 p.m., as well as weekends and holidays. While his wife was living, this was not an inconvenience for Major Jones. In addition, as a military officer, Major Jones is always faced with the possibility of mobilization in the event of a military crisis.

As a result of this schedule, the Army has required Major Jones to sign a document stating that he has taken adequate steps to assure the Army that his family obligations will not interfere with his ability to work odd hours or mobilize on short notice. In effect, this document states that Major Jones' parental responsibilities will not inconvenience the Army or affect his job performance.

Failure to sign the statement will result in Major Jones being forced to resign from the Army or face discharge. Furthermore, failure to perform his shift work could also result in discharge. This, of course, would mean the loss of 17 years earned toward a pension as well as the right to use military facilities such as the commissary, PX, etc.

So far, Major Jones has not missed any of his duties. The girls are in school during the week, but Major Jones is having a great deal of difficulty finding someone to watch his daughters on week nights and weekends. Major Jones is trying desperately to be reassigned to an office where the hours are more stable.

Questions

1. Is Major Jones being discriminated against because of his single parent status?
2. When Major Jones was required to sign the statement about the care of his daughters, was this an invasion of his privacy?
3. Did the Army bring undue pressure upon Major Jones by asking him to sign the documents under the threat of an immediate discharge?
4. Obviously, an argument could be made for the Army's view if it were a wartime situation. However, since the U.S. is at peace, does the Army or any employer have the right to delve so thoroughly into an employee's personal life, especially when the employee's job performance is satisfactory?

Equal Pay for Equal Work

A local hospital is directed by a single administrator. Due to the growth of the facility several years ago, she changed the organizational structure, organizing the hospital into four divisions: Professional Services, Ancillary Services, Nursing Services, and a Financial Division. Each of these divisions was headed by an Assistant Administrator. It was the responsibility of each of these individuals to appoint department heads to manage the areas within their responsibility. For example, the Assistant Administrator of Ancillary Services had department heads for Engineering, Housekeeping, Laundry, Materiels Management and Safety and Security. Each of these department heads had the title of "Director" of their area of responsibility; i.e., Director of Housekeeping. Thus, the terms "director" and "department head" were used interchangeably.

Within the Nursing Services division, the Assistant Administrator was also considered Director of Nursing. She had, therefore, designated her department heads as supervisors in order to have a distinction of titles. Although called supervisors within their division, they were designated department heads on the organization chart. The function of these supervisors was identical when compared to the directors in other divisions, and the job description was the same. However, the department heads in the other divisions were all males while the supervisors (department heads) in nursing were all females.

The hospital salary scale identified department heads as a Grade 16, while supervisors were a Grade 14. During the growth of the hospital, much contact was necessary between divisions. The department heads in Nursing Service began to realize that confusion was being caused by the fact that they were called supervisors while their counterparts in the other divisions were called directors. As a result, titles were changed; responsibilities remained the same.

As the Assistant Administrator of Nursing Service was writing her report of the change to the Administrator, she discovered that her department heads were being paid less than department heads in other divisions. She included this information in her report with a request that the salaries be changed.

The Administrator reviewed the report and called a meeting of all Assistant Administrators and the Director of Human Resources. She was concerned with possible violation of the Equal Pay Act of 1963 and Title VII of the 1964 Civil Rights Act.

Questions

1. If you were the Human Resource Director, what would your recommendation be regarding the salaries?
2. If an increase for the Nursing Services supervisors is in order, should the change be retroactive? If so, to when?
3. Has the hospital violated the 1963 Equal Pay Act or Title VII of the 1964 Civil Rights Act?
4. What should be done regarding the various titles?

The Fair Labor Standards Act and Eligibility
for Unemployment Compensation

Bob worked at a fast-food restaurant. He knew he was being taken advantage of by the manager, his boss, because he often was asked to work overtime but only got his regular pay, $4.10/hr. Bob never really gave this much thought until a friend told him he should demand his right to the minimum wage, if not time-and-a-half, for overtime work. He was not earning any tips during this overtime since such time involved vacuuming, cleaning counters, etc., after the business was closed for the night.

Bob finally decided to get his nerve up the next time the boss insisted he work overtime. Sure enough, two days later he was asked to close up, which meant another two hours of work after an eight-hour day. Bob went to his boss and asked him if he could get minimum wage, or time-and-a-half, for working overtime. After all, $4.10/hr. and no tips wasn't enough to live on. The manager didn't agree to this. Instead, he just laughed and said Bob should be glad he got paid at all for overtime since "some places make you work for free."

Bob was very angry. The next time he was called to come in to work, he told his boss he quit. The next day he was talking to a friend who also worked in a fast-food restaurant, and the friend told Bob that he got a little over minimum wage for overtime work. Bob was even more angry now. How could his boss tell him some places made employees work for free?

He decided to call and find out if he was eligible to get unemployment compensation while he looked for another job. When he told the state employment office why he quit, they told him he did not qualify.

Questions

1. Does Bob have the right to receive overtime pay?
2. Does his boss have the right to conceal the possibility of getting overtime pay, or is he legally required to tell Bob that he was entitled to it?
3. Must Bob receive minimum wage?
4. In your opinion, is Bob qualified for unemployment compensation under the eligibility requirements of the Social Security Act?

Implicit Overtime Under the
Fair Labor Standards Act

Glen Miller became the Assistant Pro to Head Pro Melvin Rowe at the Holly Hills Golf Club about three months ago. Mr. Rowe had hired Glen on an informal basis. The terms of employment were all verbal. However, Glen had been working about sixty hours a week and not receiving any overtime compensation. Every two weeks, Glen received the salary that he and Mr. Rowe had agreed upon for a normal forty-hour work week. Glen wasn't the least bit upset about the long hours as he felt it was just part of the job.

One evening after work, a group of the members asked Glen to play gin rummy at the clubhouse. Glen welcomed the chance to get to know the members better. As the evening progressed, Glen innocently mentioned to a member the long hours he was working. The member became rather upset and began threatening to turn Melvin Rowe into the Labor Department. Glen thought the gentleman was just kidding.

The next day Glen saw the member and was told that a formal complaint had already been sent to the Labor Department! Glen panicked at first, but he eventually calmed down and decided it was best to remain silent about the entire situation.

About two weeks later, Melvin Rowe found out about the complaint and became angry and concerned. Mr. Rowe called Glen into his office and chastised him severely. Glen tried to explain that he had no part in filing the formal complaint, but this did not seem to matter to Mr. Rowe. The once close relationship between Mr. Rowe and Glen began to deteriorate as they waited for the investigation to begin.

Questions

1. What evidence would you use to show Mr. Rowe violated the law?
2. What evidence would you use if you were defending Mr. Rowe?
3. What legislation dealing with working hours is Mr. Rowe violating, if any? Explain.

Job Grade and Eligibility for Overtime

Mason, Davis & Dulaney (MD&D), a successful civil engineering firm based in northern Virginia, currently employs over four hundred civil engineers and supporting staff. As with any large company, MD&D has, for legal and administrative purposes, set dollar compensation limits relative to individual jobs. That is, a detailed wage structure has been computed for all jobs. In addition, in compliance with federal regulations and their own wage structure, certain job types pay overtime at the rate of one-and-one-half times the normal hourly rate. Other job types allow for overtime pay at the normal hourly rate. Finally, salaried management staff receive no overtime pay at all.

MD&D performs annual job evaluations and uses these as supportive information for the salary reviews that follow shortly thereafter. As of the last salary review, several individuals reached the base-pay dollar mark (maximum level), sending them out of the first overtime pay category and into the second, which pays overtime at a straight time rate. These individuals are not professionals nor do they have supervisory status. Furthermore, they do not work independently.

All five individuals involved refused to continue working the overtime that management insisted had to be done to meet the demanding production schedule. Their refusal stemmed from the fact that they would lose money by continuing to work the same number of overtime hours, but at the lower rate. This seemed, on the face of the matter, to be a *bona fide* complaint, even in light of the recent increase in their base pay as of the date of the salary review.

For these individuals, their base pay was not what made their job monetarily worthwhile but rather the abundant supply of overtime pay. The employees felt that they deserved not only a base pay increase for a job well done but also to be left on time-and-one-half for overtime.

Questions

1. Do these individuals legally have to be paid time-and-one-half for overtime work?
2. What can be done to keep the employees happy, to keep the government happy, and to maintain the wage structure set up by the company officials?

Compensatory Time and
the Fair Labor Standards Act

A small government contracting firm has a staff composed of technical engineers, clerical support personnel, and administrative employees. Because of the government restriction against reimbursing a contractor for premium overtime pay, this organization instituted a policy of compensatory time for overtime work. All employees, regardless of salary level, position, or responsibilities, earn one hour of compensatory time for each overtime hour worked. Earned compensatory time is available for use as time off at a later date. Both overtime and compensatory time require prior approval by supervisory personnel.

All personnel hired by the company, including clerical employees who are normally classified as nonexempt in other organizations, have the compensatory time policy fully explained prior to commencing full-time employment.

The firm's compensatory time policy comes into direct conflict with federal and state wage and hour legislation. Such laws classify employees of companies within their jurisdiction into exempt/ nonexempt categories according to specified criteria, including job responsibilities, salary level, educational background, and degree of working independence. Regardless of the company's overtime policy and the acceptance of this policy by the employees, the wage and hour laws direct that employees meeting certain criteria must be paid premium overtime pay.

While the firm was technically in violation of the wage laws of the state in which it conducted its business, there was no problem until a dissatisfied nonexempt employee registered a complaint. When this complaint was registered against the company, a total review was conducted by the state Wage and Hour Division of the three preceding years, including all overtime worked by employees determined to be entitled to premium overtime pay. The company was forced to pay a substantial sum of back wages to the employees affected - even to individuals who had left the firm months or years before.

269

Questions

1. Should the company be bound to the state minimum wage laws, even though:
   (a) the majority of employees prefer to earn compensatory time?
   (b) the federal government will not reimburse contractors for overtime premiums?
2. What would you recommend the company do about what has taken place?
3. What would you recommend regarding the company compensation policy in the future?

Abuses of Compensatory Time

The Sperry Univac Corporation sells, rents and services electronic data processing equipment and employs a large staff of service people to keep its customers' equipment in order. The 30 service people who work out of the St. Paul district office (which covers most of the Midwest) all live in the St. Paul area and are often required to travel to customers in distant locations. They usually travel by air.

A given trouble call may take several hours or even days of work. When an assignment is completed, the workers fly back to St. Paul and often arrive home late in the evening or even after midnight. Under these circumstances, management has always allowed the service people to report to the office late the next day.

Recently, there have been signs that the workers have begun to abuse this privilege. A few people have developed the habit of taking the entire morning off after every out-of-town trip even if they arrive back at their home by 5:00 p.m. the previous evening.

Management has considered requiring all service people to report for work at 9:00 a.m., regardless of what time they arrived the night before. They realize that in some cases this would impose an obvious hardship, and it might encourage the employees to spread their work out so that instead of finishing their job in the afternoon and returning home late, they would work through the next morning, returning home in the afternoon.

Above all, management is anxious not to adversely affect the employees' high morale and interest in their work. These service people are paid a salary, receive liberal fringe benefits, and are treated almost like members of management.

Question

1. What action, if any, would you recommend?

Increased Responsibility
Without Compensation Adjustments

Late one afternoon, Don Chamberland began to think about his future. Don was a staff Operations Researcher and had worked for Transoil for about a year. He had been hired by Dave Scott, Director of the Analysis Department. About three months later, Scott was replaced by Jack Townsend, another staff member in the department. A replacement has been hired to fill Townsend's old position. Don Chamberland thought he was going to be selected for Townsend's old position which would have been a promotion. He was feeling a bit confused about his place in the organization and was thinking of resigning.

During the first eight months of Townsend's tenure as Director of the Analysis Department, his relationship with his immediate supervisor, Ralph Ortega, blew hot and cold. Ortega had a high regard for Jack's technical skills and experience but was dissatisfied with his lack of attention to office matters. Ortega had commented to his secretary, "I recognize Jack's shortcomings, but in a pinch, he will come through for me. We will just have to watch that he tends to business."

Jack Townsend had steadily grown to rely on Don Chamberland to take care of normal office matters. Jack traveled frequently and, when in the office, provided only general guidance to Don or worked on projects which Ortega personally assigned to him. Don made sure that all finished projects leaving the office were reviewed and approved by Jack.

Don found himself in a rather peculiar position. Other offices were beginning to interface directly with him. Don often represented Townsend at staff meetings but felt uncomfortable under what he thought was Ortega's disapproving eye. Ortega had once stopped the staff meeting and asked directly, "Where is Jack this morning?" Don mentioned the comment to Jack. Townsend responded, "Don't worry about it. You're doing a good job, you keep me informed, and Ortega's getting the service he needs." Don recalled almost telling Townsend then that he was bothered by doing work which was not his responsibility and for which he did not get the recognition.

Townsend has been given permission to hire an Associate Director. He called Chamberland in and told him the news. "I know you have been loaded down with your own work plus the things I've sort of delegated, but maybe the situation will soon improve. I'm going to talk to Ortega about promoting you to the Associate Director position. We will hire somebody else to fill your job."

Two weeks later, Townsend announced the hiring of Dr. Herbert Warner. Jack told Don that Warner was an old friend who was technically very good but that he would need help learning office procedures and the details of the department's business. Townsend commented, "I know you're probably a bit disappointed. I'll do what I can to get you a raise within the next six months. Can I count on you?"

Question

1. What would you do if you were Don Chamberland? Explain why.

Alteration of the Basic Workweek

Jack Armstrong, President of Pinetree Plastics, Inc., decided to initiate a new work schedule. Instead of the 5 day, 40 hour work week, he is going to have a three-day, 13½-hour per day work week. Industrial engineers and management consultants have assured him that it will be 50% more economical and 25% more efficient.

Pinetree employs 2,500 non-management people from a town of 8,900, and many are upset with the new schedule. If they quit, there is a good chance they will not find jobs anywhere else. The town's other major employer, the Chrysler Parts Plant, is already furloughing people. Armstrong felt he was being very fair and equitable. Anyone and everyone who could not work the new schedule would be dismissed.

The employees, who were not unionized, selected a group to approach Armstrong with their grievance. He agreed to set up a day-care center for parents whose children had no place to stay, or person to stay with, before and after school. Their other requests he rejected. They were:

1.   Time-and-a-half for more than 8 hours worked in a day. (Armstrong said he could not afford to pay any more since he would probably have to let people go anyway.)
2.   The establishment of a seniority system in case workers had to be let go. (Armstrong said it would impair the firm's efficiency. Selected cuts in less crucial departments would be more economical to the firm.)
3.   Employee input into which 3 days and which 13½ hours would be worked. (Armstrong felt it was his prerogative.)
4.   Cost-of-living wage increases. (Armstrong argued that he could not afford them.)

The employees were even more upset after this meeting with Armstrong. They brooded over their alternatives:

1.   They could ask for a vote to unionize, and let the union air their grievances.
2.   They could stage a full or partial "wildcat" strike (but Armstrong hinted that if this happened, he would lock them all out and then slowly and selectively hire them back later).

275

Questions

1. What course of action should the employees take? Why?
2. What would you do if you were Jack Armstrong?
3. Are there any other viable alternatives?

Education and Experience-Based Pay Differentials

Joanne Drew was hired by a medium-sized firm as a sales representative. She was hired for the government sales department, due to her extensive contracting background. Her salary for the six-month training period was $1,000 per month.

Joanne became very friendly with Jonathan Carter, a commercial sales representative, who had begun working for the company within two weeks of her starting date. Jonathan had a college degree, which Joanne did not, but he had no sales experience. His salary for the training period was $1,500 per month.

When Joanne discovered the discrepancy in their pay, she was sure an error had been made. She went immediately to her supervisor. He promised he would look into it.

Two weeks later, Joanne approached her supervisor again. Her previous government sales experience had served her well and she was doing very well in the program. Her supervisor hedged a bit, then attributed the pay discrepancy to Carter's college degree and to the fact that he was in commercial, not government sales.

"But that's ridiculous," Joanne exclaimed. "His degree is in biology, and I have had six years of experience in the field. It isn't fair."

"Don't make waves," her supervisor advised. "At the end of your six months training, you will be on straight commission. Then everything will appear more equitable."

Questions

1. Is there discrimination being practiced here?
2. What further recourse does Joanne have?
3. Do you think Carter's college degree is a valid reason for the pay differential?

Eligibility for Worker's Compensation

William Bower was employed by Howell Tractor and Equipment Company as a field mechanic for four years. Howell was in the business of selling, renting and servicing various types of heavy equipment such as cranes and bulldozers.

Bower and a co-worker were told by their superiors that a road resurfacing machine had broken down in Logansport, Indiana. They were instructed to pick up the repair parts at O'Hare Airport in Chicago and drive to Logansport to repair the machine. Because of the degree of damage to the machine, they were unable to complete the repairs.

At the request of the customer's foreman, they telephoned Howell's field service manager and requested permission to remain overnight at Logansport. They then went to the Ben Hur Hotel in Logansport and obtained rooms. After washing up, they went out to dinner with the customer's foreman. After dinner, they went to a bar and had two or three drinks, remaining there until approximately 11:30 or 11:45 p.m. The customer's foreman then took them to another bar where they remained, again talking about the machine and other topics, until closing time at about 1:30 in the morning.

As the tavern was closing, the customer's foreman and Bower's fellow worker suggested they go out to breakfast. Bower, however, wanted to go back to the motel. He went to the restroom and when he returned to the table, the foreman and his co-worker were gone. The latter testified that they had waited some ten or fifteen minutes in the truck for Bower and then drove around the block and returned to the tavern, leaving only when Bower could not be located.

Although he had never been to Logansport, Bower decided to walk back to the motel. He did not utilize any of the available taxi services, nor did he ask anyone for directions. After walking a few blocks, he realized that he was lost. Shortly thereafter he came upon what was apparently an abandoned railroad station. He thought he had remembered crossing some railroad tracks on the way from the motel, and he started walking alongside the tracks in the direction he thought the motel was located. He testified that a train started to pass him and that some part of the train made contact with him and dragged him along backwards. He held on for as long as he could with his left arm but finally had to let go. He apparently fell onto the tracks and the train ran over his left leg. He began yelling for help and put his belt around his leg as a tourniquet. A police officer responded to his call and later testified that, in his opinion, Bower was not intoxicated.

The company contested the claim and at the hearing that followed, Bower testified that he has been out of town on several occasions to repair equipment for Howell. He also testified that the company never had given him instructions or placed restrictions on his conduct after he left the job site. On a number of previous occasions, he had gone out with customers after work for a few drinks. On one such occasion, he had sold a customer a piece of equipment and the company paid him a bonus for the sale.

As a result of the injury, Bower's leg was amputated above the knee. He filed a claim requesting worker's compensation.

Question

1. Would you award Bower worker's compensation? Why or why not?

Eligibility for Leave Under
the Family and Medical Leave Act

Veronica Stone has been employed by the Smithfield foundation for eight years. For a period of two weeks, she experienced lower back pain at the end of the day.

She scheduled an appointment with her physician and was told that she had a kidney infection which required one day of treatment and two days rest every week for the next ten weeks. The doctor provided her with a note documenting the illness and the course of treatment.

After the first four treatments, she had exhausted her sick leave and requested relief under the Family and Medical Leave Act.

Questions

1. Is the Smithfield Foundation required by law to extend leave in this situation under the Family and Medical Leave Act?
2. Will Veronica's medical insurance be maintained if the leave is granted?
3. How much compensation must Veronica receive while on leave according to the Family and Medical Leave Act?

Multiple Leave Requests Under
the Family and Medical Leave Act

Will and Lisa Smith are married. They have two children, Connie, age 4, and Mick, age 6. In addition to taking care of them, the Smiths look after Will's maternal grandmother, Samantha Oats. She lives by herself in an apartment about five miles from the Smiths' home. Will is the only relative living close to her. Will and Lisa both tend to her needs; they buy her groceries, take her to doctors' appointments, have her to dinner at least twice a week, and so on.

The Smiths both work for Zookeepers Inc., which is a toy manufacturer with over 700 employees in offices around the country. Will and Lisa work at the same worksite, along with 100 other employees. Will, age 40, has been employed there for fifteen years and is a Budget Analyst. He is very efficient in his position and enjoys his work. He has a flexible work schedule which allows him time to be with his children and his grandmother. The entire family's health benefits are deducted from Will's pay.

Lisa, age 38, has been employed at Zookeepers Inc. for ten years; she is the Vice President of Community Outreach. As a member of the executive staff, Lisa's salary is in the company's top ten percent. She must attend many meetings and be available to address any issues the President may have for her. This limits her schedule's flexibility. Zookeepers Inc. has a benefit that allows employees to set aside pre-tax dollars for child care. The Smiths take advantage of this set-aside and have these funds deducted from Lisa's salary.

At her recent doctor's appointment, Mrs. Oats was told she was seriously ill. She will need bed rest and twenty-four hour care for a while. She is very scared and does not want to stay in the hospital or a nursing home. She wants to come stay with the Smiths.

Questions

1. Under the FMLA, may either Will or Lisa take unpaid leave to care for Mrs. Oats?
2. If Mrs. Oats were Will's mother, what rights would Will and/or Lisa have? Could they each take FMLA leave?
3. If Mrs. Oats were Lisa's mother, what rights would Will and Lisa have?
4. If one of the children became seriously ill, instead of Mrs. Oats, could Will and Lisa take leave under FMLA? How much time could he and/or she take? What would be their reinstatement rights?
5. In each scenario above, what is the maximum amount of unpaid leave that can be taken?

The Timing of Leave Under
the Family and Medical Leave Act

Fred is an employee with a large county on the east coast. The county employs around 20,000 people in their administrative, public safety, and school systems. Fred is a first line supervisor with over four years of service.

Fred and his wife, Jessica, are planning on having their first child in early April. Fred let his supervisor know of the pending birth in early February. He also told him of his intention of using the Family and Medical Leave Act (FMLA) provisions for an unknown period of time after the birth.

Fred's wife delivered on the date expected and there were no problems. Fred thought he might take about eight weeks off to care for his wife and new child. However, two weeks after the birth of his child, his mother became seriously ill.

In mid-April, Fred's seventy year old mother was admitted to the hospital. After several days of testing, the doctors determined that she had lung cancer. They recommended radiation treatments.

The doctors completed the cancer treatments on Fred's mother in early June. Fred had already taken eight weeks of leave at this point to care for his wife and child. After a follow-up visit with the oncologist, the doctor determined that Fred's mother had between two and six weeks to live. Fred's mother passed away on July 23.

Questions

1. Is Fred eligible to use FMLA benefits?
2. How much time can Fred take off?
3. Did Fred give enough advance notice of his desire to use the FMLA?
4. Is Fred required to be specific about how much time he wants to take off after the birth of a child?
5. If Fred exhausts his FMLA benefits for the birth of the child and wants to spend time with his mother until July 23, does FMLA allow him to use benefits twice in one year, since they are for two different incidents?

Individuals Covered Under
the Family and Medical Leave Act

Jason is a five year old who has been diagnosed with cancer. Jason will require constant care and attention. Jason's mother and father were divorced when he was two years old. He currently lives with his mother and her new husband. Jason's father is remarried and lives fifteen minutes away. Jason's mother and father have joint custody, and there is no animosity between the two families.

The two families have decided that they cannot afford to hire a full-time nurse to care for Jason. Each member has agreed to request a twelve week leave from work to care for Jason in accordance with the FMLA.

Questions

1. Is Jason's father entitled to twelve weeks of unpaid leave in accordance with the FMLA even though his son does not live with him?
2. Is Jason's stepfather entitled to twelve weeks of unpaid leave in accordance with the FMLA because Jason lives with him full-time?
3. Is Jason's stepmother entitled to twelve weeks of unpaid leave in accordance with the FMLA because Jason's father is her husband and he has joint custody of Jason?

The Limits of the Family and Medical Leave Act

Jane had been in her current position with Deco Graphics for nearly four years. The only person that had more seniority or was paid more was the Print Shop Supervisor, Hank. Jane had worked for small printing companies for eight years while she attended night school in pursuit of a degree in graphic arts. She had chosen to major in this field after being exposed to computer graphics design at one of her first jobs. Jane had been doing all of the design and layout work at Deco Graphics for nearly three years before receiving her degree.

Upon completion of her degree, Jane and her husband Tom decided to start a family. Jane planned to continue working after their child was born. Deco Graphics assured Jane that she would have a place with them when she was ready to return to work.

Jane's pregnancy was very difficult. She required many doctor's visits and tests, all of which were scheduled with Deco's knowledge and consent. In her seventh month of pregnancy, Jane had to be hospitalized due to complications. She remained in the hospital until Tom, Jr. was born - exactly one year to the day after her commencement exercises. Jane then wanted to take a full twelve weeks to be with her newborn son.

Fortunately, Deco paid 75 percent of the health insurance premiums for their employees. Tom's company did not provide health coverage. It was difficult for Tom to continue to pay the remaining 25 percent of the premium while Jane was not working, but he managed.

Upon returning to work after being gone for nearly 20 weeks, Jane found that Deco Graphics had not held her design and layout position open. They had replaced her with Jack, who had recently received his degree in graphic arts but had little experience. Jack had been with Deco now for nearly three and a half weeks. Deco offered Jane a position as Office Manager at the same salary she was receiving before. This position would put Jane in charge of Jack as well as three other office personnel. The twelve Print Shop personnel would still report to Hank.

Jane was not pleased with her new position. Her desire was to do design and layout. She did not feel that Office Manager was an equivalent position. Jane declined to go back to work for Deco Graphics. Jane was also considering filing a complaint under the Family and Medical Leave Act.

Questions

1. Do you believe Jane has a case under the FMLA?
2. Was Deco legally obligated to give Jane 20 weeks' leave?
3. Can Deco recoup the portion of the insurance premiums they paid while Jane was on leave?
4. Was the Office Manager position equivalent to her old position, as required under the FMLA?

Resistance to Safety Management

Mr. White has recently been appointed Safety Director of Atlas Steel, Inc. Atlas has approximately 1,000 unionized production and maintenance employees at its plant in Detroit, Michigan.

As the Safety Director, Mr. White is very concerned over the high accident rate the company has been experiencing for the past several years. To help solve the problem, a better program of machine guarding and plant maintenance has been initiated. While this program did reduce the severity of accidents, it did not reduce the number significantly.

Mr. White decided to analyze all of the work injuries that had occurred over the past year. He found that in a majority of instances most of the injuries were due to (1) failure to follow safety rules, (2) incorrect use of machines and hand tools, and (3) sloppy cleaning of work areas. Furthermore, Mr. White looked into some literature concerning industrial safety and found some research studies that proved employee attitudes, emotions and knowledge greatly influenced accident rates on the job.

Mr. White concluded that a plant-wide employee education program needed to be initiated. To educate employees in safety, Mr. White decided to have each foreman hold a safety meeting with their employees once a month. He found that the foremen vehemently objected to the added burden, claiming the extra time needed for the meeting would slow down production.

Questions

1. How should Mr. White handle the foremen who refuse to conduct the safety meetings?
2. What, if any, involvement should Mr. White seek from the union?
3. What is the employer's legal responsibility under OSHA if the employees and foremen refuse to attend the meeting?

OSHA Compliance

XYZ Company is a manufacturing firm with 820 employees. Approximately one-half of these employees work in the shop and are represented by a small, but strong, local union. Although the present union contract has 28 months to run, an issue has arisen which could lead to a union walkout.

Occupational Safety and Health Act (OSHA) standards direct the use of noise-suppressor equipment when decibel readings in the work area exceed a specified level. The purpose of this ruling is to prevent hearing impairment. It is the employer's responsibility to purchase, issue and enforce wearing of noise suppressors in areas identified as exceeding OSHA noise levels.

XYZ Company has been meeting part of the OSHA standards by purchasing and issuing earmuff-type noise suppressors. It has been less than successful insuring that the suppressors are worn by employees. In XYZ's latest attempt to insure compliance, it has announced that employees found not wearing noise suppressors where required will be suspended for the balance of the workday without pay. Additionally, as an incentive, employees who are not cited for violations will be given a twenty-dollar bonus each month.

The union's reaction to the company's policy has been negative. Although in favor of the monthly bonus as an incentive for employee's compliance, the union claims the company's action was unilateral and violated a clause in its contract. The clause called for joint agreement between labor and management on changes of company policy directly affecting employees at work. The union also claims that the majority of workers responsible for wearing the devices feel they are cheaply made, uncomfortable, and of no real value.

The union has threatened to walk out unless the company immediately rescinds its noise policy and agrees to meet with union representatives to discuss the entire issue.

Questions

1. If the company rescinds its current policy, how will it justify not meeting OSHA standards?
2. What would be a likely union position if and when attempts are made to formulate a new policy?
3. Would it be wise for the company to inform OSHA that its standard is being violated, through no fault of the company?
4. What are alternative incentives that the company might offer to induce the wearing of noise suppressors?
5. Was the company correct in unilaterally imposing its hearing protection policy?

OSHA Non-Compliance and Seniority

TMW Corporation produces 3/4 of the world's micro-synchronizers. The corporation has plants mostly in the Midwest, although a few are scattered on both the east and west coasts. Employees are members of the Electronic Workers' Union. The union contract became effective last August and is for three years.

Last year, an OSHA official visited the St. Louis plant and found several safety violations. These included the absence of safety goggles on employees whose job it is to weld tiny wires together, and the lack of an automatic shut-off switch on the wire-splicing machine. TMW was issued warnings and was told if they were not corrected the next step would be drastic fines.

The company immediately set about correcting the problems. They had to shut parts of the plants down in the Midwest on a rotating basis to take care of the wire-splicing machines. The union members were quite upset, because the employer laid off older employees, not the new trainees on the machines. They threatened a walkout.

Another problem arose when the company addressed safety goggles. When told of the need to wear their goggles, the welders refused, saying they were not able to see as well. The welders said they would take the responsibility for not wearing them. The union backed the welders in their refusal.

Questions

1. If the union members walk off the job, must they be given their jobs back when the problem is settled?
2. Can the company force the welders to comply with the wearing of the safety goggles?
3. If an accident occurred to a welder because of the non-compliance with OSHA would TMW be responsible, even though the welders and union said that they would assume the responsibility?
4. Can the OSHA official fine TMW for their employees not wearing the goggles?
5. Can the OSHA official fine the union for their members not wearing goggles?

The Limits of OSHA

Mr. Templeton, an employee of ACME Chemical Company, filed a complaint with OSHA. He felt that the air in his working area was both unhealthy and unsafe. After speaking with Mr. Templeton, the OSHA inspector, Mr. Sanyo, obtained a warrant to investigate the complaint.

Mr. Sanyo, upon entering Mr. Templeton's work area, noticed a very strong odor of organic vapors. He continued his investigation by taking air samples for on-site analysis of vapor concentrations. He determined that the concentrations were considerably above OSHA standards. Mr. Sanyo then spoke to the plant manager and the plant engineer. He asked them what type of ventilation system the plant had, because it seemed to be inadequate for the work being performed.

Mr. Sanyo called in two more investigators, and together they uncovered some severe problems with ACME's ventilation system. First, the batch mixing being conducted was done in open-top containers. This allowed a lot of evaporation. Mr. Sanyo strongly suggested that ACME close their containers because of employees' health and safety and, of course, because of OSHA regulations. He expressed his concern about a possible fire due to the fumes in the air.

The second problem dealt mainly with the plant structure. It was found that the floor-level exhaust fans were blocked by solvent drums which were being stored in the room. Mr. Sanyo said that they could not keep flammable stock in a room where it might ignite and that it would be best for the drums to be stored in another building. Next, Mr. Sanyo found that the exhaust fans were too small for the room size. (There is a minimum regulation-sized fan, 24 inches, for that particular room size.)

Finally, Mr. Sanyo found that there was no ceiling exhaust system and that fans and ducts needed to be installed to allow for such a system. Both the ceiling and floor exhaust fans had to be vented directly to the exterior of the building.

At present, the air conditioning system that serviced the batching room was just recirculating the "polluted" air and was not exhausting it. This problem caused inadequate air turnover in the room. The plant manager explained to the OSHA inspectors that the air flow throughout the entire plant was engineered in that particular way due to the processes that were performed. The room had to maintain an overall positive pressure.

Installing exhaust fans the way OSHA suggested would cause difficulties in product runs.

Mr. Sanyo told the plant manager to air lock the room, because there was no way to get around the regulations and standards. The plant manager said he would investigate the possibilities.

Questions

1. Does Mr. Templeton have the right to go directly to OSHA before speaking to his immediate superior or the plant manager?
2. What are the implications for Atlas Steel if they refuse to comply with the suggestions of Mr. Sanyo?
3. What would you do if you were the Human Resource Director for Atlas Steel?

OSHA and Small Business

A small family-owned warehouse firm, the George & Mason Storage Company (G&M), located in an industrial park with some national and regional firms, was unexpectedly visited by an OSHA inspector. The inspector was officially inspecting the facilities of Company A, going from warehouse to warehouse. As part of this inspection, the inspector passed by the warehouse of George & Mason on her way to one of Company A's other warehouses and happened to notice that there were no handrails leading up the steps of the G&M loading dock. Since this was her first solo inspection, she took time out to take a quick look at the G&M Facility.

The inspector entered the G&M warehouse through the loading dock area, where she told two employees who she was and that she wanted to walk around "just to take a look." The employees, who were about to break for lunch, told her to go ahead. The inspector noted the following conditions:

- Loading dock stairway had no handrail
- One fork lift was leaking oil onto the floor
- Numerous lights in the ceiling were out, making seeing difficult
- Fire extinguishers were blocked by open cartons and miscellaneous packing materials

At this time, the inspector was approached by the owner's youngest son who asked if he could be of any help. The inspector told him who she was and what she was doing, at which time the son responded by going to get his father. About five minutes later the father found the inspector. The inspector informed the father of the hazardous conditions which she had seen and asked to see the safety logs and reports for the firm. The father heatedly responded that the inspector should go inspect the "big guys" in the industrial park - that G&M was too small to be covered by OSHA. The inspector told the father that he would be receiving a report stating the OSHA standards that were being violated and a time limit for their correction - at which time she left.

The father told the family at dinner about what had happened. His eldest son stated that there was no need to worry since the inspector had:

- forgotten to present her credentials
- not asked to meet a company representative upon arrival
- not had the company representative present during the walk through the warehouse
- not given the employer a copy of the applicable laws
- not stated the scope of the inspection

Questions

1. Is the eldest son correct in his belief that the conduct of the inspector was improper? If so, does this relieve G&M from compliance until a proper inspection is conducted?
2. Are there any limits to the applicability of OSHA standards such as sales volume, number of employees, etc., which could exclude G&M from coverage?

Reasonable Accommodations Under the Americans With Disabilities Act

Dick's Sales is a family business which distributes electrical supplies through a network of independent sales representatives. The business was started by Dick Johnson five years ago.

Dick's office was a two-story house which was built twenty years ago. Dick owned the house and the land it was situated on. Dick and his wife lived and worked in the house until they decided to expand and hire a full-time staff to help with the daily operation of the business. They converted the second story of the house into office space and the first story into warehouse space. Dick and his wife moved into a new house.

Several years later, Dick's Sales expanded again. This time he built a new warehouse next to the house/office and converted both stories of the house into office space. When Dick built the warehouse, he had to make it accessible to wheelchairs to comply with local building codes. Because of the size of the warehouse, he was also required to put in a wheelchair accessible bathroom - which he did.

Early last year Dick hired Pat, who was confined to a wheelchair, to work in the warehouse doing quality control and labeling of products. Dick believed he was in compliance with all provisions of the Americans With Disabilities Act. However, after working for Dick's for several weeks, Pat began complaining that Dick was discriminating against handicapped individuals.

Pat's complaint was that to get to the kitchen, which was located in the first story of the office, one had to go outside the warehouse and around the side of the office to get in. Pat also complained that the second story of the office was not accessible to handicapped individuals because there were no ramps. Dick explained to Pat that because of the age and elevation difference of the building and warehouse, there was little he could do to make it more accessible.

Pat did not feel that Dick had responded to the complaints to her satisfaction. Pat contacted the EEOC.

Questions

1. Did Pat have a case against Dick's Sales under the ADA?
2. Had Dick made reasonable accommodations under the ADA?

The Limits of Reasonable Accommodations
Under the Americans With Disabilities Act

John Smith is a Systems Analyst for ABC Information Systems Company. ABC Information Systems contracts with businesses from Washington, D.C. to Richmond, Virginia. John's responsibilities as a Systems Analyst require him to travel all over the region to establish systems or troubleshoot any problems. John has been with ABC for five years.

Last January, John was working at a chemical company in Richmond. He had respiratory arrest and had to be rushed to the hospital. Doctors believed that this was caused by a severe reaction to burning chemicals. John was released from the hospital but was prohibited by the doctors from working at that particular chemical company in Richmond. ABC took John off the account and assigned another analyst.

About six months later, John again had the same episode at an accounting firm. Doctors did not know why this incident had occurred. They ordered environmental tests but found nothing harmful. Doctors ordered John to only work at his office in Washington, D.C. for the next six months as a precaution. ABC accommodated John and gave him a temporary assignment in Washington.

Approximately one month after John had returned, he had another episode while in his office. He remained in the hospital for several weeks while doctors tried to determine what could be causing these reactions. John had never experienced this problem while at home.

Once again, environmental tests were done and nothing was discovered to be causing this reaction. Doctors concluded that John had a spontaneous respiratory reaction, possibly caused by stress.

ABC felt that John could not be reasonably accommodated because all of the positions in the company are stressful. As a result they informed John that he was being dismissed.

Question

1. Given the "reasonable accommodation" requirements of the Americans With Disabilities Act, do you believe ABC Information Systems was justified in terminating John's employment?

Reasonable Accommodations
and Travel Requirements Under the
Americans With Disabilities Act

Jackie is a 30-year old African American woman who is a paraplegic. She has been employed by a major corporation for the past five years as a customer service representative. This position involves responding to telephone inquiries from customers and working as needed at the walk-in service desk. Her job performance has been consistently rated as excellent by her supervisor, who has also commented on her wide-ranging knowledge of the company and its products.

A new position has opened in the Sales Department and Jackie has applied. This job involves calling on customers at their place of business with very little time actually spent in the office. Jackie has a personal attendant who brings her to the office and picks her up daily but is unavailable during the day.

The Sales Manager is quite impressed with Jackie's work record with the company but is concerned about her physical ability to perform the job of salesperson. For this reason, he did not select her for the position.

Jackie has filed a complaint under the Americans With Disabilities Act (ADA) stating that, given reasonable accommodation, she could have performed the essential job functions.

Questions

1. Do you believe Jackie has a valid complaint under the ADA?
2. What do you think would have been "reasonable accommodations" under these circumstances?

The Americans With Disabilities Act
and Public Safety

A large county Fire Department utilizes volunteer and career personnel in fire and rescue operations. Before being hired, both types of personnel must take a physical examination, meet physical agility standards, and pass the Emergency Medical Technician's Certification examination.

A young man applied to be a volunteer paramedic. He took the physical agility test and passed and was already certified as an Emergency Medical Technician. He took the physical examination and failed because he was deaf. He appealed to the county's Medical Review Board and was again denied approval to be a volunteer paramedic due to his hearing disability.

He has sued the county under the Americans With Disabilities Act stating that he has been discriminated against and that, with reasonable accommodations, he can perform the essential functions of a paramedic.

Questions

1. Has this young man been discriminated against because of his disability?
2. Does the ADA address public safety positions?
3. Who determines reasonable accommodations in this case?
4. Do you believe that this young man should be allowed to volunteer as a paramedic? Why or why not?

Implementing Management by Objectives (MBO)

The All-Good Products Corporation was founded by Mr. Donald B. Johnson in 1963. The company was formed to provide a variety of household products that would be sold door-to-door. Products included such items as cleansers of all types, floor wax, furniture polish, mops and brooms, plastic mixing utensils, and shoe polish.

The company was organized into six regions throughout the United States with from six to ten districts in each region. District Managers hired sales personnel to cover specific areas within their district. Districts, regions, and the company's main office, located in Chicago, each had Departments of Human Resources, Training, Sales, Distribution and Accounting. Sales personnel reported to the District manager who, in turn, reported to the regional Vice President. The regional Vice President reported to the President.

The company expanded rapidly after it was initially founded, but by 1994, the volume of sales had started to level off. In 1995, total sales decreased by 2 percent from 1994. Even though the philosophy of the company was to promote a spirit of entrepreneurship, the top management came to realize that more and more managers down the line looked to higher headquarters for decisions.

Early in 1995, attitude surveys were given to regional Vice Presidents, District Managers, and sales personnel. Results of the survey revealed that subordinate managers and sales personnel viewed headquarters as a paternal figure who seemed to always have the right answer. The President, Mr. Johnson, responded by issuing policy statements and monthly informational newsletters to subordinate managers and sales personnel in an attempt to foster the spirit of entrepreneurship and pride in achievement.

These attempts at communicating with the employees had some positive results. Sales during 1995 increased by about 4 percent over the previous year; however, the President still was not satisfied with the situation. Consequently, he and his staff met with some Organization Development (OD) experts from the University of Chicago.

What followed was an intensive effort to diagnose the major problems and select methods which would help the company attain its sales objectives. A management by objectives (MBO) program was devised, stressing that employees establish specific objectives or goals. Even though the company had established a broad goal of increasing sales volume by 8 percent by

1997, top executives wanted to insure that each salesperson established personal objectives which, in turn, were to be reported to the District Manager. Reports indicated that salespeople responded enthusiastically and 87 percent of them had established objectives exceeding the company goal.

The year-end results for 1997 revealed that sales volume had increased by 7 percent - just short of the company goal. More significantly, the results for the first six-month period of 1998 indicated that the year-end sales volume increase might exceed the 10 percent mark. Top management was pleased with the indicators and felt that after only two years, managers and sales personnel were actively participating in attaining realistic, specific sales objectives.

Questions

1. What can top management do in this case to ensure that the MBO program continues to be a success?
2. What can first-line supervisors do to ensure it continues to be a success?

An Employer's Social Responsibility in Fair Employment Practices

The Variety Store Company operates a chain of retail stores throughout the southwestern states. The company has been operating for more than 40 years and has become a well-established firm in the region. The firm has become increasingly aware of the problems facing minorities and has always hired proportionate numbers of minorities in every location, in accordance with fair employment regulations.

In one store, the manager has been asked to answer the local Fair Employment Practice Commission's charges that the store had been discriminating against minorities by placing them in only the lowest paying jobs. The manager was deeply concerned, yet felt the store had done nothing wrong. The manager was aware that minority group members did not appear in management positions but at the same time felt the applicants from the minority groups have not been qualified to assume such positions.

He plans to tell the commission that members of minority groups will be hired into management positions as soon as they become qualified. He feels that it is not his responsibility to make sure that minority groups appear in such positions.

Questions

1. Is the manager's reply legally acceptable and/or reasonable?
2. What steps would you take as Director of Human Resources for the Variety Store?

Sick Leave and Pregnancy

Jane Doe is a 30-year old registered nurse who is employed in the Critical Care area of a modern acute-care facility. The hospital is located in the suburbs of a large city on the East Coast. Jane had accepted the position as a charge nurse on the evening shift of one of the hospital's Adult Intensive Care Units because she had been impressed with the quality of patient care, and she felt the employee benefits were good when compared to other hospitals in the immediate area.

Jane quickly adapted to her new position and was respected and well liked by all her co-workers. She shared her views and suggestions with her Head Nurse and Supervisor without hesitation. During the first six months of her employment, she made several positive changes. It was apparent that she had become an influential member of the nursing staff. Jane's former position had been in a large hospital in California where the nurses were highly organized and very involved in changes in the nursing service.

Approximately a year after she began employment, Jane was happy to discover that she and her husband were going to begin their family. Jane's first few months of pregnancy were uneventful, and she continued to work as before. During her fifth month of pregnancy Jane developed a slight complication and her physician advised her to remain in bed for several days. Not wanting to risk adversely affecting her pregnancy, she complied with the physician's instructions. She called the nursing office, advised the appropriate individual of the situation, and informed them that she would be out of work for the next three days.

After contacting her physician and being assured that all was well, Jane returned to work. Her performance was not affected by her pregnancy, and she continued to perform all the duties of her position. However, when Jane received her paycheck on the following payday, she realized she was missing three day's pay. She knew she had sufficient sick benefits to cover the three days of illness she had experienced, so she inquired in the nursing office as to whether an error had been made in her paycheck. She was informed by the payroll clerk that her three days of illness were the result of her pregnancy, and no sick benefits would be paid. The payroll clerk informed Jane that hospital policy stated that sick benefits would not be paid for pregnancy or illnesses related to pregnancy. Jane felt that this

313

was unfair since she had sufficient sick leave to cover her illness, and she believed pregnancy should be covered by such leave.

Jane knew that the hospital had a grievance procedure which would be available to her, but she felt this required stronger action. The following morning she contacted a lawyer and explained her situation. The attorney informed her that he would contact the hospital and make an appointment to see the Human Resource Director. Having heard what the attorney wished to discuss at the appointment, the Human Resource Director notified the appropriate administrator who, in turn, asked the Director for advice.

Question

1. As the Human Resource Director, what advice would you give? Why?

Selection for Promotion

The ABC Corporation is a large merchandise chain with retail stores throughout the country. Headquartered in Minneapolis, ABC has twelve regional offices. Within each region are five districts, each with a sufficient number of subdistricts to control the activities of the approximately eight hundred outlet stores.

The ABC Corporation has a "promote from within" policy whenever possible. Retirement has led to a regional office directorship vacancy in the New England region. The Human Resource Department at ABC Corporation headquarters has been tasked with nominating qualified candidates to a special selection board for the purpose of choosing the new New England Regional Director. Two candidates, Mr. Smith and Mr. Jones, have been recommended to the special selection board. Both candidates have been informed of their nomination.

Seven factors were identified by the selection board as critical. These factors were made known to the Human Resources Department, which scored each candidate on each factor. Below is the data pertaining to Mr. Smith and Mr. Jones.

Critical Evaluation
[Weighted 1 - 10 (low - high)]

Factors	Smith	Jones
1. Years with firm	10	8
2. Sales performance (last 5 years)	10	10
3. Appraisals by superiors	10	10
4. Opinions of subordinates	9	7
5. Personal qualities (health, personality, social)	7	8
6. Education (beyond high school)	7	8
7. Training with ABC Corporation	<u>10</u>	<u>10</u>
	63	61

Having been notified that he was a candidate for the New England Regional Directorship, Jones wrote to the selection board. He expressed his gratitude for his name being placed in nomination. He further mentioned that since the ABC work force was 17% minority, yet not one Regional Director was a minority, consideration should be given to the fact that he was African American.

Questions

1. How would you defend the selection of Smith?
2. How would you defend the selection of Jones?

Management Development and Job Rotation

For the last several years, the Acme Production Firm has been using job rotation in its management trainee program for young college graduates. This management development program was designed to teach the trainees the managerial policies and practices of the firm. The program was only partially successful, because the trainees were confused by the varied teaching techniques of senior managers, lack of an adequate feedback system, and poor attitudes of some of the senior managers.

You, as the Management Development Officer in the Human Resource section, realized the need for a better systematic training program for the trainees, as well as for the trainers. You decided to use the "mentor system" to assign a trainee to a senior manager for six months. The manager would be responsible for planning and conducting the training program. The relationship between the two was to be very informal and supportive, and a performance evaluation was to be conducted after the third and sixth month.

After five months, the "mentor system" has not produced satisfactory results. Trainees are requesting transfers to other sections or quitting. Some managers are requesting reassignment for their trainees.

The standard reasons given by the trainees, as well as the managers, for quitting or asking for reassignment are, "we just don't get along with each other," "personality clash," and "mismatch." Currently, the trainees' and the managers' morale is low. One trainee stated that he didn't care for the "understudy assignment."

You have questioned your supervisor concerning the recruiting methods used from the college campuses and how he selects trainees. He has told you the firm uses the same method of recruiting and selection as other firms. That is, they pick highly motivated top graduates with a Business Administration background. He also informs you that the firm does not have funds available for a formal, centralized training program and that the next group of trainees will start in three weeks.

Question

1. What course of action would you pursue at this point? Why?

Educational Requirements for Promotion

Carla Devon had been employed at the Mercantile Savings and Loan for nine years. For the last four years, she had attempted to obtain promotion to the position of Assistant Manager at any of Mercantile's 30 branch offices. Due to her inability to obtain such a promotion, she felt compelled to lodge a complaint with the state Civil Rights Office.

In an interview at this office, it was learned that Carla had made good career progress since joining the company as an Assistant Teller. Within five years, she had been promoted from Assistant Teller to Teller, Head Teller, Loan Officer, and Senior Loan Officer. Upon hearing rumors that a number of vacancies existed in other branch offices, Carla sent a letter to management notifying them of her desire to be considered for any such openings. During the next four years, Carla sent numerous letters to Mercantile's management on this same subject but received no response. During this period of time, a number of Assistant Branch Manager vacancies occurred, but the vacancies were consistently filled by men.

Mercantile's management was shocked and outraged that Carla would feel compelled to file a complaint. In response to the complaint, the Director of Human Resources indicated that in all instances in which an individual had been promoted into, or hired into, the position of Assistant Manager of a branch office, the qualifications of that individual were in compliance with the standards set by Mercantile. Carla did not meet the standards. The qualifications were: 1) the attainment of a Master's degree in Business Administration; 2) five years of banking experience; and 3) good job references. Carla could meet all except the degree requirement.

Mercantile's Human Resource Manual did not contain promotional procedures or qualifications. The investigation, initiated in response to Carla's complaint, disclosed, however, that every Manager and Assistant Manager did possess an MBA. In attempting to learn the reason for the MBA requirement, the individual conducting the investigation was told that Mercantile felt that every manager in the organization should possess the MBA because it provided flexibility in personnel movement.

The Human Resources Director stated that while he was confident that Carla was familiar with Mercantile's operations, he felt that she did not possess the needed flexibility to hold down the position of Assistant Branch

Manager. He stated further that Mercantile did not feel any responsibility to respond to Carla's repeated requests for consideration.

The Commission conducted interviews with several Assistant Branch Managers and learned that these individuals considered their main function to be assisting in the daily supervision of the branch. Any important, long-term policy decision was referred to the central office. In addition, a number of those interviewed had, previously in their careers, held jobs identical to those held by Carla - jobs such as Teller and Loan Officer. Lastly, it was learned that only three out of the 30 Assistant Branch Managers were female and that all management positions above that level were filled by males.

Questions

1. As the Director of Human Resources, how would you deal with Carla?
2. In your opinion, was the MBA requirement for promotion to Assistant Branch Manager a BFOQ (*bona fide occupational qualification*)?
3. If the answer to question two is "no," what, if any, legal difficulties does Mercantile now face?
4. If the answer to question two is "yes," what, if any, legal difficulties does Mercantile now face?

The Availability of
Office Records to Employees

Over the years, salespeople in the ABC Company had developed the habit of perusing office records. They claimed they needed such access to check particular customer accounts, learn new customer histories, etc. Management was anxious to discourage this practice for fear that a salesperson, who had become intimately familiar with company costs and customers, might accept a position with a competitor.

The problem was intensified when new offices were constructed, separating the salespeople's quarters from those occupied by the office staff. The salespeople were now expected to request necessary information from the office staff over a four-foot high counter and were never to enter the new premises. However, it became apparent that the salespeople were determined to preserve the practice of looking at the records.

At first, the salespeople tried to think of every conceivable way to "break the barrier." It became a matter of pride to see if they could enter the office and walk around. Management reacted by making the rules against infiltration even more rigid. All salespeople were absolutely forbidden to enter the office other than for exceptional reasons.

This time the response from the salespeople was even more severe. The most common complaint was that they had to enter the area because the receptionist was not giving them all their messages. Next, they began to find fault with their new quarters. Verbal confrontations broke out between the salespeople and the Sales Manager, and the salespeople began to make aggressive remarks about the office staff. This further intensified the separation and alienation between the salespeople and the office staff.

Question

1. How would you, as Director of Human Resources, handle this situation?

Sexual Identity Problems and Employment Rights

Larry Miller has been working as a store decorator for the past six years at the J. T. Penn Company, a large national department store chain. He has little contact with the public other than to be seen doing a window display, etc. Larry's job performance has always been above average with little time lost for illness or tardiness.

It is widely known among the store employees that Larry is very effeminate. In truth, Larry feels his life would be more meaningful as a woman, and he is planning to have a sex change operation to achieve this end. Larry has made his desire known and is the subject of much gossip throughout the store. Larry has adequate sick leave and vacation time available to take time off from work to have the operation. Larry has requested a transfer to another store, to be effective upon his return as a woman.

Company management has made it clear to Larry that they would be unwilling to let him return to J. T. Penn after the operation. They have also stated that if he is somehow allowed to return, he would be reassigned to the same store. Management's hope is that the embarrassment of facing his former co-workers will force Larry to quit.

J. T. Penn management has also stated that under no circumstances would Larry be allowed to return with his previous seniority and benefits. In effect, he would be treated as a "new hire." This, of course, means less pay, vacation time, etc.

Questions

1. Does the company have the right to refuse Larry employment after the operation?
2. Does the company have the right to insist Larry return to the same store?
3. Does the company have a right to deny Larry his seniority and other benefits if he is allowed to return?
4. How would you handle this situation if you were the Human Resource Director for J. T. Penn Company?

Employee Appraisal During
Times of Supervisory Turnover

Late one Friday evening, Jason Shell was pondering what to do about his office secretary's request for help. Jessica Savage had just received an annual performance rating. She thought the rating was unfair and would seriously damage her chances for promotion.

Shell worked in a staff position for a large government organization. Day-to-day activities involved highly technical subjects. Due to the formal organizational structure and frequent inter-agency communications, a large part of the office output consisted of notes, letters, reports and visual aid materials.

For the past year, the office staff consisted of Shell, his boss (Don Jenkins) and two secretaries. Marsha Benson was recognized as Jenkins' secretary. Jessica Savage was assigned to the other staff members - Shell and two other positions which had been vacant for the past year. Because of the vacancies, Savage had acted almost as Shell's personal secretary. Benson was to assist when the workload piled up. However, Benson made it clear that her assistance would not be routine.

Three months ago, Jenkins resigned to take a new position. Ralph Cranston was hired as his replacement. The other two staff positions were also filled at the same time. When interviewing for Jenkins' position, Cranston had been told by various people (including Shell) that Marsha Benson did not measure up and should be removed. The allegations were that Benson was slow, didn't do tasks assigned which she didn't like and had a rather untidy appearance. Savage was described as pleasant, willing to accept most any task, but not the most efficient or accurate secretary. Shell had commented, "you better read what she types very carefully."

Over the past Christmas holidays, Benson took an extended vacation. During that time period, Savage served as Cranston's secretary as well as doing almost all of the office's typing, reproduction and telephone answering. Shell remembered this time period as hectic. But with patience and cooperation, the office had functioned reasonably well. Cranston had been able to get another office to assist with his personal typing.

Three weeks ago, both new staff members indicated plans to leave. As a result, mail and office correspondence were piling up. Shell had asked Savage if she would like to work overtime on Saturday to sort out the critical items requiring office attention and to work on the filing.

Savage approached Shell on Saturday morning with her problem. Company regulations required a yearly performance appraisal covering at least seven areas. Performance was to be rated for each area as *rarely accomplishes*, *almost always accomplishes*, and *always accomplishes*. Both the supervisor and the employee were to sign the appraisal. Cranston had just submitted Savage's appraisal with about one-half in the "almost always" column and one-half in the "always" column.

Savage told Shell that she had begun to think about the performance rating. She admitted that she had not taken any exception to the rating when Cranston provided it for her signature. However, she said, "I know I did a good job for him when Marsha was on vacation. The appraisal really hurt me. I want to apply for another position with the organization. With that rating, Human Resources will just toss my application in the trash can. Mr. Shell, what should I do? How can Mr. Cranston rate me when he has been my boss for only three months?"

Questions

1. Does Savage have a valid complaint?
2. What recourse might she have?
3. How should Shell respond to Savage?

A Question of Security

Mr. X works as a GS-5 civilian guard at Government Agency A; Dr. Y works as a GS-13 professional at the same office.

Dr. Y's working hours are 1:00 p.m. to 9:00 p.m. Dr. Y's wife usually brings him to work and returns at night to pick him up. Since the activity is secured at 4:30 p.m., the guard working at the front gate (Mr. X) normally calls late-working employees to confirm that a visitor is expected before allowing the visitor on the grounds.

Mr. X has been calling Dr. Y to tell him that his wife has arrived to pick him up but has grown to feel that it is no longer necessary. As a result he stopped doing so a week ago. Mr. X feels that calling Dr. Y to announce his wife's arrival is not a security matter but a courtesy.

Dr. Y has complained to Mr. Z (Mr. X's supervisor) that Mr. X is not properly performing his job. He needs the phone call from Mr. X so that he can go downstairs from his office and unlock the front door to the building and let his wife in to wait for him while he finishes what he is working on. He cannot observe his wife's arrival from his office window.

Mr. X counters that Mrs. Y should call Dr. Y when she leaves home. Dr. Y knows the travel time necessary and could look out another office window to see when Mrs. Y actually arrives.

Mr. Z supports Mr. X. When he suggests to Dr. Y that Mrs. Y call him when she leaves home, he found out that Mrs. Y used to do this but too often did not actually leave when she had called. That left Dr. Y standing downstairs waiting for his wife rather than upstairs finishing his work.

Question

1. How would you handle this situation?

Employer and Employee Coverage
Under Sexual Harassment Regulations

Roberta Johnson worked for a large genetic research firm in Langley, Virginia. The firm employed many female and minority employees, most of whom enjoyed working at that facility. Each year the firm would get all of its employees together for a picnic at a lake near Langley. Last year Roberta was in charge of the organizational committee for the picnic. She spent long hours lining up the entertainment, activities and the food.

Roberta chose a local catering company called "Dolgoffs' Fine Cuisine." The general manager of Dolgoffs, Frank Tate, assisted Roberta in the selection and distribution of all food and drinks at the picnic. Roberta was glad that her boss, Melissa Henderson, gave her full autonomy in organizing the picnic. Melissa was very busy and didn't have time to worry about "details." Roberta and Frank met often, but never at Roberta's work.

Frank was very crude and was always telling jokes demeaning to women and minorities. Roberta was offended but did not want to tell Frank because the picnic was drawing nearer and Roberta wanted everything to go smoothly. Finally, Roberta could not tolerate Frank's insults anymore. The day before the picnic she told him she was upset by his remarks and did not want to hear them anymore. Frank got angry with Roberta and told her there was no way he was going to work with a "feminist."

Roberta tried to line up another catering firm for the picnic, but it was too late. She told Melissa about the situation. Melissa became very upset and told Roberta it was all her fault the picnic was ruined. She even told her she was considering giving her a letter of reprimand.

Questions

1. Was Roberta sexually harassed?
2. Was Roberta working in a hostile work environment?
3. Does Roberta have a legal claim of sexual harassment against the catering company?
4. Does Roberta have a legal claim of sexual harassment against her own company?

A Question of Sexual Harassment

Maive, a business analyst in her mid-twenties, was hired for an entry level position. Shortly after starting her new job, she received and accepted an invitation to dinner from a male colleague in a senior-level, non-management position.

Although Maive politely declined her co-worker's next invitation, his invitations did not stop. Maive finally confronted the co-worker and explained that she was not interested in a relationship, especially one with a co-worker.

After this confrontation, Maive began to receive notes and computer messages from her co-worker trying to convince her that they were right for each other, and Maive should give him a chance. This continued for approximately one year, during which time Maive declined all invitations and limited her contact with this co-worker.

One day Maive received a message stating that her co-worker would leave the company if Maive would agree to give a relationship between them a chance. Maive decided that this had gone too far. She was uncomfortable around this co-worker and had become afraid to be alone in the office building after hours. She confided in a friend, who was a manager within the company, but requested that he not act on the information. Her work environment became increasingly stressful.

Maive went to her manager and explained the situation, but requested that he not do anything until after she had a chance to confront the co-worker one more time. They agreed that Maive would explicitly request that her co-worker refrain from having any non-business communications with her. If he agreed and acted accordingly, they would let the issue die; if not, her manager would take the issue to the Director of Human Resources.

Questions

1. Are the actions of Maive's co-worker an example of sexual harassment even though they began when Maive accepted an invitation for dinner? If so, which of the two types of sexual harassment is this an example of?
2. Did Maive's manager respond correctly to Maive's situation?
3. Could Maive's manager be held responsible if Maive decided to press charges against the company, even though she requested that he not do anything?
4. Could Maive's friend be held responsible because he had knowledge of the situation, even though he was requested by Maive not to act on the information?
5. Even though the Human Resources Department was not informed of the situation, could the company be held liable because two of its managers had knowledge of the situation?

Unfair Labor Practices

Tom Jackson has worked on the autoblock assembly line at the Cleveland, Ohio, plant of the American Metal Manufacturing Company for 13 years. During this time, he has been quite active in union activity, doing things like helping to organize workers, performing investigative work into health and safety standards and talking with other employees about problems they are having.

One investigation of health and safety standards by Jackson resulted in charges being brought against the American Metal Manufacturing Company for violation of the 1970 Occupational Safety and Health Act. Jackson testified before members of the agency regarding violations of the standards, some of which included improper ventilation, lighting, operation of equipment and excessive heat in the welding department. His testimony was largely responsible for the American Metal Manufacturing Company being assessed a stiff penalty and a warning of future fines if conditions did not improve.

Shortly after Jackson's testimony, he was told he was being promoted to the newly created position of assistant foreman of the day run. He was promoted even though there was a person in his department who had greater seniority than he did. His major responsibility was to take over for the foreman during his lunch period and on his days off and to help distribute work orders and keep track of employee mistakes. He had a few other small duties but had to confirm everything with the foreman and in all activities was under the foreman's control.

Now that Jackson had become an assistant foreman, he was put on a salary instead of getting an hourly wage and was also told that he would have to drop his union membership because, according to Taft-Hartley, supervisors and foremen cannot belong to a union.

This action on the part of management thoroughly enraged Jackson, as he felt that while the promotion was a step up in prestige, the job offer was simply a method management had used to get him out of the union. He felt that they had done this because of his recent testimony on safety matters and his continuous union activities over the years. Jackson went to the union and told them of his predicament and asked them to file an unfair labor practice charge with the National Labor Relations Board. The union agreed to file and represent Jackson.

The arguments each side presented before the NLRB were as follows:

Management:

1. The position of assistant foreman was created because of the need for someone to take over when the foreman was absent.
2. Tom Jackson was the person with the most seniority.
3. Since Jackson's job is now that of a foreman, according to Taft-Hartley, he must give up his membership in the union.

The union and Jackson countered these points by stating:

1. That while the job of assistant foreman may be needed, the duties being performed by Jackson do not contain any actual responsibility, because he needs to check out everything with his foreman. Thus he is not in *actuality* a foreman.
2. Jackson was promoted over a more senior employee for the purposes of getting him out of the union.
3. That the above constitutes an unfair labor practice under the Wagner Act because the company was discriminating to discourage membership in a labor organization.

The case went to the NLRB and is scheduled to be heard next week.

Questions

1. Is management discriminating because of Jackson's membership in a labor organization?
2. Are the responsibilities of the job sufficient to make Jackson a part of management?
3. If he is, in fact, part of management, must he relinquish his membership in the union under Taft-Hartley as management contends?

Unfair Labor Practices During
Union Organizing Attempts

John R. Snelt and Sons had been a non-union shoe factory since its inception in 1967. Lately, numerous supervisors had been reporting to their managers that talk of joining a union by the employees had been overheard. The owners were upset by this and a little puzzled as to why the employees would want a union. Mr. Snelt felt he had always paid competitive wages, provided good benefits and had been open to employee suggestions. He knew the business had changed dramatically since 1967 but didn't feel these changes warranted the need for a union.

Joe Snelt noted for his father that over the past five years they had hired a number of new employees and that the few employees left from the inception were now a minority. Perhaps these newer employees were the initiators of the union, Joe suggested.

Mr. Snelt decided that not only he and his managers, but also his first-line supervisors, should talk to the employees and see if they would be able to change their minds about needing a union. A few of the supervisors decided they would get to the heart of the problem and did so immediately. They proceeded to ask the employees under them what they thought of all this union talk and if they were going to join.

As the weeks went on, it seemed to Mr. Snelt that the union discussions were getting very serious. Supervisors were reporting that union literature was being passed out in the parking lot areas and that authorization cards were being distributed.

As the talk became more and more serious and a large number of the employees were signing authorization cards, the same group of supervisors decided to visit some of the homes of their friends who were employees to discuss the pros and cons of joining a union.

These employees reported to the other employees that management said many of them would be losing jobs if the union came in. However, these employees also claimed that the supervisors told them if the union didn't come in, management had made promises of raises and would try to promote a few more employees.

When the union organizers heard what was going on, they filed an unfair labor practice claim with the NLRB. They also argued that because of what had happened, the union should be recognized even without the election.

Mr. Snelt, of course, disagreed and demanded an election.

Questions

1. Does the union have grounds for their unfair labor practice charge? If so, what are they?
2. Is it possible to have a union represent this group (or any group) without an election?

Distribution of Union Literature
on Company Property

John Smith had been warned by his supervisor that if he were late one more time, he would be fired. The day after his last warning, John came to work at 7:45 - 45 minutes late. At 7:46, he was fired. He was told that his final pay would be ready around noontime.

As a rule, discharged employees were allowed to remain on the premises until receiving their final paycheck. After staying in the lunchroom for a half hour, Smith left the plant. Shortly afterward, he returned to the lunchroom with an NLRB pamphlet and some union literature.

During the morning coffee break, as the former employee was discussing the NLRB pamphlet with other employees, he was interrupted by a supervisor. The supervisor said that it was illegal to have the literature on company property. The supervisor threatened to have Smith arrested unless he left the plant and took the material with him.

Questions

1. Was Smith within his rights in handing out the NLRB pamphlet? In handing out union literature on company property?
2. What difference, if any, does the fact that Smith is no longer an employee make in the answers to Question 1?

Employee Discharges Preceding
Union Representation Votes

A Midwestern department chain store called Plus Value was opening another unit in its chain. A reason for the location choice of the new store was that management knew the unions were not strong in that particular area. Some of Plus Value's stores were union and some were not, and the management strongly wanted the new store to be non-union.

Management undertook a massive recruitment campaign through advertising in the newspapers. After testing and interviewing all of the applicants, people were hired as sales clerks, cashiers, and loading dock clerks. As the company grew, the threat of a union organizing the workers was ever present. Upon opening, Plus Value hired about 40 people to handle the big crowds at the store's grand opening. About 30 of the 40 employees were originally hired as permanent help while the other ten were temporary.

About two weeks after the store had opened and the ten temporary employees were let go, union organizers came to the store and started to encourage the employees to sign authorization cards. Eventually, the union claimed it had at least the 30% necessary to call for a union election. The management, having only 30 employees, had a good idea who most of the pro-union employees were, and they also knew there were probably 12-15 employees who were against the union. Management knew it would be a close vote.

About a week before the election, a disciplinary incident occurred between the Assistant Manager of the store and one of the men on the loading dock. They had an agitated verbal exchange which climaxed in a shoving match. The cause of the fight was not clearly known, but the dock clerk was known to be very verbal about his pro-union views. As a result of this incident the employee was dismissed. In protest, two of his friends, who also were dock employees and were at the scene of the fight, quit their jobs. They said their friend's dismissal was not just, and he did not deserve to be fired. Management did not discourage the other two from quitting because they knew they were also pro-union.

Management was faced with 3 loading dock vacancies and 3 less pro-union employees. They realized the advantage they had gained in the union vote. Therefore, without hesitation, Plus Value hired three replacements from the pool of the ten temporary employees who were previously let go. These three happened to be anti-union.

Finally, when the vote for the union did come, the union only received 42% of the vote. The union was very upset about the outcome and claimed that Plus Value had staged the incident with the dock employee.

Questions

1. Does the union have a legal issue in questioning the firing of the pro-union employee?
2. Can the union bring charges against Plus Value for using unfair selection practices for hiring the three new anti-union employees?

Favored Employees, Discrimination, and Unfair Labor Practices

About two weeks following the end of a strike of the registered nurses at St. Luke's Hospital, the hospital administrator sent a note of appreciation to the registered nurses who continued to work during the strike and to the extra RNs who were transferred from St. Mary's to help cover the shifts of the striking nurses. In the letter of appreciation, the RNs were praised for their hard work and long hours, and for "overcoming hardships and personal sacrifice in a definite gesture of dedication to duty." The letter indicated that nurses should be concerned with taking care of the sick rather than striking for higher wages.

For all the nurses who worked more than one shift during the strike, the chief nurse gave compensatory time or a day off. In addition, the LPNs were given time off with pay for their efforts in assisting in patient treatment during the strike, because without their services, the hospital would not have been able to meet patient needs, according to management.

The union filed an unfair labor practice charge with the National Labor Relations Board alleging that the hospital had infringed upon their right to strike and shown partial treatment in the working conditions afforded their peer employees. The union also alleged that they should have been consulted before other nurses were granted time off and the resultant change in work schedules was made.

Questions

1. Has management violated any part of the National Labor Relations Act?
2. Has management discriminated against the union members?
3. Can the NLRB force the hospital staff to grant days off with pay to all RNs, including the nurses on strike?

Selection of Union Members for Supervisory Positions: A Conflict of Interest?

Wagner Auto parts is in the business of producing and selling quality automobile parts for American-made cars. It started as a family business over 50 years ago and is still run by the son of the original owner. Its central management and research headquarters is located in St. Louis and its two manufacturing plants are located in Detroit and Newark.

All of the laborers within the plants are unionized. One of the unwritten rules between management and the union concerns seniority. It was well understood that promotions within the plants would be based on seniority. When it came time for a new foreman to be hired, the production worker who had the best combination of merit and seniority was traditionally promoted to fill the vacancy.

This method proved to be less and less effective. The foreman invariably remained a member of the union, most often becoming one of the officers. Despite his new status and position within the management of the company, it usually seemed that his major priority was to work for the goals of the union and the workers rather than those of the company as a whole.

Two weeks ago, a foreman position in the Newark plant became available. The union members within the plant immediately began to speculate about who among them would be chosen. The union had their candidate pretty well picked out when management announced their plans to hire someone from outside the plant. By the time the new foreman showed up for work the next day, members of the union had already held a meeting and decided to strike. They demanded that a clause be written into their contract guaranteeing that all foremen would be chosen from within their membership. Management attempts to compromise with the union failed and three days later, the workers in the Detroit plant went on a sympathy strike.

Questions

1. Did the union members have a right to demand that the foreman be chosen from within their membership?
2. Did management have the right to choose the person whom they felt would best fill the job, regardless of whether or not he was a union member?
3. What are some of the possible implications of the strike?
4. Discuss possible alternatives and solutions to this problem.
5. Discuss what steps you would suggest be taken to guard against such a problem arising in the future.

Conflict: Low Turnover and EEO Goals

The Greater Odenton Widget Manufacturing Company employs a staff of thirty-five and is involved in interstate commerce. Turnover in the organization has always been very low. The firm's employees are quite content with their relationship with management. Consequently, union organizing has never seriously been considered. Workers identify with the firm and display enormous pride in the family-like atmosphere. Respectable profits are reported annually. The company's president attributes the steady growth of the company to the high quality of work performed by each and every employee. In return, management rewards employee efforts by liberal yearly bonuses and cash awards for employee suggestions that are implemented.

Initial hiring when the organization was founded accurately reflected the demographic composition of the vicinity. However, over the last few years, there has been a large influx of ethnic minorities. Consequently, the company's work force no longer represents the geographic region from which they can be reasonably expected to hire.

The firm has now been charged under Title VII of the 1964 Civil Rights Act with having a disproportionate number of white males employed relative to the community profile. The firm was instructed by the Equal Employment Opportunity Commission to place a greater emphasis on the hiring and promotion of minorities. If this were not done, the company was told it would face fines and possible legal sanctions.

The company found itself in a difficult position. The low turnover rate limited the number of vacancies each year. Moreover, these spaces, even if totally filled by minorities, would not correct the imbalance. Personnel practices soon became numbers-oriented. The end product was that less-than-fully qualified applicants were selected and that a number of employees who otherwise would not have been considered were advanced in grade or promoted to supervisory positions.

Question

1. How would you have handled this situation if you were the Director of Human Resources?

Alcohol: A Disqualifier for Worker's Compensation or Unemployment Compensation

A male applicant, age 47, was hired by a local banking institution as Chief Collection Officer. His wealth of knowledge was vast and at age 34 he had been the President of the tenth largest bank in the United States. Alcohol had been his downfall, however, and it was only after extensive medical treatment that he was able to again pursue a career.

The local bank has approximately 180 total employees in seven offices throughout the state. It is a state-chartered institution and is insured by the Federal Deposit Insurance Corporation.

The Chief Collection Officer's principal duty was to offer advice and enter into "sticky" situations. He proved so successful that after one year, the President of the bank also made him a member of the Board of Directors.

After approximately fifteen months on the job, he came to work swaying slightly and smelling of alcohol. While walking down the office stairs, he slipped and fell. The President, who was walking behind him at the time, rushed up to the employee and immediately had an ambulance summoned. X-rays revealed three broken ribs and a mild concussion. A blood test was taken and the results showed the employee had a very high concentration of alcohol in his system. At this time, the employee was dismissed.

The employee filed for both worker's compensation and unemployment compensation.

Questions

1. Is the employee eligible for unemployment compensation given the guidelines set up by federal legislation?
2. Given that alcohol was involved, does the employee qualify for worker's compensation?

The Legal Position on Dismissal for Personal Appearance

A large northeastern university hired a new law professor, Allan Johnstone, to teach criminal law. He had spent five years as an attorney with the Department of Justice and was considered quite competent.

After four months, complaints began to be heard in the dean's office regarding the professor. A petition signed by fifteen senior professors was submitted to the dean finding fault with Mr. Johnstone's "lax teaching and academic habits and, in general, a demeanor degrading and unworthy of the profession." These professors urged Mr. Johnstone's dismissal, and some threatened to resign if he remained.

The dean consulted most of the professors and then summoned Mr. Johnstone to his office. Mr. Johnstone expressed the opinion that the other professors were not so much against him professionally, but personally. He felt they held a grudge against him because he sported longish hair and a beard and did not dress as they did. Mr. Johnstone argued that the professors had lost touch with the "real world" and that they were "decadent and archaic in nature and thought."

Having heard both sides of the argument, the dean informed Mr. Johnstone that he would be dismissed at the end of the semester, though he still had two-and-a-half years left on his contract. Mr. Johnstone went back to his office to ponder his alternatives.

His first thought was to sue for breach of contract. He calculated his chances as 50-50, since the university was a State school and the courts usually ruled against plaintiffs unless they were tenured. He also felt the school had weighed these facts beforehand and knew the odds were really more in their favor. He figured the best he could do would be a judgment for a portion of his future salary.

Mr. Johnstone felt he would have a better chance by pursuing a different route. He knew the EEOC under Title VII would not handle the case because it did not involve discrimination, *per se,* based on race, color, sex, religion or national origin. He did know the university held certain federal training contracts and thus, under the OFCC, had an affirmative action program. He felt he could sue for reinstatement since he was, in effect, a minority of sorts. He was a veteran, he came from a culturally and socially disadvantaged background, and he was one-eighth American Indian.

Questions

1. Does Mr. Johnstone have a case under Title VII of the 1964 Civil Rights Act?
2. If you were the Human Resources Director for the university, how would you handle this situation?

Just Cause for Separation

Mary Johnson had just graduated from the University of Florida with a Bachelor of Science in Business Administration. She moved to Miami immediately after graduation and looked for a job in retail management. She had worked as an Assistant Manager for a boutique in Gainesville for four years while she attended college and felt she was now qualified to be a manager.

Mary was hired as Manager of a fashionable boutique in Miami Beach. The boutique was part of a Florida-based chain and had a reputation for its high fashion merchandise and expensive accessories. Mary had the duties of a regular manager, as well as the responsibility for all hiring and firing of personnel. Although Mary had a degree in Business Administration, she had not majored in management and had taken only one basic human resource management course. Yet at the time she accepted the position as manager, she felt she would have no trouble handling the personnel responsibilities.

The chain of boutiques that Mary worked for was owned by a husband and wife who visited the stores approximately once a month. On their first visit since the hiring of Mary, they were quite pleased with the shape of the store. Sales figures were good and the store was making ever increasing profits under Mary's management.

A problem came up, however, when reviewing the new employees that Mary had hired. It seemed that two of the women that were hired did not fit the image of what the owners wanted for their sales personnel. Their merchandise was high fashion and expensive, and the salesgirls had to have "a special look." In other words, the two people in question were just not attractive enough. Mary was called into the back room and was told that she had to fire the two salespeople. Mary was upset over the situation, but had no choice in the matter. Either she fired the two young women or the owners would do it and replace Mary as well.

Mary made up some story to tell the salespeople about having to cut back the staff and informed them they would have to be the first ones let go. A month later the two girls found out from friends still working at the boutique the real reason they were fired. They considered filing suit against the boutique for wrongful dismissal.

Questions

1. Under what law, if any, could the two saleswomen have claimed discrimination?
2. Were the two young saleswomen entitled to Unemployment Compensation?
3. If Mary had refused to fire the employees, could she have legally been fired by the owners?
4. If Mary had been fired, could she have received Unemployment Compensation?

Implicit Company Policies and Discharge

Alice, Betty and Carol are three of fifteen employees of a private-school cafeteria in a large eastern city. Alice is American-born and has worked at the cafeteria for five years. Betty and Carol were born in the West Indies and have been at the cafeteria one year.

Betty and Carol were observed taking leftover food home one afternoon. Taking leftover food home was not an unusual occurrence in this kitchen, but the pressure to hold down costs had caused management to decide to try to stop it. As a result, Betty and Carol were fired for stealing.

Betty sued for reinstatement claiming discrimination against her because she was foreign-born. She did not deny taking the leftover food but claimed that Alice had been observed doing the same thing and had not been fired. Management countered that while Alice may have been observed taking food home, it was before the decision to crack down, and thus no discrimination was intended. Betty and Carol were simply the first ones caught after the decision had been made.

Questions

1. If you were hired to arbitrate this case, what would your decision be?
2. Should Carol, who did not sue, be entitled to whatever relief, if any, Betty receives?
3. What can management do to avoid being sued again - without assenting to stealing?

Last Hired, First Fired

In 1992, Diane Smith, a former Labor Department administrator, was hired by Gescorp, a large manufacturing firm, to establish and implement the company's court-ordered affirmative action program. In its decision, the court has found Gescorp's hiring policies in violation of Title VII of the Civil Rights Act of 1964. Furthermore, the court ordered that an affirmative action program be instituted to insure that African Americans would comprise at least ten percent of the company's work force and that this ten percent be distributed evenly through all job levels.

Initially, it was felt that the implementation of this program would be met by stiff resistance from the company's predominantly white work force, but by August 1994, the affirmative action goals had been met through careful selection of replacements following normal attrition. No whites had been laid off or fired, and the new workers filled positions at all job levels when they became available.

Due to her success in implementing the affirmative action program, Diane was promoted to Director of Human Resources. Her new duties included the administration of the company's labor-management relations. Although the company had had its share of labor difficulties, they were viewed as nothing out of the ordinary. The union, which had been at Gescorp for ten years, had never caused much trouble.

It was not until early in 1995 that problems developed. Gescorp's Board of Directors had decided that due to declining sales ten percent of the company's work force had to be laid off for an indefinite period of time. It was the duty of Diane, as Director of Human Resources, to determine which employees and jobs would be cut.

The union contract contained a seniority clause which specifically said that layoffs would be conducted under the principle of "last hired, first fired." To comply with the union contract would mean eliminating nearly the entire African American portion of the company's work force. Diane did not know what to do.

Questions

1. What do you feel Diane should do?
2. What are the legal consequences of laying off white workers with seniority?
3. What are the legal consequences of laying off the African American workers hired under the court ordered affirmative action plan?
4. Is there a compromise and, if so, what is it?
5. What, if anything, does Title VII say about union seniority systems?

Seniority vs. Ability in
Layoff Determination

Lancor Tool and Maintenance Company has had a history of promotion from within based on longevity with the company. Employees were hired as apprentice workers and were promoted to better jobs as they learned skills and gained more experience.

The more established workers with the company were eager to get a job driving a company truck of their own and answering trouble calls to surrounding areas when these calls came into the Lancor Company. This traveling repair service was considered more desirable than staying on the premises of the Lancor Company and accepting and repairing equipment from off-the-street customers.

Recently, the company became concerned with the fact that the more senior workers could not repair the new, more sophisticated equipment as well as the younger, newer workers. Complaints were coming into Lancor concerning problems in the field. The older workers could not repair the equipment on the spot and were forced to bring it back to the in-house service department of Lancor so that the younger workers could complete the job.

The company finally negotiated an agreement with the union permitting it to use ability and skill tests in the selection of new repair crews. The older workers were no longer able to bid on the more desirable jobs. For the first time, Lancor was able to go outside the organization and hire young students just out of trade school. These students learned quickly and had the knowledge and understanding to work on the new equipment. After a while, the older repairmen who had come into their jobs prior to being screened were shifted to less desirable shop jobs.

The problem that now faces the Lancor Tool and Maintenance Company is one of declining business forcing a cutback in the size of the repair department. Since layoffs are based on seniority, nearly all of the relatively new and more able younger employees will be laid off if the present decline continues. Lancor fears the loss of their young, skilled workers will further erode their business and that, eventually, competitors will begin making inroads.

Question

1. What alternative courses of action are available to Lancor? What are the implementation problems and possible implications of each?

Transition and Turnover Problems
Caused by Technological Advances

A large firm that manufactures stereophonic equipment and specializes in amplifiers has been a leading regional distributor for over 25 years. Until a few years ago it had been continually expanding due to ever increasing profits. In the past few years however, it has experienced a substantial reduction in sales and profits as a result of increased competition from foreign markets.

In an attempt to increase efficiency and sales, the main office called in consultants to advise on updating equipment. Based on their recommendations, new equipment was purchased and it was decided that several hundred employees would have to be laid off. The new machinery was to increase production and decrease staff by requiring a higher level of skills. Management felt if the new machinery had to remain idle during the training period for the present staff, it would cause further delays in production and that the process of training some employees and gradually reducing the staff would be too costly and too slow.

Since the older employees were unfamiliar with the new machinery, it was advised that an outsider be hired to oversee the training. A supervisor from a competitive company was offered an attractive salary, to which she agreed, and when she came she brought her own staff of operators. The new staff caused a further decrease in older employees and created conflicts between them and the new people. Many departments had a difficult time maintaining morale in light of the changes that were taking place.

After several months, the new staff and new machinery were working smoothly, but expenditures were still higher than the consultants had predicted. Suddenly, one day the main terminal broke down and production had to be halted until the parts arrived. If something were not done immediately, production would fall behind schedule, resulting in financial losses to the company. The only alternative was to return to the old machinery, even though it was slower and could probably not meet contract deadlines.

A problem developed because the new skilled employees were unfamiliar with the old machinery and there weren't enough of the older employees remaining to do the job. Pressed for time, the remaining older employees were asked to work nights and the following weekend.

Questions

1. Should management have dismantled the old system and dismissed the staff before the new machinery had all the bugs out and the new staff proved efficient?
2. How could the old system have been utilized to prevent production slow-down and company loss?
3. How could the impact of the machinery on the employees have been minimized?

Wage Garnishment and Eligibility
for Unemployment Compensation

Two years ago, Mike Taylor got married. At that time he purchased a new car and a home through a finance company. The car payments were $495 a month and the payments on the house were $2,350 a month. Although this was quite an expense, Taylor was able to make the payments because he and his wife both worked.

Nine months after their marriage, Mrs. Taylor had twins and could not return to work. In November and December of last year, Mike Taylor did not have the money to make the car payments. In January, the finance company had the car payments deducted from his salary.

Taylor's employer, Mr. Johnson, did not like this. He was, however, aware of Taylor's situation and did not say anything. Five months later, the finance company called again saying Taylor had failed to make the last three payments on his house. Johnson called Taylor into his office and told him he would have to make the payments on his own because he was not going to be troubled with having to deduct the money from his paycheck.

Taylor had exhausted his savings and could not afford to make the payments. When the legal documents arrived requiring that the payments be withheld from his pay, Johnson fired Taylor.

Taylor did not have any luck in finding another job. He filed for unemployment compensation, but when he went to the state agency, they informed him that he was not eligible to collect.

Questions

1. Was Johnson justified in firing Taylor? Why or why not?
2. Is Taylor eligible for unemployment compensation? Why or why not?

Eligibility for Social Security Retirement Benefits

Alexander Smith was born in 1941 and currently works and resides in Springfield, Virginia. Alexander began working in 1957 part-time and began full-time employment in 1962 after completing his undergraduate college education. Since that time, he has been employed on a full-time basis, thus paying his share of Social Security tax (FICA) as required by the Social Security Act. Alexander now has numerous grandchildren and would like to retire and spend some quality time with them.

Questions

1. What is the earliest possible age that Alexander may retire and receive Social Security without a reduction in his benefits?
2. If Alexander chose to retire early, when could he do so, and how much of a penalty would he incur?
3. If Alexander were to delay retirement, would his benefits increase as a result? Explain.

About The Author

Dr. Kenneth A. Kovach is a Full Professor in the School of Business at George Mason University where he has been voted Outstanding Faculty Member and received the Distinguished Faculty Award. He specializes in Human Resource Management/Labor Relations research and has published eight books, over sixty articles, and over two hundred cases in these areas.

Dr. Kovach is also a consultant to numerous local and national firms, including the U.S. Department of Defense, American Red Cross, and the American Council on Education. He is on retainer with numerous employer and labor organizations in the areas of contract negotiation, mediation, arbitration, diversity and sensitivity training, employee motivation, etc.